# Religion and Modernization in the Soviet Union

## Westview Replica Editions

This book is a **Westview Replica Edition**. The concept of
Replica Editions is a response to the crisis in academic and
informational publishing. Library budgets for books have been
severely curtailed; economic pressures on the university presses
and the few private publishing companies primarily interested in
scholarly manuscripts have severely limited the capacity of the
industry to properly serve the academic and research communities.
Many manuscripts dealing with important subjects, often representing the highest level of scholarship, are today not economically viable publishing projects. Or, if they are accepted for
publication, they are often subject to lead times ranging from
one to three years. Scholars are understandably frustrated when
they realize that their first-class research cannot be published
within a reasonable time frame, if at all.

Westview Replica Editions seem to us one feasible and practical solution to the crisis. The concept is simple. We accept
a manuscript in camera-ready form and move it immediately into
the production process. The responsibility for textual and copy
editing lies with the author or sponsoring organization. If
necessary we will advise the author on proper preparation of
footnotes and bibliography. The manuscript is acceptable as
typed for a thesis or dissertation or prepared in any other
clearly organized and readable way, though we prefer it typed
according to our specifications. The end result is a book produced by lithography and bound in hard covers. Edition sizes
range from 200 to 600 copies. We will include among Westview
Replica Editions only works of outstanding scholarly quality or
of great informational value and we will exercise our usual
editorial standards and quality control.

*Religion and Modernization in the Soviet Union*
edited by Dennis J. Dunn

To the surprise of many students of the Soviet Union, religion has shown itself to be a force still powerful in Soviet
society. In contrast, the impact of religion in developed
Western societies has declined. Dr. Dunn points out that the
study of this antinomy can shed light on the entire concept of
"modernization" in the U.S.S.R. The study of the Soviet case
can reveal the effect of religions and religious problems on
Soviet modernization, and vice versa, and can also provide insight into the question of whether religion and modernization
are compatible--or whether the advance of the latter signals
the demise of the former.

This pioneering examination of the relationship between
religion and modernization in the U.S.S.R. brings together the
work of top international specialists in the fields of Soviet
religions and intellectual history.

Dennis J. Dunn is associate professor of history and
director of the Institute for the Study of Religion and Communism at Southwest Texas State University. He has recently
completed *The Catholic Church and the Soviet Government,
1939-1949,* to be published this year as part of the East European Monograph Series.

# Religion and Modernization in the Soviet Union

edited by
Dennis J. Dunn

Westview Press
Boulder, Colorado

*A Westview Replica Edition*

Published in 1977 in the United States of America by

    Westview Press, Inc.
    1898 Flatiron Court
    Boulder, Colorado  80301
    Frederick A. Praeger, Publisher and Editorial Director

Library of Congress Card Number:  77-86372
ISBN:  0-89158-241-X


Printed and bound in the United States of America

# CONTENTS

Page

vii

# PREFACE

The idea of this volume was conceived at an international symposium on religion and modernization in the Soviet Union which was organized at Southwest Texas State University in March 1976 by the American Association for the Advancement of Slavic Studies. The contributors to this volume were participants in this symposium. They represent not only an array of disciplines, but also the best scholarship available for analyzing the relationship between religion and modernization in the USSR.

This collection of essays ultimately is a team effort and it stands as a tribute to selfless scholarship and to the commitment of both publisher and researcher to the advance of knowledge. The book was produced via the relatively inexpensive off-set method of publishing and all royalties, small though they may be, will be given to the Research and Development Committee of the American Association for the Advancement of Slavic Studies to fund further conferences delving into unexplored or still puzzling problems of Slavic studies.

The book owes a deep debt of gratitude to the Research and Development Committee of the American Association for the Advancement of Slavic Studies, then chaired by Professor George Hoffman of the University of Texas. Both Professor Hoffman and Professor S. Frederick Starr, also a member of the

Committee and the Executive Director of the Kennan
Institute for Advanced Russian Studies, Washington,
D.C., were of immeasurable help in organizing the
conference. Professors Alfred Levin, V. Stanley
Vardys, Alexandre Bennigsen, and William C. Fletcher
provided many valuable insights and much encourage-
ment at the early stages of this project. Professor
Sidney Monas did the same at the end of the under-
taking. The idea for the meeting was planted two
years before by Bohdan R. Bociurkiw during a visit
to San Marcos, Texas. He is to be commended sing-
ularly for his leadership in the field of church-
state relations in the Communist world.

The conference could not have been held or executed as smoothly as it was without the full support
and cooperation of Southwest Texas State University.
In many ways the hosting of this international gathering marked the emergence of Southwest Texas State
University as a center of scholarship in the southwest. A special note of thanks goes to Frederick
Praeger and Lynne C. Rienner of Westview Press for
their interest and support in bringing the conference papers to print. I extend my appreciation to
my wife, Margaret, who provided me with the time so
crucial to scholarship. Linda Catoggio did the su-
perb job of typing the final manuscript. Exercising
the editor's prerogative, I wish to dedicate this
volume to Bohdan R. Bociurkiw, a man of uncommon insights into the problems of religion in the Soviet
Union.


San Marcos, Texas                          D.J.D.
June, 1977

Chapter 1
INTRODUCTION

Dennis J. Dunn and Donald W. Treadgold

<u>DEFINITIONS AND SUMMARIES</u> by Dennis J. Dunn

The relationship between religion and modernization in the Soviet Union is an overlooked subject.
There are multiple books on the problem of Soviet
modernization and also on Soviet religions but none
on the nexus between them.  For many Western observers the term "modernization" conjures up ideas of
huge factories, bulging cities, and secularized education, almost anything but religion, churches, and
believers.  If, per chance, religion does impinge on
the image, it usually would be thought of as something like a human appendix, interesting but not of
much perceptible value.  It has, of course, been recognized with regard to the USSR that religions have
suffered a certain oppression, but, notwithstanding
such persecution, Western scholars, like Walter La-
queur, still conclude that religion has not been a
significant factor in the past fifty years of Soviet
history.[1]  Religion and religious concepts seem, in
the eyes of not a few Western social scientists, to
be waning in and to have little relevance to the
modern society.[2]
Such assumptions undoubtedly have played a role

in discouraging a meaningful analysis of the relationship between religion and modernization in the
USSR.  In addition, such preconceptions, based upon
such unreliable developments as the decline of
church attendance in Western modernized states, must
be used quite reservedly in examining Soviet society.
To the surprise of many Sovietologists religion within the past few years has shown great tenacity and
even resurgence to the point where Robert Tucker entitled an article "Religious Revival in Russia."[3]
Given the patent discrimination against Soviet believers and the lack of data on Soviet religions, it
is problematical whether religion actually has revived only within the past few years or whether it
has been a powerful if latent force throughout the
course of Soviet history.  The pith of the presently
observable influence of religion in the USSR suggests
that it has deep roots.[4]

Be that as it may, there is little question
that today religion is a significant factor in Soviet
society and this is underscored by the veritable tor-
rent of religious samizdat reaching the West since
the late 1960s.[5]  In that sense the Soviet Union de-
fies those who have assumed that religion would decline in a modernized state, or else it provides evidence that the USSR is not really modernized.  Since
no one has yet charged, including the authors in this
book, that the Soviet Union is not a modernized
state, the Soviet experience is a paradox for those
who believe that religion and modernization are incompatible and that the advance of the latter is syn-
onymous with the denouement of the former.  Accordingly, the religion or religious problems in Soviet
society merit close scrutiny for what they can reveal

generally about modernized countries and specifically about Soviet society.  In addition, investigation
of the connection between religion and modernization
in the Soviet Union is of interest because Russia was
a latecomer to modernization and, once the process
did start, it evolved in a cultural atmosphere that
was strongly religious as well as multi-religious.
As such the Soviet case can reveal the effect of a variety of religions and of religious problems on Soviet
modernization and vice versa.

Modernization is a controversial concept.  Those
who react to it rarely agree upon its definition and,
indeed, its value.  Donald Treadgold refuses to allow
the word, as if it were dripping with cholesterol,
into his "intellectual diet," preferring instead the
term "Westernization."[6]  His choice, however, is dis-
gorged by Cyril Black, a pioneer in the study of modernization, since the term Westernization "implies
that Western or European institutions are themselves
the essence of modernity and that other societies
may forget their historical heritage and adopt modern values and institutions in their Western or European form as they might abandon the ox cart for the
automobile or the fez for the hat."[7]  Sidney Monas,
on the other hand, sees the concept with its emphasis upon science and progress as an archaic vestige
of the enlightenment.  "Scientism, positivism, belief in the Idea of Progress--who among us," he asks,
"reposes much confidence in them any longer?"[8]
Charles M. Fair, in the same vein, portrays modernity with its scepticism and secularism as a return to
animality, a lapse into a new Dark Age so many times
worse than the "late Roman" experience because of
modern society's "fearful instruments."[9]

I shall not attempt to judge the worth of the
concept of modernization or, indeed, whether or not
the societal processes which it describes (chiefly
industrialization, urbanization, and secularization)
are the harbingers of an approaching apocalypse.
Those questions, to do them justice, should be treated separately and at length.  The attempt here is
simply to set out the concept of modernization as it
was defined for the authors and, thus, to provide the
reader with the reference point to which the authors
were reacting in their essays on religion, and, se -
condly, to summarize the major themes of the essays.
Donald Treadgold, in the second part of the introduction, addresses directly the question of whether
or not religion and modernization (or to use his term
"Westernization") in the USSR are incompatible.

In the conference proposal which was placed before the authors, modernization was defined as the
process of change from an agrarian to an industrial
society that resulted (and results) from the growth
of man's knowledge and his increasing control over
nature.  It is the means "by which societies have
been and are being transformed under the impact of
the scientific and technological revolution."[10]  Rec-
ognizably emerging in the West in the course of the
eighteenth century, modernization (or Westernization), borne on the shoulders of Western missionaries, explorers, emigrants, traders, and soldiers,
sped forward during the nineteenth and twentieth centuries to embrace the entire world.[11]  A social,
economic, political, and cultural cataclysm, it was
and is, nonetheless, a transformation desired by most
people.

In a very general sense, a model of a modernized

4

society would include a pattern of structural development encompassing urbanization, factories, centralized government, professional elite, technical and
scientific education, increased capital investments,
division of labor, expansion of trade, environmental
pollution, growth in social diseases such as delin-
quency and alcoholism, smaller and disorganized families, individual alienation, mechanized agriculture,
developed systems of transportation and communication, and a modernizing ideology.  The modernized society would also comprise a cultural transformation
whereby native culture is modified (sometimes abandoned) to harmonize with the imported Western ideas.
In Russia the modernizing process was initiated by
the tsars in the middle of the nineteenth century
and then in this century, the process was dramatically accelerated by the communists.  In dealing with
the above definition of modernization, the authors
reflected the general debate which surrounds the concept.  Each one handled the term differently, some
concentrating on one or another of the various aspects of the concept, some modifying or criticizing
it for one reason or another.  Virtually all agree
that in the USSR the crucial fact in church-state relations in a modernized context has been direct state
interference in religion's ability and/or desire to
modernize.  All also agree that religion is quite
strong in the Soviet Union and that while secularization has advanced significantly the masses and a
growing number of intellectuals are involved, in one
fashion or another, with religion.  Alfred Levin, in
describing through the Duma debates church-state relations on the eve of the revolution in 1917, presents the fascinating thesis that both westerners

5

and slavophiles were close on religious matters and
that both hoped to recall a vital church that had
provided a true leadership for the national spirit
in times of past crises.  Walter Sawatsky sees the
growth of the principle of separation of church and
state as a positive by-product of modernization and
argues that this trend had been going on in Russia
since at least the time of Peter the Great.  Sidney
Monas, a Viconian by nature, does not think of modernization as a forward development but rather as a
cyclical regression in human history.  He does point
out the increasing curiosity in religion among the
Soviet intelligentsia and interestingly calls attention to the fact that religion is the one level on
which the intelligentsia and the masses, so aliented
from one another during tsarist times, might now find
common ground.  The question then will be, as he
says, "who will transform whom?"  David Powell devel-
ops the theme of secularization in Soviet society and
argues persuasively that antireligious cartoons, one
major dimension of the regime's antireligious efforts, have little effect on believers and that their
primary functions seem to be to entertain and reinforce atheists.

In Part II, in taking up the experiences of
specific religions, William C. Fletcher claims that
the state forced Russian Orthodoxy into a position
of complete subservience and, thus, shackled the
church's ability to adopt modernizing characteristics.
He argues, though, that if survival and growth in a
modernized country are the earmarks of modernization, then the subservient Russian Orthodox Church
has modernized.  Alexandre Bennigsen in dealing with
Islam also emphasizes that the state prevented Soviet

6

Islam from modernizing and simultaneously attempted
to russify the Muslims. Nonetheless, he writes, Soviet Islam persevered by identifying its conservative
traditions with the Muslim way of life and now it is
on the threshold of major change with both the modernist and conservative trends strong and present.
Professor Bennigsen thinks that the Soviets have
given up hope of russifying the Muslims and that this
fact could eventually lead, if accurate, to the victory of religious reformers over religious conservatives since the latter's role as protectors of Islam
would be passé. Zvi Gitelman writes that while Judaism has been intellectually and institutionally
thwarted by governmental force in terms of its response to modernization, it has nonetheless persisted
because of the deadness of the materialist ideology,
the apathy among the secularized population toward
religious believers, and the close relationship between Jewish ethnicity and Judaism. Modernization,
though, was as powerful, if not more powerful, an influence on Judaism than the government. He now
thinks that because of the persistance of religion in
such a modernized country as the USSR that religion
must be viewed on a cyclical rather than a linear
path in a modernized context and that the crucial
question now is what will be religion's role in post-
modern society.

   V. Stanley Vardys makes the point that the Catholic Church in Lithuania was adjusting to modernization between the wars, but that since the Baltic
States have fallen under Soviet control, the government has prevented the church from developing. His
point is that there is no contradiction or essential
conflict between religion and modernization. Bohdan

7

R. Bociurkiw argues along a similar line in discussing the Ukrainian Autocephalous Orthodox Church,
suggesting that one of the main reasons the Soviet
authorities suppressed the church was that it was
adapting handily to modernization and, thus, represented a more sophisticated danger than other religions to the party's desire for an ideological monopoly. Andrew Blane, in the concluding chapter, con-
tends along with so many of the authors, that the
state rather than industrialization, urbanization,
or education has been the egregious factor in the
Protestant sects' reaction to modernization. He emphasizes that the sectarians' most difficult time
with the government was during the transformation to
modernity and suggests that this can be explained by
the fact that latecomers to modernization, such as
Russia, needed extensive political control and coordination.

RELIGION AND MODERNIZATION IN THE USSR by Donald W.
Treadgold

A hoary anecdote dealing with the early period
of post-revolutionary education in the USSR has an
examiner and his student engaging in the following
exchange:

> Q. What is God?
>
> A. God is a superstition by which the
>    exploiters delude the laboring
>    classes by leading them to place
>    their hopes for rescue from their
>    misery in a nonexistent after-life
>    rather than in the life they are
>    actually living.
>
> Q. Well, you have passed.
>
> A. Thank God!

8

In this anecdote is posed the problem of the relation
between religion and "modernization," as well as the
way in which it is complicated by the interplay between the conscious mind and unconscious reflexes
produced by cultural conditioning.

I shall take the term "religion" to refer to the
higher religions represented in the USSR in any numbers:  Eastern Orthodox Christianity, Islam, Judaism,
and Buddhism; the religious aspect of Communism,
though in my view a vital topic, may be left to be
discussed on other occasions.  "Modernization" is
defined above by Dennis J. Dunn as "the process of
change from an agrarian to an industrial society that
resulted from the growth of man's knowledge and his
increasing control over nature."  Alternative definitions may, of course, be found; I choose more or
less at random Josefa Saniel's, in her article on
Japan in Religion and Progress in Modern Asia, ed.
Robert Bellah (New York:  Free Press, 1965):  modernization is transformation of traditional systems
into modern systems.  That won't do, because it is
tautological.  She goes on to add that that means
"systems ideally characterized by the highest possible degree of efficiency"--that is, "the rationalization" of traditional systems.  But rationalization,
indeed, has often been thought to be the precise innovation made by the capitalist system, which by any
reckoning is at least several centuries old.  Let me
put on record my own view, that "modernization" is
not a useful term at all; that it contains various
implicit but often quite well concealed value judg-
ments of a sort I do not share, an additive I do not
want to have smuggled into my intellectual diet; that
it is conceptually in origin a form of confusion, in

9

that those who use it most often have in mind three
things:  first, industrialization, a process originating in the West; second, the transplantation of the
products of the mid-twentieth century technology of
the West to places whose own industrial base can not
in the foreseeable future be expected to produce such
technology on their own; third, Westernization in
broadest sense, including not merely industrial and
technical importations but also political, philosophical, and other values and ideas drawn from the
United States and Western Europe.  Even these three
things need to be conceptually distinguished.  I have
urged such objections before to valued colleagues of
mine who say "modernization" when they mean Westernization; the reply has been to cite such examples as
that of China, which was influenced by Japan's modernization; my retort has been that what they are
talking about is Westernization mediated by Japan.  I
shall now drop that subject, having no hope that the
term "modernization" is going to disappear from dis-
course.  It will not even disappear from my own dis-
course, because it was never there to begin with.

     I propose, then, to address the question of con-
flict or compatibility of religion and Westernization
in the USSR, focusing chiefly on Russian Orthodox religion and Westernization viewed under such headings
as cultural in a broad sense, political, and technological.  I begin by distinguishing two groups:  the
Orthodox ideologists, if I may so speak, such as A.
E. Levitin-Krasnov and Boris Talantov, and the Orthodox writers, chief among them Alexander Solzhenitsyn.

     Levitin-Krasnov's views are examined in Barbara
Wolfe Jancar's interesting article in Dissent in the
USSR, ed. Rudolf Tokes (Baltimore:  John Hopkins

University Press, 1975). She writes that his views
contain overtones of "traditional Russian messianic
mysticism." For all I know Levitin-Krasnov may in
fact be a mystic or a propagandist for mysticism, but
there is no evidence available that he is either one.
"Mysticism" is unhappily often used by writers un-
familiar with the subject as simply an equivalent for
religious belief or elements of religion which do not
depend on reason. Levitin-Krasnov speaks of "Holy
Rus" as accounting for the deepest historically
formed characteristics of the Russian people, such as
"love, goodness, and suffering" which survive today
"only" among believers. It sounds as if he is concerned exclusively with the Russian Orthodox community, but it is he who has called perceptively for
"free religion and free atheism" in the USSR, calling
attention to the fact that the atheism of the Soviet
Union is no more free than the religion is, even
though it is officially favored, and that the atheist
is no more unable to ignore the imperatives of ideological conformity than the believer. (In this respect the position of contemporary atheism in the
USSR is somewhat comparable to that of Russian Orthodoxy under the Empire. It was likewise officially
favored, but not free, though the constraints placed
on it by the state were milder--as tsarist constraints in general were--than those imposed by the
Soviet regime.) His positive prescription is for
what he terms "neohumanism," a "stateless, truly
free, classless society," which would be a true "theocracy." But the main thrust of Levitin-Krasnov's
writing seems to be more immediate in focus; he sup-
ports the priestly dissenters such as Eshliman and
Yakunin and indicts the hierarchy for cesaropapism.

As for Talantov, who is now dead, his attention also seemed directed at the alleged failings of the leadership of the contemporary Orthodox Church in the USSR. His essay "Serveivshchina" (The Wicked Deeds of Sergei, referring to the Metropolitan, later Patriarch) attacks the submission to the state made by Sergei in 1927 on the basis of a distinction between ecclesiastical and governmental spheres. Talantov has written letters to President Podgorny in the USSR and Pope Paul VI regarding the disabilities the Orthodox suffer.

Of the ideologists, as we have termed them we may find them so deeply involved on the barricades of religious dissent that their perspectives for the future are difficult to characterize. Krasnov is a democrat of sorts, concerned with what democrats abroad think, and he is an Orthodox Christian concerned with possible reconciliation with Roman Catholicism, implying an admiration of the latter as contrasted with the unhappy situation of Orthodoxy for much of its history that recalls Chaadaev. (What other of the "ideologists" think about such matters may not be very clear.) It is interesting, however, that Krasnov clearly regards much of the world outside as what used to be called the "free world" and looks to Western Christianity as being in as enviable a position compared with that of the Russian church as the West is politically in contrast with the USSR.

If we turn to the writers, in particular Solzhenitsyn, we find a less clearly Westernizing tendency, partly to be sure because he is in the midst of the West and all its troubles, though he made sharp remarks about Daniel Ellsberg and Ramsay Clark before he was involuntarily exported to Frankfurt.

Here I make no attempt to contribute new knowledge of Solzhenitsyn, but make a few remarks which risk being obvious on the one hand and controversial on the other--or even wrong. His pilgrimage to the United States did not help his public relations; the liberal press some time ago discovered that he was not a liberal, and after properly reprimanding him for that deficiency for some months seemed to lose interest in him. I imagine a Politburo scenario just preceding his exile that runs as follows: Suslov says, can't we make an exception and execute him? Andropov says, no, a labor camp, I have a nice one in mind for him. Brezhnev says, no, no, the cost to détente would be too great; I know, let's send him to the West and let the liberals carve him up for us. Seconded, and passed unanimously.

To say that Solzhenitsyn is not a liberal is not to say what he _is_, and of course he may change his views further, as may Sakharov. We should remember that both men were good Marxist-Leninists, as far as we can tell, fifteen or fewer years ago, and the evolution of both to their present positions--Sakharov as Westernizing liberal, Solzhenitsyn as Orthodox Christian thinker--presents subjects that have not yet found their historians.

Let me offer my own characterization in a word: Solzhenitsyn is a syncretist, the chief figure in our time to exemplify the movement whose antecedents, I have argued in a recent book, included the plurality of groups supporting Alexei Petrovich when Peter the Great was deciding whether to kill him; scattered figures during the hundred and twenty-five years who resisted forced Westernization, but not the learning or technology of the West; the slavophiles, driven by

13

German philosophers to look for and with astonishment discover the fact that the Russians had a heritage of their own; Dostoevsky and Soloviev; the flowering of diverse schools of literature and the arts in the reign of the last tsar; _Vekhi_.

It has come to be widely noted that Solzhenitsyn acknowledges his own debt to _Vekhi_ in Chapter Two of _August 1914_, when by reporting influence of the book on his father ("Sanya Lazhenitsyn") he implies cultural paternity--rather than dealing with paternity of blood. A distinguished Soviet dissident, soon after he emigrated, was recently questioned by an audience at a great Eastern university. He was asked what positive ideas inspired his fellow dissidents; he replied, "Well, we are looking again at _Vekhi_." The obvious puzzlement of the largely contemporary-oriented audience was sufficient that a senior literary specialist had to rise and explain what that was, and many scholars may still be confused about the nature of the influence in question.

There has been a good deal of talk about Solzhenitsyn's debt to Tolstoy; in the realm of ideas there is very little. The Tolstoyans in _August 1914_ are dolts in the Stavka and court who believe that God will not let anything bad happen to Russia. His literary debt to Tolstoy, Dostoevsky, and other Russian writers is of course quite another matter. He has also exhibited the influence of Western writers. To cite only an example or two, the devices of John Dos Passos's _USA_ have been freely borrowed in _August 1914_; _The First Circle_ has a structure (not merely a title) that hangs on Dante. Solzhenitsyn writes for mankind and draws on the experience of mankind, not only Russia.

14

However, his foremost concern is indeed Russia, and his adherence to Orthodox Christianity defines much of that concern. Solzhenitsyn's attitudes to the Orthodox church past and present are not all simple. He defends the Old Believers against the established church of the day, perhaps there venturing onto thin ice historically in his specific observations. He defends the Orthodox Church of today in the USSR against some of the criticisms of Russian Orthodox émigrés; on the other hand, he indicts the church in the Soviet Union for inadmissible forms of cooperation with the state. His depiction of the pre-revolutionary church is in black enough colors that he concludes that its condition at the beginning of the twentieth century was one of the main causes of the Revolution.

He offers not merely an assessment of the Russian past, however, but also a specific program for the USSR, set forth in his letter to the Soviet leaders. The ten points he enumerates may be summarized as follows: abandonment of official Marxism at home and abroad; abolition of the collective farms and establishment of a government based on law and civil liberties; reduction of armaments; concentration on the domestic economy with special stress on the development of Siberia; temporary retention of the authoritarian aspect of the state; renewal of the Russian cultural tradition, based on the family and church. Sakharov, one may recall, agreed with six out of the ten points and disagreed on the others, but that fact does not suggest that any of the religious dissidents take a route other than Solzhenitsyn's, for Sakharov is not religious but rather has become a Western-style liberal.

15

The program of Solzhenitsyn just discussed, in connection with other statements of his, has evoked certain misunderstandings. He has been unjustly accused of wishing to impose religious conformity. He does not; his antecedents in this respect go back to Christian leaders of the fourth century who opposed the edict of Theodosius I making Trinitarianism the faith of the Empire. Solzhenitsyn has been accused of nationalism, inaccurately to the extent that an "ism" is to be regarded as placing ahead of everything else whatever precedes that suffix; he puts first not the nation, or Russia, but God. In an essay in From Under the Rubble he writes, "no people is eternally great or eternally noble." We Russians, he says, are not traversing the heavens in a blaze of glory but sitting forlornly in a heap of spiritual cinders. The word "messianism" has been applied to Solzhenitsyn, but he looks for no earthly messiahs.

On the basis of our brief examination of certain of the Orthodox ideologists and writers, it may be possible to proceed to address the question, does Russian Orthodoxy involve conflict or compatibility with Westernization? (If specifically theological reasoning is used, or the psychological manifestations of folk religion are considered, one may to be sure come out somewhat differently.) Some of the views of Solzhenitsyn or any other Christian may be rooted in his Christianity; some may be compatible with Christian faith. Christianity is not an ideology and in many ways it may be best interpreted as the relentless enemy of any ideology. On issues affecting government, the Christian is left with empirical problems to solve like anyone else, though approaching them on the basis of commitment to certain values.

Culturally, Russian Orthodoxy may be open to
various syncretist solutions, combining admiration
for Western culture and use of its fruits with a consciousness of the cultural achievements of the Russian
tradition and a mastery of them.  There is no necessary contradiction here at all.  Many examples exist
of Russians who have been proud of their own past and
at the same time deeply interested in the past and
present creations of Western culture.  The World of
Art (<u>Mir Iskusstva</u>) group was equally fascinated by
the rediscovery of the ancient Russian icon and by
news of the latest Paris fashions in art.

Politically, it becomes more difficult to say
what Westernization is.  It was once thought that the
West and democracy were inseparable, that one implied the other.  As the number of democracies shrinks
and democracy as a system seems to exhibit ever more
intractable problems, some people seem to stress socialism or simply effective government as ingredients
of the West's political production for export.  The
issue of whether democracy might come to Russia accordingly loses some of its poignancy.  Solzhenitsyn
questions whether it is likely to do so.  In a recent
interview he told Maurice Nadeau:  "In objecting to
my proposals, no one has suggested an alternative
solution that is even remotely practical.  Andrei Sakharov has objected by saying:  'No, we need immediate
democracy.'  I shake him by the hand.  I agree.  We
do need democracy.  But where are we to get it from?
You [the West] won't give it to us. . . .  And, if we
start to seize it by force, this will be the beginning
of our total destruction."  Any observer may conclude
that, considering the immediately preceding decades,

17

Russia is less prepared for instant democracy in 1977
than it was in 1917, though instant democracy is
scarcely in prospect for the USSR.  But Solzhenitsyn's program for putting the rule of law and individual rights first may commend itself to those who
wish democracy for Russia, even if he himself dares
hope for little more in the foreseeable future.

Technologically, Solzhenitsyn and Western en-
vironmentalists seem to speak the same language.
Neither, as far as I know, is in favor of tearing up
power lines.  The Russian peasant may be dark, but I
know of no evidence that he objects to electric
lights.

Technologically, the Soviet regime is avidly
eager to benefit from the West's offerings.  Culturally and politically, the ban on "ideological coexistence" will stop any importations it can.  Like Nicholas I, Brezhnev wants "fire that will not burn."
In the long run he will not get it.

The long run and the short run, to be sure, need
to be distinguished.  The Decembrists' constitutional
thinking was irrelevant to Russia in 1825, very relevant to 1905 and 1917, though ultimately shunted
aside and defeated.  Supposing someone had reported
from Minsk in 1898 that a group of nine men had just
held there a clandestine meeting from which would
come a movement that in half a century would rule a
third of the world.  He could scarcely have hoped
that his editor would print the dispatch, and medical treatment or a nice long vacation might have been
suggested instead.  What matters to the prospects of
religion and Westernization is not how Solzhenitsyn's
thoughts look in 1976 but rather how they may look
several decades hence.  Will Solzhenitsyn's grand-

children or Khrushchev's granchildren win out? Which-
ever group does, the West of today will be part of
what happens. Solzhenitsyn reflects one kind of what
Toynbee called "apparentation and affiliation" with
the West, Khrushchev another. The difference is
great, but it is not total.

Solzhenitsyn writes that the task of the writer--
and one might add, of the religious person whatever
his profession--is not to defend or criticize one or
another form of economy or state organization. "The
task of the writer is to select more universal, eternal questions [such as] the secrets of the human
heart, the triumph over spiritual sorrow, the laws of
the history of mankind that were born in the depths
of time immemorial and that will cease to exist only
when the sun ceases to shine." The flush toilet and
the Fiat may flourish and grace many societies, and
one need not despise their contributions to human
happiness and liberation, but the fundamental issues
will be decided in the midst of the values and commitments of individual human beings.

## NOTES

1. *New York Times Review of Books*, February 28,
1971, p. 4.

2. Paul Hollander, *Soviet and American Society:
A Comparison* (New York: Oxford University Press,
1973), pp. 186-87. Cf. *New York Times*, June 1, 1969;
March 5, 1970.

3. Robert C. Tucker, "Religious Revival in Russia" in Alex Inkeles and Kent Geiger, eds., *Soviet
Society: A Book of Readings* (Boston: Houghton Mif-
flin, 1961), pp. 424-28. Also see this writer's "Religious Renaissance in the Soviet Union," *Journal of
Church and State* (Winter 1977), pp. 21-36.

4. Dunn, "Religious Renaissance."

5. The most complete collection of religious samizdat (self-published) materials is at Keston College (Centre for the Study of Religion and Communism), London.

6. See pp. 9-10 below. For a fuller treatment of Treadgold's views, see his The West in Russia and China, 2 vols. (Cambridge: Cambridge University Press, 1973).

7. Cyril E. Black et al., The Modernization of Japan and Russia (New York: The Free Press, 1975), p. 8.

8. See p. 121 below.

9. Charles M. Fair, The Dying Self (Garden City, New York: Doubleday & Co., Anchor Books, 1970), pp. 246, 250 passim.

10. Black, Japan and Russia, p. 3.

11. For general studies of the cultural Westernization of the world, see William H. McNeill, The Rise of the West (Chicago: University of Chicago, 1963); Arend Th. Van Leeuwen, Christianity in World History (London: Edinburgh House Press, 1964). Also see of course Max Weber's The Protestant Ethic and the Spirit of Capitalism, trans. Talcoot Parsons (New York: Scribner's Sons, 1958)

# PART I

## RELIGION AND SOVIET SOCIETY

# Chapter 2
## TOWARD THE END OF THE OLD REGIME:
## THE STATE, CHURCH, AND DUMA

### Alfred Levin

On October 25, 1910, in the Fourth Session of
the Third Duma, Ivan Semenovich Kliuzhov, Octobrist
Deputy from Samara, rose to speak in defense of the
section of bill offered by the Committee on Public
Education removing parochial schools of the Orthodox Church from the jurisdiction of the Holy Synod
to that of the Ministry of Public Education--a delicate matter indeed.  The debate was fierce, the
atmosphere tense, and the speaker worthy of no little attention.  He was the grandson of one of the
chief figures who had engineered the major educational reforms of the 1860s.  He had dedicated some
thirty-five years to the question of reform and development of the primary school system as a village
teacher, an inspector of public schools, and had
sat as a member of school committees in uiezd and
guberniia zemstvos and in the city councils.  His
folksy, salty manner and his clarity and simplicity
of delivery caught and held the attention of all
elements in the Imperial Duma.[1]  For he was more
familiar with the problems and day-to-day functioning of the primary schools than any of his fellow
deputies.  He was, at the moment, explaining with a
sense of shock, that one village priest had divided

23

primary school pupils into "ours" and "theirs." He
had blessed the "ours" and referred to the "theirs"
as "nemtsy" (foreigners). Kliuzhev knew that under
pressure from the upper hierarchy priests had to attack zemstvo schools and after hearing through the
sermon, a bit too vituperative for his tastes, he
inquired of the priest, "How is it not a sin for you
to censure one school or another here?" The clergyman replied somewhat diffidently, "I'm sorry Ivan
Semenovich, I didn't know you were here."[2]  Then
Kliuzhev remembered that when he was about to leave
the village of Khoroshenko he was appalled by the
request of a local priest.  "Ivan Semenovich, insist in the school council that all girls study in
our schools and the boys in your zemstvo schools."
The deputies giggled.  In reply Kliuzhev asked him
how on earth he or the school council could require
a peasant to send his daughter where he had no heart
to send her.[3]  Kliuzhev was reflecting on matters
that were common knowledge to the deputies:  the
deep divisions and hostilities in Russian society
that had developed around the zemstvo and church
schools in the last two decades of the Old Regime;
the intense pressure on the lower clergy from their
hierarchical and official superiors; and their
parochialism and general level of ignorance.

I shall not dwell here on the condition of the
Orthodox Church at the end of the Old Regime:  the
complete centralization of control over matters of
faith and administration in the Holy synod; the un-
conscionable overburdening of the provincial bishops
with bureaucratic paper and red tape; their frequent and arbitrary transfer from province to pro-

24

vince; the virtual control over their decisions by
their consistories; their impersonal, frequently
harsh, attitude toward the generally semi-literate
village clergy whose small remuneration was supplemented by charges, for sacramental duties, considered exhorbitant by the peasantry; the lifeless
formalism of their services and the spirit of much
of the hierarchy.  These have been documented more
than adequately by intensive studies in the past
four decades.  I will concern myself here with the
attitudes toward the Orthodox hierarchy and its
faith as they are reflected in the Duma debates by
elements of Russian society who had a significant
influence on the course of its development--the
state, representatives of church officialdom, their
supporters and the Duma opposition.  I have always
felt that the chief significance of the Duma lay not
in its accomplishments--these were relatively limited in its brief existence--but in its reflection
of the Russian mind, Russian civilization, at the
beginning of the twentieth century.  It was far from
representative, but the most influential elements
had their spokesmen in it. And it is in that context that I will consider the debates on the church.
Keep in mind that the extreme left was a miniscule
element in the Third and Fourth Dumas when major issues concerning religion were debated.  The Social
Revolutionaries boycotted the Duma.  The Marxists
were a relatively minor quantity and their attitudes
have been too well scouted to be considered here.

  While the Duma's efforts in the area of religious reform were not inconsiderable, its successes
were not particularly great.  The Russian constitution of 1906 and the statutes on the Duma and

25

Imperial Council, modelled largely on German and
Austrian systems, limited parliamentary activities
on budgetary matters relating to the armed forces
and the royal family and in foreign affairs.  But
more seriously, the Duma faced the veto of the semi-
appointive, conservative, sometimes unregenerated
upper house, the Imperial Council, as well as that
of the tsar, always oversensitive about his prerogatives.  Two Weltanschauungen confronted each other
and the powerful "autocracy" and <u>chin</u> proved re-
markably heedless and myopic.  Serious proposals for
change were well nigh equated with revolution or
the threat thereof.  Hence, badly needed renovation
of the church from within, in a universal council,
was postponed and the Duma's major efforts were rejected by the upper house and the tsar.  The state
strove to retain a maximum of its heretofore un-
limited prerogatives in the traditional statist concept while the Duma majority, the opposition in the
debates on religious matters, sought to broaden the
rights of the Orthodox clergy and non-Orthodox
faiths in the name of the civil rights of the individual.  The state applied the strictest interpretation to older laws and the concessions it yielded
in the post-1905 period, while the Duma saw broader
implications in the meaning of the laws and did its
utmost to keep the regime to its original promises.

The Duma's chief successes lay in its efforts
to improve the salaries of the clergy--from about
twelve and a half million rubles in 1908 to almost
nineteen million rubles in 1915--and it raised the
appropriations for the parish schools from about
nine and a half million rubles in 1908 to twenty two

and a quarter million in 1914.[4]  But in most key
ventures its endeavors proved frustrating and fruit-
less.  The "establishment" was unyielding when faced
with the loss of some power to the lower hierarchy
or of the favored position of the established church.

It is not my purpose to follow the weary and re-
petitive debates on all questions concerning religion but rather to concentrate on those which best
reflect the attitudes of the major socio-political
elements in the Duma to provide some inkling of the
intellectual environment--or lack of it, as the
case may be--for the condition of the church and
religion in the few years immediately preceding the
revolutionary and Soviet periods and which did indeed influence the philosophy of the church under
the Soviet regime.  The Imperial Council expunged
some amendments liberalizing the right to change
from one faith to another and efforts at compromise
in a joint committee failed.[5]  Changes by the Duma
in a measure issued under Article 87 of the Fundamental Laws to facilitate the rights of Old Believers to form congregations, worship and preach were
rejected by the Imperial Council and the matter
rested.[6]  No agreement could be reached between the
two houses on uniting all schools funded by the government, including the parochial, under the uiezd
school councils with a budget assigned to the Ministry of Public Education.[7]

The measures concerned were considered and
their fate determined in the course of the Third
Duma, 1907-1912, heavily weighted by the constitu-
tionally questionable Electoral Law of June 3, 1907
in favor of aristocratic, propertied and Russian

elements. Yet this was the most productive of the Russian parliaments largely because it operated under relatively normal circumstances. Under the aegis of the Premier and Minister of the Interior Peter Arkad'evich Stolypin, behaving for all the world like a right wing Octobrist, the administration introduced a series of bills to guarantee the freedom of religious conscience promised under the law of April 17, 1905 and the more general Manifesto of October 17, 1905 guaranteeing religious liberty. Even the Kadets acknowledged that the bills had a liberal ring and were acceptable enough. But efforts by the Duma Committees on Religious Affairs, Old Believer Affairs, Affairs of the Orthodox Church, and Public Education to further liberalize the measures brought irreconcilable splits in these committees and in the Duma.[8]

The most significant bill, on the right to change one's faith, was introduced early in the Third Duma, on November 11, 1907. It proceeded naturally from the law of April 17, 1905 and was based on that decree. It sought to define more exactly the conditions permitted for those who would leave Orthodoxy for a non-Orthodox faith or forsake one non-Orthodox confession for another. Briefly, the bill provided that any Christian reaching the age of 21 might transfer to any other Christian faith without restriction. Those Christians over 21 who had converted to Christianity and whose parents and grandparents were non-Christian could revert to their original faith and all mutual obligations between them and the church they left were considered cancelled. The Committee on Religious Affairs, reporting April 10, 1909, made some significant revisions. It allowed any person over 21 to transfer from any religion to any other provided it was not outlawed. A minor reaching 14 was allowed the same rights if he had permission from his parents or guardians to transfer, and these determined his faith if under 14 years of age. All changes had to be registered by the police within 40 days after submission of a petition therefor. Persons gravely ill were excluded.[9]

Stolypin defended his measure succinctly and forcefully and he thought primarily in terms of the legal relations of church and society to the state and the privileged position of the Orthodox Church under the Fundamental Laws.[10] He warned the Duma of the complexity of the problem since civil and religious relationships of the state with the Orthodox Church were not clearly demarked by law yet they were closely interwoven. The higher the position of the church the more it entered into the state organism, and he fell back on the classic caesaropapist concept. The church had given the state spiritual strength and this had, in turn, lent strength to the church. The state left to the church the right to regulate its dogma and internal affairs, but it had the right to define the political, property, civil and criminal norms arising from the religious conditions of its subjects. The state should strive to bring about a balance between the various interests of religious freedom and the predominant church. And the Duma should ponder its legislation with these considerations in mind. Here Stolypin's characteristic, innate Great Russian

nationalism colored his argument. The demand that
the church run its own affairs apart from the state
arose from the suspicion of the state--and only when
non-Orthodox elements began to participate in the
government. For now the Duma had a part in determining religious policy but the "aliens" (inorodtsy)
in it were to concern themselves only with their own
needs and not purely Russian matters. This was
directly in the spirit of the Manifesto of June 3,
1907 which he had proudly authored. He had studied
the Committee's bill and could support its theoretical precepts, but good theory did not necessarily
mean good practice in the hard realities of the Russian cultural environment. For placing non-Christian faiths on level with Christian would run counter to basic Russian sensibilities.[11] "You will be
guided, I am sure, by considerations of how to reform, how to improve our life, according to new principles without harm to the vital foundations of our
state, the popular spirit united and uniting millions
of Russians . . . . Our task is to adapt Orthodoxy
to the attractive theory of freedom of faith within
the limits of our Russian Orthodox state."[12]

Bishop Evlogii, an archconservative, at least
on matters concerning the privileges of the Orthodox
Church, generally concurred with Stolypin. But he
levelled a special attack on the provision allowing
persons 14 to 20 years of age to leave the church
as provided in the Committee's project. They were
simply not mature enough to make decisions for themselves or their children, should they marry, and he
cited the masses in Cholm who had forsaken Orthodoxy
to rejoin the faith of their forebears, the Uniate

Church, under intense "propaganda" and "terror."
He also assailed the Committee's provision for a
decision within 40 days rather than at the termina-
tion of that period which the Holy Synod had requested in the hearings. And he was especially apprehen-
sive over the exclusion of gravely ill persons from
the requirement; it was an obvious loophole that
could annul the whole bill unless it were more specifically defined. He was considerably disturbed by
the possibility that draftees might change their
faiths while in service. Although the Committee had
refused to drop this provision it would be a cause
of considerable distraction for the soldier and might
generate religious hostility among the troops. In
general, he warned that the bill might bring insta-
bility in public life.

The church could support the government's bill
and certainly its attitude of cautious reform and a
degree of paranoia toward change. Close union of
church and state--shades of Joseph of Volokolamsk--
and a vigorous effort to save what it could of the
privileges and power of both, resting on traditional
statist concepts, marked the attitudes of state and
church officialdom.

The Committee's bill spoke for itself. Its majority which managed to "contain" the reactionary
and moderate, nationalist right, ranged from the mid-
dle-of-the-road Octobrists through the Progressives
and Kadets. Their purpose, with varying degrees of
reservation was to assure the realization of the
rights of the individual in a society with a long,
authoritarian tradition. Emphasis on individual
choice and a minimum of government regulation of

31

religious affairs in its own interests were the basic theses of the bill.

Early in his explanatory statement the reporter for the Committee on Religious Affairs, its Chairman, P. V. Kamenskii, warned of the danger to society inherent in maintaining the statist tradition. He held that in the past, as the church became a major support for the state structure--a royal instrument-- tolerance came to be regarded as a heresy. This had led to military struggles, the death of millions, and repression. And only long and bloody experience brought back a saner sense of toleration.[14] And the liberal leaders hammered away at the theme that hesitation by the state on religious toleration not only confused matters, but brought a weakening of the moral fiber of society. The renowned liberal lawyer, V. A. Maklakov, argued with the precision of a jurist that by refusing to allow change of religious belief the government had long ago accommodated itself to the hypocrisy it begot by forcing an individual to acknowledge a faith which he did not accept. And Kamenskii urged that the concept of freedom of faith would promote sincerity and justness.[15]

The Kadets saw only a negative impact from the policy of state support for one church in its own interests. The deputy from Enissei Oblast, the lawyer A. V. Karaulov, maintained that neither the state nor the church had a need for intolerance. And Makalakov observed that favoring one creed or another on the basis of trustworthiness and permissibility in the state had led not only to the use of inadmissible force but would create confusion in policy concerning the predominant church. For if the state allowed change to Catholicism or Lutheranism, Christian faiths, but not to paganism, it thereby equalized other Christian denominations with Orthodoxy. The Kadet leader, P. N. Miliukov, saw tolerance in Russia as an occasional spark quickly doused by the close union of church and state "on the basis of their mutual service to each other." He concurred with Bishop Mitrofan that matters of faith could not be decided by a majority opinion, the Orthodox. The state simply could not interfere in matters of conscience as in matters material and when it became selective it begot such distorted effects as the identification of the Dukhobors as insupportable anarchists. And the Dukhobor flock would be considered most desirable subjects under normal circumstances. Russia had lost what Canada gained.[16]

The Octobrists emphasized the overwhelming benefits to society and the church that would be garnered from unfettered freedom of faith. D. A. Leanov held that suppressive legislation had brought only wide religious indifferentism and indifference ultimately killed faith. Orthodoxy needed only preachment of love and peace, a high spiritual example demonstrated by the Orthodox clergy, and self government in the parish which brought the church close to the population. "Our Church," Dr. M. Ia. Kapustin added, "does not need the protection of the government, the police, the courts etc., but the vital examples of the apostles must truly permeate our popular life, live in the parishes . . . . From this viewpoint the new principles pronounced by the Monarch and now reinforced [in the Duma's bill] should call forth a regeneration of Our Orthodox faith."[17]

33

The representatives of the national minorities, particularly the Poles, were highly skeptical about the prospects for real liberalization of their religious status. A. I. Parchevskii recalled the fierce repression of the Uniates in the relatively recent past. "Over this area (Cholm) there hangs the bloody nightmare of heavy memories and restrictive laws cannot dispel them. They can be dispelled only by the peaceful, legal course of life." He held that even after the publication of the Law of April 17, 1905 freedom of change was severely restricted by local officialdom. And Father S. G. Matseevich was certain that the pressures, threats, exhortations to which an applicant for change would be subjected in a forth day waiting period would be unbearable.[18]

The obvious alternative to the traditional, authoritarian religious policy, and the major theme of the opposition throughout the debates on religious legislation, was the right of the individual to select the confession of his choice; to declare it and promote it openly. The reporter Kamenskii immediately brought this attitude into focus. Every normal individual reaching maturity "should be allowed the right to believe as his conscience instructs him to select a religious teaching according to his own inner conviction." Miliukov argued vigorously in the classic liberal tradition that "only that state possess real freedom of conscience which offers it as a personal matter for the individual, opening thus full freedom of choice but [also] of creating a private individual viewpoint."[19]

Kamenskii took every opportunity to stress the major differences between the Duma and government bills. The Committee on Religious Affairs had eli-

minated the administration's limitations on the right
to change beliefs.  It did not require any kind of
permission from civil authorities provided the beliefs of a dispensation were not punishable under
the criminal code.  Because the government's bill
violated family interests by not providing for permission to change between the ages of fourteen and
twenty-one the Committee gave parents the right to
make that decision.  And the Committee considered
the period of clerical admonition of backsliders only
as a "bare prinicple" without any obligation whatever
on their part.[20]  Parchevskii preferred the characteristic observation of the ethnic minorities that
the whole matter of religious freedom was closely
bound up with the question of official legality.[21]
Yet he was only expressing one of the fundamental
frustrations of all elements of Russian society that
saw the need for some kind of "renovation."  The
state made its own rules of the game and as frequently violated them.

In his formal presentation to the Duma, the premier had forcefully warned against rash action which
might offend the sensibilities of the Russian people.
The reaction in the Duma ranged from a lament on the
woeful ignorance of the peasant to an assault on the
government for its special concern for Russians and
Orthodox to the exclusion of other ethnic and religious groups, and a denial that the Russians were all
that sensitive.  Miliukov deplored the division of
Russians and Poles into "latins" and Orthodox in 1898
and the tendency to lay the proliferation of sectarian denominations at the door of "aliens."  Speaking
for the Jews N. M. Fridman assailed the limitation
of rights on purely ethnic and religious grounds and

35

Karaulov doubted that sects were offensive to Russians since they were largely Russian in composition. "Proudly the bell towers of the Old Believers soar to the sky. In hail and storm the processions of the Old Believers move on. Freely and unhindered the sectarians sing their psalms and deliver sermons at their meetings and the Orthodox sensibility of the Russian people is not perturbed."[22] And Kapustin scoffed at the idea that Russians might defect to a non-Christian fold.[23]

The logical flaw in the Committee's bill was its inconsistent rejection of the right to hold no faith at all. Curiously enough this fostered no great furor in the otherwise acid debates. Kamenskii, perhaps considering Russian sensitivities, or his own, stated simply that the Committee felt that "at the present time" it could not consider the legalization of a non-believing status under the law of April 17, 1905.[24] The Kadets would naturally lead the attack. Maklakov observed that the government was quite correct in drawing the logical conclusion from the Duma's bill that the right to stand outside of religion had to be recognized, but the administration had, itself, not yet acted on that right. Or, as Miliukov noted, the administration felt that the exclusion of non-believers was not logical but they might serve as a temptation for the faithful. He felt that non-confession might be beneficial for the church. It might cleanse and reanimate it by shriving it of "spiritual corpses."[25] Perhaps the committee's outrageous conclusion was simply the kind of inconsistency that the left of center had come to expect from some Octobrists and the more frenetic elements to their right.

36

A characteristic aspect of the Duma debates and
especially on the matter of religious freedom was
the constant reference to Western models; states
where established churches were maintained. The
government and right leaned heavily on the more conservative Prussian and Austrian arrangements.[26] But
the Duma majority in these debates on bills concerning religion gazed longingly at the more liberalized
Western systems. The Octobrists and Progressives
reflected a combination of liberal and slavophile
strains that they felt in their bones could only
strengthen their "magnificent culture." Kamenskii
held up the Napoleonic code as a basis for legislation in the west. Assailing the official tendency
to combine faith and nationality, Miliukov repeated
Cardinal Newman's doctrine to the effect that "to
live means to change and to be mature means to change
frequently." And he hailed the Cardinal as a representative of a church that was able to adapt itself
to the development of the human spirit. Finally,
Parchevskii bowed deeply in the direction of the
transatlantic west. He held that "this principle
[the right to freedom of conscience] was first sol-
emnly pronounced in the eighteenth century in the
United States of North America after the War for Independence and was gradually introduced in all European countries."[27] And it was in the course of these
debates that he focused squarely on a sense of frustration surely experienced widely by students of
Russian civilization. He bemoaned the circumstance
that he could not "deny that in a difficult situation
orators sometimes appear to whose fate falls the obligation to defend such truths as in essence do not

require or need such proofs.  Among these undoubtedly solid truths, which are by now subject to no
doubt whatsoever in the civilized world, belongs the
right of each citizen to change from one faith to
another."[28]

Discussion of any measure, government or Duma,
liberalizing the status of the Old Believers was
bound to generate an explosive atmosphere and a
scramble to the podium.  The consciences of the
state, the church, and the right were disturbed by
centuries of repression of these dissident but otherwise model and Russian subjects and the Orthodox
hierarchy was more than sensitive to the snobbish
staroverets claim that they alone were the true
church.  For the Duma majority the Old Believers were
the stereotype for victims of a long-enduring, il-
liberal, official policy and an ideal springboard for
a campaign to legislate complete freedom of faith.

The very fact that the Administration's bill
was issued under Article 87 of the Fundamental Laws
(covering a critical matter while the Duma was not in
session) was in itself a considerable irritant for
the Duma.  The Ministry of the Interior submitted
its bill on February 28, 1907--to the Second Duma--
and a special Committee on Old Believer Questions received it in the early sittings of the Third Duma,
in January 1908.  It reported a project on the cre-
tion, rights and duties of Old Believer congregations
on May 8, 1909 and the Duma took it up at once.[29]
The government's bill provided for the free conduct
by the Old Believers of their religious activities
and the founding of congregations for the moral, educational and welfare needs of their members who gath-

38

ered for general prayer in a church or house of worship with the permission of the governor or city prefect. These officials might close the congregation for illegal or immoral activity with the consent of the guberniia or oblast administration. Their opinions could be appealed to the Ruling Senate. Guberniia or oblast administrations accepted or rejected petitions to establish congregations. The congregations were to be governed by a general assembly, an elected council or selected clergy. The clergy, including monks, might use special vestments and monastic and clerical garb. Civil records were to be kept by the council or designated officials and examined monthly by the congregation and annually by the guberniia or oblast administration with a penalty for improper procedure. If there were no congregation, books were to be kept by the elders, or city, or volost administrations.

The Duma made some substantive changes in the Old Believers' bill allowing both freedom of worship and preaching, the holding of conferences and declarative registration (as against permissive) for the establishment of congregations. Their higher clergy were allowed titles equivalent to the Orthodox Church and local clergy were not to be selected by local officials. They were to be designated only by the general assembly of the congregation.[30]

The reporter for the Committee, the Kadet deputy Karaulov, set forth the main terms of the bill, going far beyond his claim that the Duma was only defining the government's terms more exactly. He reemphasized the right to preach; the need for fewer petitioners than in the government's bill to form a congregation (from 50 to 12); declarative registra-

tion with the Office of Societies and Unions, not
the provincial administration; Old Believer clerical
nomenclature and local civil registry if the congregations had any reservations on the matter--all under the concept of freedom conscience.[31]

Assistant Minister of the Interior, S. E. Kry-
zhanovskii, rejoined with a hint of contempt and no
little sarcasm: "The Chairman of the Committee on
Old Believer Affairs relieves me of the task of presenting the government's viewpoint in detail; his
criticism was so comprehensive, so annihilating that
after it I can boldly state that from [the Committee's] conclusions and the charges it has introduced on these . . . .questions there remains no
stone on stone."[32] He emphasized the state's interests based on a strict interpretation of the
Ministry's bill and existing law. He objected to the
broadening of Old Believer rights at the expense of
the Orthodox Church. He rejected out of hand clerical nomenclature for persons the church regarded as
laymen. That would establish the Old Believers as
a parallel church--an unbearable situation. The Old
Believers did not preach but propagandized and un-
limited preaching was permitted only to the established church. One had to know who was given the
right to preach for the Old Believers included a
number of denominations with differing dogmas, some
dangerous to the state and society. He observed
that only the government could regulate the keeping
of their congregational records and he strenuously
objected to an item in the Duma bill which allowed
the holding of clerical or public office by persons
who had committed civil or religious offenses.[33]

Father Iurashkevich, speaking for the church
and the right offered their support for the government's stand in defense of the canonical and legal
interests of the church and the security of the
state and society.  He gave voice to the apprehen-
sions stirred among churchmen by the Old Believers.
Involved was the question of granting complete freedom to a confession which taught that millions of
Russians living and dead were not Christians, were
heretics, and that only they, the Old Believers,
were the rightful church who preserved the faith,
led by splendid people standing firmly for what they
considered sacred.  But the good father rejoined
that they were dogmatically diffuse because they
rested on a rational basis, each understanding the
truth as he saw it.  Their misfortunes, not their
faith made them model subjects.  And it was indeed
idealistic and unrealistic to regard them as developing advanced concepts moving Russian society and
state.  For they were truly dangerous to both church
and state.  He did not hold with supporters of the
Duma's bill that truth would ultimately prevail and
strengthen the Orthodox Church in competition with
the Old Believers and others.  Was it necessary to
lose millions of Orthodox souls in a struggle with
the Old Believers?  They had to be seen in their
true perspective as an element which regarded Orthodoxy as rebellious and sought to undermine it so
that it would be replaced by the cult of nihilism.
And they nourished a tradition of hostility to the
state.[34]

The Duma majority rather assailed the regime
than defend its own position.  And they rallied to

the basic concept of complete and unfettered freedom
of conscience as an inalienable right. Here, too,
on the question of the liberties of the Old Believers,
they charged the government with modifying its own
rules and retreating from promises announced by the
administration or wrenched from it in 1905. And they
argued for the broadest interpretation of the meaning
of the administration's bill. In reporting for the
Duma Committee on Old Believer Affairs, Karaulov
maintained that it had unquestionably provided for
a declarative, purely registrational procedure for
establishing a congregation, but the Ministry now
held for the right of guberniia officials to make
the final decision. It had declared that "If the
entry in the registry is not made a week after the
submission of a statement, the Old Believer congregations by this fact [of submission] is considered
active and recognized as legal." And the ministry's
explanatory statement to the Duma, accompanying its
measure in 1907 held that the guberniia administration had no right to enter into the substantive consideration of Old Believer petitions and only saw to
it that the founding of a religious society was performed legally. Any phrase in the Ministry's bill
not corresponding to the meaning of the legislator
was erroneous.[35]

The Kadet leader Miliukov vehemently concurred.
Since the government disposed of many resources to
turn declarative into permissive registration there
was, in practice, no important difference between
the two. But in principle there was a great difference "insofar as it is connected with freedom of
individual conscience, insofar as declarative con-
firmation of religious congregations is connected

42

with the proper resolution of the question of the relation of the state to religious congregations."[36]

The Octobrist spokesman Kamenskii was firm in his opinion that the Minister of the Interior had clearly demonstrated in his bill that he completely understood the meaning of freedom of faith. For he had declared that the government had an obligation "to indicate the necessary measure to assure to each person the possibility of unhindered realization in practice of the right granted by the grace of the Monarch's will" and the Minister's definition of religious freedom was classic: "Freedom of faith for each person having a sufficiently mature conscience, without hindrance and without any legal hurt, to acknowledge his faith and to present it in the external rituals of his denomination together with other persons confessing the same religious teaching." He read the administration's bill as allowing Old Believers to preach without the red tape in existing law and asked the administration to sign its own work.[37]

Professor Miliukov could not see any distinction between the right to preach and the right to propagandize, under the October Manifesto. "I think we have to realize 'bare dogma'; for propaganda and dogma were intertwined 'blood and flesh'." Non-forcible "perversion" had been eliminated from the new criminal code and the law of April 17, 1905 sought to ameliorate punishments for religious offenses. Yet but a year later, the law of March 14, 1906 in its notorius Article 90, punished by imprisonment any preachment to convert an Orthodox to another religion or sect, thus, nullifying the articles of the Code

43

and contradicting the principle it intended to realize. The farther from the moment of pronunciation of the principle of the law of April 17, 1905, the weaker and more indecisive the law on freedom to preach became and might not be realized at all. No one was calling for unconditional preaching--only that the regime hold to the viewpoint stated on February 20, 1905 that the meaning of freedom of conscience included "the right of each person to state his faith and convince those who do not belong to it to adopt the teaching preached by him." He maintained that official qualifications came under pressure from the Holy Synod in a note of December 22, 1907--a rejection of the entire principle of legislation.[38]

The adversary position was clearly presented here in terms of a consistently irritating and infuriating characteristic of the bureaucracy--a constant and arbitrary changing of grounds for action.

Several deputies insisted that freedom to practice faith, especially preaching, was in the state's best interests. Kamenskii pointed out that the church itself clearly understood that parishes, including Old Believer, were a source of strength for Russian society while exclusion from them generated sectarianism. Thus, preaching as one of their functions could not be regarded as a threat to Orthodoxy. At any rate, the Old Believers were allowed to preach in churches and hold processions under existing law. Public preaching was permitted but regulated under the law of March 4, 1906 and complete prohibition of preaching for non-orthodox would only bring legal chaos.[39]

Miliukov exhorted the Duma to put the whole

matter of Old Believer rights in the proper legal
order "for interested persons. . . . If there is no
firm basis in law the population will petition high
administrative institutions" and local authorities
who had no guidelines to apply the law of April 17,
1905. "Public order will not allow for the neglect
of several million Russians."[40] He saw no merit at
all in the argument that identical nomenclatures for
office would threaten the position of the church.
Can there be any doubt, he asked if one regards the
other with hostility? "If there is a Bulgarian tsar
is the right and position of the Russian tsar subject
to any danger or limitation? Will the population
confuse the two tsars?" It was just as difficult to
confuse an Old Believer archbishop and a Muscovite
metropolitan. They will exist, these titles, whether specifically legalized or not. And it was not
much of a step to legalize a term once it became common usage.[41]

In pressing the point that tolerance made for
an orderly society the Duma orators never tired of
portraying the Old Believers as the tsar's most desirable subjects who had been martyred unnecessarily
for promoting the cause of "the freedom of spiritual
life." The Russian nationalist Ermolaev, a staroverets, underscored his nationalist tradition. He
observed that the Most Reverend Bishop Mitrofan had
recognized "that when our fatherland underwent a
trial recently [the Japanese war] the Old Believers
forsook their closed, isolated position; for their
Russian national heart it was unbearable to witness
the debasement to which the Russian name was subjected. Hence there began an extensive drawing together of Old Believer and Russian Orthodox people. .

45

. .they acknowledged a common race and brotherhood and they went hand in hand to reform the country."[42]

The irrepressible Kamenskii quoted church authorities profusely to bear witness to the staunch patriotism of the Old Believers.  The Metropolitan of Kiev, Platon, a member of the Holy Synod, had declared in a pastoral statement that the Old Believers were not only related to the Russian Orthodox by blood, but stemmed from the same Orthodox faith. Christianity allowed for various forms of worship, and Orthodoxy only partly differed from the Old Believers in external forms.  And Archbishop Nikon of Vologda had referred to the Old Believers as "sacred preservers of sacred ancient rituals and covenants." Kamenskii asserted that any fear that freedom of preaching would lead to religious and ultimately political anarchy was least applicable to the Old Believers for they had always been loyal sons of the tsar.  In the 1860s they were not attracted by emigration or liberalism.  In 1905 they were on the side of law and order and persecution had not diminished their loyalty to tsar and country just as Avvakum had written Alexei Mikhailovich from Pustozersk Prison:  "The more you torture us the more we love you."[43]  The speaker vividly reflected a millenial Russian tradition--the identification of church and national spirit as a positive source of strength in Russian society.

The strong westernist strain emerged sharply in the exhortations of the liberal leader, Pavel Miliukov.  The history professor could not forego the temptation of an inspiring lecture.  The Russian state had changed considerably since Peter I.  Before his reign it was theocratic-patriarchal, and

now under Russian law the monarch was not its owner
but one of its organs, the head of the state, and
this evolution could not have come about without
the significant change in relations between church
and state.  The prepetrine regime was ruined together
with the theocratic view of the predominance of the
church over the state whereby its very existence was
placed under the sanction of the church which regarded the state only as its lay arm.  If that view
had prevailed the petrine reform would have been un-
thinkable.  Peter had undoubtedly damaged the church
spiritually but at the same time "he put us on the
road of civilized European nations.  We can never re-
trieve that step nor should we condemn it" and Russia could return to the church its soul "in turning
from absolute government to representative government
. . . . and when the church standing on an antiqua-
ted viewpoint, warns that an effort to introduce into
Russia. . . .a principle. . . laid down in the great
[petrine] reform, threatens ruin for the church. . .
we answer we have no fear.  The principle of freedom is a vital principle; it will give you the living
water you need so much and have needed from the time
of the petrine reform."[44]

Subtly emerging from this essentially positivist view of a church-state relationship is a firm
secular emphasis most concretely expressed by Miliukov.  In his opening statement on the Duma bill he
maintained that the entire presentation of the question should have been radically different.  "No one
has said that we should speak not as the representatives of the mission of one church or another. . . .
but that we are here in one category--as legislators,
and that on this law as on all others subject to our

47

examination we should view it exclusively from a legislative and state viewpoint." The Duma was simply not competent legally or by expertise to deal with matters arising from canon law. Like the pre-parliamentary legislators, operating on canonical grounds, it would have to consider legislation on Old Believer rights in terms of proximity or distance from the Orthodox Church and for this it would have to be guided not only by police considerations, but also by those of the Holy Synod or missionaries who alone were regarded as competent to decide on how harmful a sect might be in relation to the established church--a situation untenable for the Duma. And the professor was certain along with the Metropolitan Mitrofan that the Old Believers would resolve the question of freedom of faith exactly as did the Orthodox Church--they would simply not permit it.[45]

Another prickly item which begot acute polarization in the Duma was the section on Orthodox parochial schools of the bill reported on December 10, 1910 by the Committee on Public Education. The Ministry of Public Education had introduced a bill two years earlier, on January 8, 1908, which called on the organs of local self-government, the zemstvos and city dumas, to plan and realize an empire-wide elementary school network. It would allot church schools receiving state funds the same subsidy as those under the Ministry of Public Education. The Duma committee rejected this concept and allotted an increase of nine million rubles to the public schools over a ten year period and of a million and a half rubles to the Holy Synod for the parish schools. The clerical administration was to appoint the head-

masters of these schools and its representatives
were to sit on the county and provincial school councils of the public schools. But parochial schools
subsidized by the government were placed under the
jurisdiction of the Ministry of Public Education.[46]
This bill generated essentially the same attitudes
as those which emerged from the parliamentary wrangle
over Old Believer rights and freedom of faith. State
and church officials were concerned about the rights
of the established church and the fate of Orthodoxy.
The Duma assailed the special position of the Orthodox Church and its ineffectiveness as a spiritual
body.

L. A. Kasso, the Administrator of the Ministry
of Public Education, saw no grounds at all for uniting church and secular schools under a single administration. Uniformity was not always fruitful.[47]
The Ober Prokurator of the Holy Synod, Luk'iakov,
rested his case for the continued separation of
public and parish schools on the caesaropapist concept. In contrast to the adversary positions of
church and state in the west regulated by concor-
dats, he depicted an idyll of a church and state
acting together peacefully and beneficially for the
good of the Russian community--bound not only by
juridical norms but by moral values. Both public
and parochial schools worked toward the same educational end and to develop the same love for the
mother country. Only the clergy could instill true
moral-religious values and teaching of this order
had been a tradition of Russian, Christian society
from its beginning. He warned that the Duma's bill
would demoralize the clergy after their considerable
effort to develop the parish school system since the

1880s and he foresaw a sharp reaction from the laity who supported these schools if they lost jurisdiction over them and the great treasure they had invested in them.[48]

The chief proponents of independent parish schools, V. N. Lvov and Bishop Evlogii, insisted that there was no real clash of interest between state and church schools. That antagonism had been stimulated by the leadership of elements who felt strongly about each type of institution, and by the press. Parochial schools were necessary for the teaching of religious subjects in a religious spirit and they were a strong preventative against the dissemination of revolutionary ideas.[49] "If the priest does not convince the teacher and estranges him, if the teacher considers himself an independent competitor and not a loyal aid of the priest then the moral significance of the school is lost and can easily be turned into a danger to the state."[50] They warned, moreover, that the Duma was encroaching dangerously on the powers of the Holy Synod through which the tsar worked his will in matters religious.[51]

The Duma constitutional majority assailed the parish schools as creations and creatures of the state instituted for its own purposes. According to deputy Kliuzhev they proliferated under pressure from Constantine Pobedonostsev. After the publication of the rules on church schools on June 13, 1884 the bishoprics, school officials, and public figures were swamped with open rescripts and secret circulars calling on them to open parish schools, and governors and land captains were hard at work

setting them up.  Thus, their number rose from about
1,700 to 40,000 at the moment (1910).[52]  The Muslim
deputy Enikeev, Fridman, speaking for the Jews, and
Garusevich for Poles could see the parish schools
only as repressive instruments for the state.  Re-
lentlessly they drove hard for russification without
regard for the sensitivities of the border peoples.[53]
These minority representatives were chagrined and
frustrated by the consistent bureaucratic retreat
from relatively liberal positions on sensitive issues.  They regarded religious instruction in their
schools by teachers of other faiths as a facet of a
general russification policy and in the name of state
interests.  An effort to set up a society in Warsaw
to offer primary education for Polish workers was
rejected on grounds that it would isolate the Poles
and lead to a disturbance of public order.[54]  Enikeev asserted that "the schools that now operate
in the border areas are finished, they have been diverted into a missionary, political swarm. . . .
It's a habit of our old bureaucratic government to
say one thing and do another. . . .  In regard to
school matters the Council of Ministers has no doubt
that [it] cannot and should not pursue the goals of
russification in [the Muslim] area since the character and manner of thought of the people is developed
under the influence of religion, the family and society and not under the influence of outside knowledge obtained by instruction."[55]

Deputy Kliuzhev was especially articulate in
expressing a view widely held among the intelligentsia that the church schools were simply not doing
their job.  He observed that former Ober Prokurator,
D. A. Tolstoi, had not involved the clergy in teach-

51

ing because they were not properly prepared for it.
He quoted experts on the church schools to the effect that they were poorly educated, learned the gospel by rote and were not equipped to apply it to resolve the perplexities of their folds. To turn the
church schools over to the clergy would be a "two-
fold lie" which would only stimulate sectarianism.
The zemstvo schools of his native Samara were far
more attractive to the faithful largely because of
their competence in religious education.[56]

It was in the context of this debate on control of church schools that open and implied anti-
clericalism was most clearly pronounced in the Duma.
Professor Miliukov perhaps best exemplified this attitude in his emphasis on the long tradition, since
Peter I, of bureaucratic, that is, lay control over
the church schools. With some heat he attacked V.
N. Lvov's interpretation of Peter's Spiritual Regulation of 1721 to prove that the church alone had
regulated its schools. Lvov was thinking of Patri-
archs Filaret and Nikon, of a state within a state,
and his clericalism as an ideal for education was
truly something new; the first declaration of this
sort in the Duma.[57]

Finally, the liberal, humanistic concept of
public education emerged from the school debates
tinged more than lightly, if philosphically, with a
nationalistic hue. Kliuzhev was certain that the
fatherland would welcome any school head--clerical
or lay--who had a proper religious training for presenting religious studies. And if the schools were
unified there would be no cause for the village
priest to separate "theirs" and "ours" and he would
bless all the sons and daughters. Early in his

evaluation of the Duma's measure, Miliukov contrasted
the ritualistic and humanistic purposes of church and
public schools respectively. The parochial schools
were established for no other purpose than to compete
with the public network. "The lay school wants to
free the personality, the religious school wants to
repress it. . . . The ideal of the lay teachers. . .
is to develop initiative, to develop a conscious relationship to surrounding life, nature and society,
to instill in their students. . . .the joy of life,
to give the people a developed mind and firm will."
Spokesmen for the church schools in the Committee on
Public Education would teach Church Slavonic, religious singing and preparation for the sacraments.
The choice between them was not difficult for anyone who wanted the schools to prepare the country
with the best and most modern means in the competition between nations.[59]

The reporter for the Committee on Public Education added a further piquant touch highly acceptable
to the constitutional center. He was proud of the
fact that women were being recruited by the teaching profession. ". . . .the Russian woman has demonstrated her capabilities in pedagocial matters";
that women could act as teachers, administrators and
in educational councils to broaden the contingent of
expertise in matters educational.[60]

The progressive priests in the Third Duma represent something more than a fascinating diversion.
They offer a new perspective for participation by
men of the cloth in Russian public life in the twentieth century and a justification therefor. They
were following an old tradition, but in a new frame
of reference. There were generally five of them and

53

never more than seven (in the first two sessions, 1907-1909)--a mere handful. To realize some impact on the work of the committees they joined the Progressive Fraction, the most congenial politically. They shared its views on political questions but were somewhat more radical on social issues. They served on its bureau and sat as its representatives on the Duma's Budget, Labor and Finance Committees and on the Committees on Public Education and Orthodox Affairs. They assumed a special importance in the latter Committee with Fathers A. A. Popov as Chairman and I. V. Titov as Vice Chairman.[61]

These progressive clergy held a significant position in the religious life of Russia in the early twentieth century largely because of their emphasis on social justice as the justification for their aggressive participation in public life and in opposition to the general conservatism and Great Russian nationalism common to the hierarchy--a position which was to carry over into the Soviet period. And they sounded not unlike the pochvennik slavophiles, and later Pasternak, in their insistence that Christ first raised the status of the individual: "A person is not a slave because he is the son of God. . . ." He is no building material but a builder, he is in the image of God. He has an absolute value and should not be sacrificed to any welfare without his consent. Thus, the inviolability of person, home, correspondence could procede only with the consent of the individual through proper legal procedures.[62] And their program called for the protection of all civil liberties with the implication that true Christianity could not succeed without them, and for separation of church and state.[63]

This fistful of progressive clergy brings into
focus the whole matter of cultural standards--they
were promoting western standards in opposition to the
six-century statist tradition; standards held to be
non-indigenous to Russian civilization.

These attitudes were, of course, not unexpected
in the westernist, moderate and left-of-center liberal, constitutionalist tradition. The Third Duma
was the product of a manipulated electoral system.
Yet it continued to give support, in perhaps more
elegant and measured tones than its short-lived predecessors, to the fundamental antagonisms generated
by the policies and mores of the old regime. This
criticism could no longer be stifled but the harsh-
ness of its tone surprised the bureaucracy. The main
body of the Octobrists was "lefting" and the Kadet
leadership could be unmistakably, if subtly, nation-
alistic--somewhat in the Decembrist tradition. And
in the combined assault on the regime, His Majesty's
opposition--both loyal and suspect--gave voice in
these debates on the relationship between church and
state and society to propositions that had been the
order of the day since the French Revolution in
Western Europe. Some, as the Polish deputy Parchev-
ski had observed, needed defense only in the context
of the Russian political scene--like freedom to
preach without hindrance. And the entire center insisted on at least a modicum of proper legal behavior within the parameters set by the regime itself.
But in this struggle for the acceptance of essentially basic freedoms for the expression and defense
of individual dignity, the constitutionalist element

55

in Russian society stood pretty much alone in promoting freedom under parliamentary government as the road to a politically and spiritually stronger society. They delved deeply into the traditional Russian past to recall a vital church that had provided a true leadership for the national spirit in times of crisis--a source of positive strength in Russian society. The westernists and slavophiles were not that far apart in 1910.

NOTES

1. Gosudarstvennaia Duma, Stenograficheskie otchety, tretii sozyv, sessia 4, (St. Petersburg, 1908-1912), p. 420. (hereafter cited as SOGD, III)

2. SOGD III, 4, pp. 422-423.

3. Ibid., p. 435.

4. John S. Curtiss, Church and State in Russia; the Last Years of the Empire 1900-1917 (New York: Columbia University Press, 1940), pp. 347, 349-350.

5. Ibid., p. 325.

6. Obzor deiatel'nosti gosudarstvennoi dumy tret'iago sozyva, 1907-1912 gg. Chast' vtoraia. Zakonodatel'naia deiatel'nosti sostavlen kantselariei gosudarstvennoi dumy (St. Petersburg: Gosudarstvennaia tipografiia, 1912), vol. 2 p. 51 (hereafter cited as Obzor deiat.).

7. Ibid., pp. 423-424, 426; Gosudarstvennaia duma, otchet Frakstsii Narodnoi Svobody vol. 5 (St. Petersburg, 1908-1912) p. 69 (hereafter cited as Otchet Fr. N. S.).

8. Ibid., pp. 32033.

9. Obzor deiat., pp. 55-56; Curtiss, Church and State, p. 323.

10. SOGD III, 2, p. 1754.

11. Ibid., pp. 1755–1767.

12. Ibid., p. 1767.

13. Ibid., pp. 1765–1777.

14. Ibid., pp. 1741–1742, 1981.

16. Ibid., pp. 1784, 1882, 1900–1901, 1907–1908.

17. Ibid., pp. 1777–1778, 1779, 2070–2071.

18. Ibid., pp. 1880–1881, 2048–2049.

19. Ibid., pp. 1740, 1906.

20. Ibid., pp. 1740, 1741, 1746, 1750–1751, 1752.

21. Ibid., p. 1881.

22. Ibid., pp. 1744, 1884–1885, 1903–1905, 1921–1922.

23. Ibid., p. 2070.

24. Ibid., pp. 1748–1749.

25. Ibid., pp. 1748–1749, 1983, 1906.

26. Ibid., pp. 1762–1763.

27. Ibid., pp. 1743, 1874, 1902–1903.

28. Ibid., p. 1873.

29. Obzor deiat., pp. 58–60.

30. Ibid., pp. 60–61.

31. SOGD, III, 2, pp. 1006–1010.

32. Ibid., p. 1025.

33. Ibid., pp. 1023–1029, 1413–1416, 1419–1420.

34. Ibid., pp. 1031–1036.

35. Ibid., pp. 1410–1412.

36. Ibid., pp. 1224-1225.

37. Ibid., pp. 1042-1044.

38. Ibid., pp. 1222-1224.

39. Ibid., pp. 1045-1046.

40. Ibid., p. 1218.

41. Ibid., pp. 1220-1221.

42. Ibid., pp. 1035, 1037-1038.

43. Ibid., pp. 1046-1048.

44. Ibid., pp. 1226-1227.

45. Ibid., pp. 1214-1216, 1225-1226.

46. Obzor deiat., pp. 423-424, 426; Otchet Fr. N. S., 3:66, 4:56-57; SOGD, III, 4, p. 6.

47. SOGD, III, 4, pp. 6-7.

48. Ibid., pp. 165-180.

49. Ibid., pp. 17-44, 121-128.

50. Ibid., pp. 130-131.

51. Ibid., pp. 36-42.

52. Ibid., pp. 421-422.

53. Ibid., pp. 308-310, 317-318, 329, 334-335, 534.

54. Ibid., pp. 305-317.

55. Ibid., pp. 332-333, 334-335.

56. Ibid., pp. 424, 427-434.

57. Ibid., pp. 101-104.

58. Ibid., p. 436.

59. Ibid., p. 99.

60. Ibid., p. 15.

61. Voprosy viery i tserkvi v III-ei gosudarstvennoi dumie. Otchet gruppy progressivnykh svia-
shchennikov gosudarstvennoi dumie (St. Petersburg:
1912), pp. 79-80. Father I. V. Titov replaced Father
A. A. Popov in the Budget Committee when he left the
Duma after the second session when the church un-
frocked him. Fr. P. N. Ispolitov sat on the Finance
Committee and on the Committee for Orthodox Affairs
as did Fr. V. S. Sokolov along with Frs. M. I. Sin-
derko and V. D. Solukha until they left the group.
Fr. V. V. Klimov was in the Labor Committee and Fr.
Titov sat on the Committee for Public Education,
Ibid., pp. 36-37, 79-80.

62. Ibid., pp. 40-41, 81-82.

63. Ibid., pp. 8-14.

Chapter 3
## RELIGIOUS ADMINISTRATION AND MODERNIZATION

Walter Sawatsky

In June 1975 the basic "Law on Religious Associations" passed in April 1929 was amended.[1] Although a quick initial reading of the changes produced puzzled stares among several experts, a careful examination reveals several major changes. Of greatest significance is the fact that the Council for Religious Affairs (henceforth CRA) set up in 1965 and long criticized by Soviet dissidents as lacking a legal foundation, has now had its existence and functions legitimized in law. Technically speaking it was not acting illegitimately before this, since a series of 1962 amendments to the 1929 law provided it with a legal foundation, but these were not made public.[2] It might now be correct to consider the Council for Religious Affairs the legal successor of the Permanent Commission on Religious Matters created in 1930 whose authority was written into the 1932 published amendments of the "Law on Religious Associations." At any rate the CRA's existence, powers, and functions are a matter of public record and having been written into the basic "Law on Religious Associations", one can now expect this administrative unit to share in the longevity that the basic law itself has come to enjoy.

Although the 1975 amendments clearly indicate the general powers and functions of the CRA, another striking feature of the amendments is the tendency at several points to be less specific than formerly, giving wide-ranging discretionary powers to the CRA instead. This means that the CRA not only has wide powers on paper, it exercises even more influence in practice and inclines one, therefore, to inquire more closely into its structure and into the personalities who head it. An authoritative interpretation of the "Law on Religious Associations" as amended in 1975 appeared in October 1975.[3] This is somewhat more forthcoming than the law itself regarding the CRA's structure, but it is still true that the CRA maintains an unnecessarily low public profile. An inquiry into the structure and personalities of the CRA must rely rather heavily, therefore, on the piece-meal information provided by samizdat (self-published) and oral sources.

From the time of its inception in late 1965 as a combination of the Council for the Affairs of the Russian Orthodox Church under the USSR Council of Ministers (hereafter CROCA) and the Council for the Affairs of Religious Cults under the USSR Council of Ministers (hereafter CARC), the CRA and its predecessors have been charged by Orthodox and Baptist dissidents with violating Soviet law by engaging in activity contrary to its public proclamations. When the CRA's predecessors were set up in 1943-44, Georgi Karpov, who headed CROCA from 1944-60 described its function vaguely as maintaining

> contact between the Government and the
> Patriarch of Moscow and All Russia in af-
> fairs requiring Government decision. While

61

> interfering in no way in the internal
> life of the Church, the Council contri-
> butes to the further normalization of re-
> lations between Church and State, super-
> vising the correct and timely implemen-
> tation of Laws and Decrees of the Govern-
> ment concerning the Russian Orthodox Church.[4]

The emphasis appeared to be that it was a body for
conducting liaison between church and state and that
it was responsible for ensuring that state laws were
kept. In their famous letter to President Podgorny
in December 1965, the Orthodox priests Eshliman and
Yakunin charged, however, that the Council for Orthodox Affairs during 1957-64 had "radically changed
its function from being an official department for
arbitration. . . .[and] had become an unofficial and
illegal control over the Moscow Patriarchate."[5]
These and sharper criticisms have also been made of
the CRA since then, a recent samizdat publication
designating it "an organ for terrorizing priests and
interfering with their work."[6] Orthodox critics in
particular have demanded that the CRA observe Soviet
law, implying that the council, if properly performing its duties, could serve as guarantor of freedom
of conscience. With the publication of the 1975
amendments to the "Law on Religious Associations"
which provide the CRA with a constitution, the state
has fulfilled the Eshliman-Yakunin request "to place
all activities of CROCA under the conditions of legal
publicity," although perhaps not "to submit it to
systematic public control," as was also called for.[7]
In light of these recent developments what prospects
are there for a "return to Soviet legality" and can
one view the CRA as the administrative device for
guaranteeing freedom of conscience?

It would be wrong to seek an answer to this question by restricting oneself to Soviet history and the ideologically motivated struggle to overcome the last vestiges of religion that have managed to survive in a communist state committed to "scientific atheism." Several of the fundamental problems an administrative unit, such as the CRA, is intended to solve go back in history at least to the time of Peter the Great. Therefore, it is proposed here to set the question of state administration of religion within the framework of the long term modernization of the Russian Empire.

Modernization and modernity are terms lacking in precision but probably no less useful than the historian's short hand reference to earlier periods such as the Renaissance. In this book it is used to indicate a general pattern of development from an agrarian to an industrialized society thanks to the growth of man's knowledge and his increasing ability to harness the forces of nature. Modernization contains the element of _dirigisme_ well described in Marc Raeff's definition of modernity as:

> society's conscious desire to maximize all
> its resources and to use this new poten-
> tial dynamically for the enlargement and
> improvement of its way of life. The po-
> tential of resources included not merely
> material products and riches, but intel-
> lectual and cultural creations as well.[8]

As applied to the subject of state administration of religion, Raeff's general line of argument is quite apropos, for he argues for the beginning of an implicit modernizing ideology under the absolute despots, those enlightened rulers who had come to the conclusion that "the subjects' welfare and prosperity would increase productivity. . . .which in turn would rebound to the benefit of the state and the ruler's power. . . ."[9] Thus, he traces the development of interventionist and regulatory police states (polizeistaat) with rulers attempting to refashion existing corporate bodies and institutions into efficient tools for centralized planning and administration. The "well-ordered police state" was able to develop most rapidly in those countries in which the power of the church had been broken, that is, particularly in Protestant lands. The rulers benefitted as well from cooperation with Protestant clerics who sought to foster general education and who now viewed work in the secular sphere as a calling.

## PETRINE AND ALEXANDRINE MODERNIZATION ATTEMPTS

The Great Reforms of Tsar Peter I were thoroughly imbued with this type of a modernizing ideology. Central to his reforms was the creation of a strong army with a functioning governmental administration to support it. Peter's Russia, however, lacked the necessary corporate bodies and institutions for carrying out the grand reforms, most of which were simply copied from German models. The major corporate body controlling education and communication with the population was the Orthodox Church, led by a patriarch with power and prestige nearly equal to that of the tsar and certainly not committed to modernization along the Western guidelines that Peter had in mind. Peter, therefore, thought it vital both in order to secure his shaky hold on the throne and for the interests of state to break the independent power of the church.

Specifically this meant the abolition of the patriarchate and its replacement by an Ecclesiastical College. The Spiritual Regulation of 1721 which created the Ecclesiastical College and spelled out the legal basis for church administration remained in effect till 1917. It "was to be little more than the appropriate government bureau for administering ecclesiastical--as distinct from military or foreign --affairs."[10] The name was changed almost immediately to the Orthodox Holy Synod and the hierarchs tried in various ways to raise the prestige of the synod above that of the other colleges, but in reality it was now "a government bureau charged with administering the church in the name of the tsar."[11]

The Spiritual Regulation of 1721 clearly placed the church under the tsar's direct control. Synod members had to swear an oath of allegiance in which they acknowledged the tsar as the "Supreme Judge" of the church. Final approval of all hierarchical appointments was reserved for the tsar. In fact the distinction between the realm of Caesar and that of God was almost entirely blurred, Peter even demanding in the Supplement to the Regulation that the priest was obliged to report the secrets of the confessional if the sins confessed, both potential and actual, were in any way treasonous or rebellious.[12] The synod immediately established a chancellery for conducting its business affairs and again the tsar specified that the _chinovniki_ in the synodal offices were to be considered a part of the general state administrative structure, receiving similar salaries and being eligible for promotion to other departments of state. As the tsar's personal represen-

65

tative to the synod, Peter created the office of
Ober Prokurator, specifying that this individual was
to be "the eyes of the tsar," reporting all synodal
discussions and decisions to the tsar and reporting
the tsar's instructions to the synod.  He was, however, not to preside; that was left to the senior
hierarch on the synod.  Within four years Peter had
died and the rulers during the remaining part of the
century lacked the power to exercise fully the rights
of control granted to them by the Spiritual Regulation.  Till 1803 the office of Ober Prokurator remained largely ornamental so that key hierarchs in
the synod ran the church, dealing directly with the
tsar and his officials.  The synodal bureaucrats
found it in their best interests to align themselves
with the hierarchs.[13]

This subordination of the Orthodox Church to the
tsar through the creation of a Holy Synod represents
a fundamental change enabling a modernizing tsar to
restrict a potential body of opposition and to re-
direct its considerable energy and influence along
lines conforming to state interests, even if at
first the reform was largely formal.  Much less well
known is another fundamental change that showed more
clearly Peter's modernist outlook.  In May 1721 Peter ordered the synod "to assume specific responsibility from the College of Foreign Affairs for all
churches of the Roman, Lutheran, and Calvinist confessions located within the boundaries of the Russian
state."[14]  The synod was to keep detailed records of
churches and clergy, ratifying the appointments of
clergy.  In fact it even found itself approving the
building of new Lutheran churches and schools in the

Baltic region, his empire now included sizable sections of the population whose religious affiliation
was non-Orthodox. With these Peter followed a policy of limited tolerance, guaranteed at first by trea-
ty. More problematic was the relationship with the
Orthodox schismatics who had broken away in 1666 and
represented more than 20 percent of the population
by the early 18th century. With these Peter followed a policy of harrassment through fines and severe penalties.[15] After Peter's death the synod's
control over the other religious confessions lapsed
except for their continuing attempts to restrict the
growth of the schismatics or Old Believers.

Thus, at the end of his reign Peter had introduced legislation placing the administration of the
dominant church under the state and made the Holy
Synod responsible for administering all religious
affairs in the empire, thereby creating a secular
state with a department for regulating religious
matters. To write and sign such legislation of this
sort may indicate a modernist outlook, but it did not
yet mean that these reforms would be put into execu-
tion that easily. In fact, these two problems--the
subordination of the Orthodox Church to the state
and the creation of an administrative unit to produce
and regulate a standard religious policy enabling the
full maximalization of resources for a well-ordered
state--have long been an important concern of the
state. The present CRA formed in 1965 is not unlike
its predecessors, sharing even the similar difficulties of enforcement and is perhaps most strikingly
similar to the Ministry of Religious Affairs set up
in 1817.

In a very real sense the great church reforms

introduced by Peter were finally realized by Tsar
Alexander I and his minister Prince Alexander N.
Golitzyn during the first quarter of the 19th century.
First of all the reign marks a watershed for the
Russian Orthodox Church for it was with Golitsyn
that the office of Ober Prokurator became the most
important in the administration of the church.  Several of Golitsyn's predecessors, particularly his immediate predecessor Iakovlev (1803) had attempted to
assert the rights granted to the Ober Prokurator by
the Spiritual Regulation without success.  Thanks to
Golitsyn's personal intimacy with the tsar and his
own considerable diplomatic skill he was able in less
than a decade to make the synod an obedient instrument of his will and that of the tsar's.[16]  Despite
Golitsyn's success at realizing more fully than ever
before the intentions of the Petrine church reforms,
his achievements were complicated and frustrated by
his and Tsar Alexander's attempt to foster a specific religious ideology, Pietist Christianity.

   With the advent of Nicholas I, Orthodoxy re-
gained its former dominant status, becoming a major
kingpin of the empire.  The slogan "Orthodoxy, Nationality and Autocracy" introduced under the new
tsar remained current till the end of the century.[17]
Administratively the other religious confessions continued to be administered by a Department for Religious Affairs for Foreign Confessions (under the Ministry of Interior), part of the Dual Ministry introduced by Golitsyn in 1810.  Although Golitsyn himself was frustrated, the office of Ober Prokurator
remained powerful and was in fact given ministerial
status in the 1860s.  Legally the Russian Orthodox
Church was still referred to as the "Greko-Russian

Confession," another change introduced by Golitsyn
to reduce Orthodoxy to a position of equality with
other religions.[18]

## DUMA AND PROVISIONAL GOVERNMENT GOAL:  FREEDOM OF CONSCIENCE

What was implicit in Golitsyn's approach to
church matters finally became explicit in 1905 when
the state finally decided it was in its best interest
to grant freedom of conscience.  Specifically it
meant that the non-Orthodox confessions and sects
were granted legal rights, particularly several sects
whose membership was ethnically Russian.  Theoretically it meant that the religious confessions could
no longer rely on artificial state support to prop
up their institutions and citizens of the empire had
the right to make a free choice between the various
religious ideas and communities offered to them.[19]

According to official statistics for the year
1897, the government claimed that 69.4 percent out
of a total population of 125.6 million belonged to
the Orthodox Church.  This included, however, all
Old Believers which Ober Prokurator Pobedonostsev
had estimated as totalling 13 million in 1895.  That
would mean that the ruling Orthodox Church represented only 59 percent of the population and even then
one is inclined to suspect these official figures as
being inflated.  These figures clearly indicate that
by 1900 state support of the Orthodox Church meant
that it was ignoring the wishes of at least 41 percent of the population.  There was a detailed break-
down of membership in other confessions but significantly, no category for atheists.  That might have
reduced the Orthodox majority still more.[20]

In 1904 Metropolitan Antony Vadkovskii, presiding member of the synod, appointed a committee of liberal professors to work out suggestions for reform. The resulting memorandum was presented to Count Witte who made full use of it. A key question put in the memorandum was: "would it not be better to allow the church to manage its own affairs and so increase its vitality?"[21] In March 1905 thirty-two parish clergy signed a manifesto with the approval of Metropolitan Antony in which they said:

> The forthcoming liberation of the religious conscience from external restraint is welcomed with great spiritual joy by all true members of the Orthodox Church. The Church will at last be cleared of the heavy charge of violating and suppressing religious freedom. This was formerly done in her name under the pretense of defending her, but it was done against her will, and against her spirit.[22]

There was a fairly widespread feeling in the church in favor of reform although churchmen differed on the direction it was to take. To a degree liberals in favor of freedom of conscience and democratization of the church administration were most influential during 1905. In subsequent Dumas the conservatives, more strongly represented in the hierarchy, took over and reform discussions began to center on the recreation of the patriarchate. Actual work on reforms had fizzled out by 1912 but the question was confronted anew under the Provisional Government. As on other policies, the Provisional Government was extremely slow in introducing changes into the religious sphere, the law granting full religious liberty finally coming on July 19, 1917. A month earlier the office of Ober Prokurator had been abolished and

70

a Ministry of Confessions created in its stead.  The
last Ober Prokurator, A. V. Kartashev, became the new
Minister of Confessions.[23]

The Minister of Interior had at first worked out
a project of wider scope which would have allowed religious communities completely free internal administration, restricting the Ministry of Confessions
to general oversight with regard to functions such as
the performance of marriages which involved questions
of legality.  The government did propose, however, to
support the churches, its officials, and institutions
financially but by means of a lump sum, specific use
to be determined by the church.  This proposal was
not approved by the Provisional Government.  Instead
they simply approved the creation of a Ministry of
Confessions.  This ministry was to deal with all confessional matters and included in its jurisdiction
all duties regarding Orthodox affairs formerly handled by the Ober Prokurator of the Holy Synod and also the affairs of the other confessions which had
till then been under the control of the Department
for Religious Affairs of Foreign Confessions under
the Ministry of the Interior.  The offices of Ober
Prokurator and Associate Ober Prokurator were abolished, instead there was to be one minister with two
associates.  So the new Ministry of Confessions
marked no radical change for it was merely the Ober
Prokurator under a different name performing the same
duties--a state official deeply involved in internal
church matters.[24]

Some Orthodox leaders feared a possible separation of the church from the state and, in particular,
they wanted to guarantee the primacy of Orthodoxy.
For example, they insisted that the head of govern-

ment and the Minister of Confessions must be Orthodox. This the Provisional Government resisted on
principle.[25] At a sobor the position of conservative
Orthodox won out in favor of the creation of a patriarch, although it must be noted that the delegates
present for the final voting no longer represented
a full quorom and of those present slightly over
half voted in favor of a Patriarchate.[26]

Particularly among the hierarchy, it is striking
how little their attitudes had changed from those hierarchs who sought the overthrow of Golitsyn because he had reduced the Orthodox Church to a position of equality with other confessions. It, therefore, seems highly unlikely that had the Russian
government evolved gradually toward more democratic
forms as envisioned by the Kadets, that the Orthodox Church would ever have agreed to disestablishment voluntarily.

## DISESTABLISHMENT DIFFICULTIES TILL 1930

With the seizure of power by the Bolsheviks,
the major problem in the religious sphere was still
the problem Tsar Peter had attacked with such fero-
cious energy. It would be necessary either to force
the leaders of Orthodoxy to rethink the church-
state relationship in favor of disestablishment or
separation of church and state, or else to subdue
the church. Only then could one think seriously of
the next step, the provision of freedom of conscience
through the equal treatment of all confessions.

The Soviet attitude to religion has been characterized by a violent antitheism which its advocates
like to style as "scientific atheism." We will re-

72

turn to this ideological aspect eventually, but it is played down here in order to highlight the more systemic aspects of religious administration. Seen from that angle, the continuities with the tsarist regime are more striking than the innovations.

The first piece of Soviet legislation on religion clearly indicated the government's intent to push forward with the establishment of a secular state fully free of religious influence or commitments to support religious institutions. The first article of the Decree of the Council of Peoples' Commissars on January 23, 1918 stated simply: "The church is separated from the state."[27] Non-Orthodox religious bodies certainly welcomed Article 3 which could be for them a Magna Charta of religious liberty. It stated "every citizen may confess any religion or profess none at all. Every legal restriction connected with the profession of certain faiths or with the profession of no faith is now revoked."[28] Further articles of the decree already indicated the government's intent to conduct a thoroughgoing purge of religious influence on government and so allowed religious associations a very narrow sphere of operation. Most restrictive was the quite unprecedented declaration that "no ecclesiastical and religious association has the right to own property. They do not have the rights of a legal entity."[29] If carried out literally this effectively fettered the activity of central religious organizations.

Administratively government action was much less radical due no doubt to the fact that the new Soviet state had to rely on existing bureaucrats till it had trained its own, and to the fact that Soviet power remained insecure during the initial years.

73

The Ministry of Confessions of the Provisional Government was abolished and once again the ministries
(now Commissariat) of Justice and of Internal Affairs
formed subdivisions responsible for implementing religious policy. The section on cults in the Commissariat for Internal Affairs was responsible for the
legalization of groups, leasing of buildings and the
granting of permission for various religious conferences. At the same time the Soviet secret police,
initially called Cheka, continued the function long
performed by the tsarist secret police, that of conducting surveillance of religious groups, looking
with particular interest for any signs of counter-
revolution in the church. The Commissariat for Education was made responsible for the more aggressive
and less secret activity of conducting antireligious
propaganda. Analysis of Soviet religious policy was
and still is difficult because of the Soviet Government's secretiveness, but it is apparent that it was
complicated from the first by jurisdictional squab-
bles and by differences of viewpoint on how best to
achieve the full eradication of religion.[30]

An embryo Council for Religious affairs was
created in 1924 when the Department of Cults in the
Justice Commissariat was abolished and its respon-
sibilities transferred to a newly created Secretariat for Religious Matters attached to the Presidium
of the All-Russian Central Executive Committee. In
1930 it was renamed the Permanent Commission for Religious Matters under the Council of Ministers and
its powers were written into the basic 1929 "Law on
Religious Associations" as amended in 1932.[31] The
permanent commission included representatives from
the Commissariats of Justice, Internal Affairs, and

Education, and from the secret police (then OGPU)
and the trade unions. With the 1932 amendments this
commission took over from Internal Affairs the power
of "sanctioning national church conferences and setting procedures for registration of and reporting by
individual organizations."[32]

From 1918-30 the different religious confessions in the USSR did not experience a common history. By 1922 the Soviets launched an all out campaign to break the power of the Orthodox hierarchy.
This included the imprisonment of Patriarch Tikhon
till Tikhon decided it would be more expedient to
cooperate with the state. State demands became more
insistent till permission for a religious organization to exist now required more than a neutral apolitical position. The state now demanded unconditional loyalty and full support of its policies. A
number of bishops imprisoned in the Solovki Islands
wrote a letter in 1926 in which they affirmed support
for full separation of church and state. They pointed out that the law on the separation of church and
state prohibited the church from involvement in politics and civil administration, but at the same time
it also meant that the state renounced all interference in the internal affairs of the church which
they understood to mean its "teachings, liturgy and
administration."[33] The state, however, was unwilling
to grant itself those restrictions and interfered
most noticeably in church administration so that the
church that began to emerge following Metropolitan
Sergei's proclamation in 1927 was a church whose independent power had been broken. Observers watched
with incredulity the pro-government statements of
leading hierarchs.[34]

While the Orthodox church was reeling under the
full onslaught of the state's suppressive powers,
the sects flourished.  Those which had suffered so
long under tsarist restrictions now experienced un-
usually extensive freedoms.[35]  Religious confessions
such as the Roman Catholic, Lutheran, Reformed, and
Mennonite which had enjoyed various privileges under
the tsars lost these privileges and were forced into
a competitive situation.  The freedoms for the sects
vanished quickly as the fledgling Soviet Government
became worried about their rapid growth and independent ways.  Restrictions were gradually imposed and
the year 1930 has come to be regarded as the beginning of greatest difficulty for all churches when the
state launched a massive campaign to eradicate all
religion from society.

The creation of the Permanent Commission for Religious Matters with responsibility for all religious
confessions reminds one of such predecessors as the
Ministry of Confessions of the Provisional Government, Golitsyn's Dual Ministry, and Tsar Peter's Holy
Synod.  Apparently the Orthodox Church had finally
accepted its loss of primacy and one state agency
could now deal with all religions on the basis of a
common policy.  Information about the activities of
the permanent commission and its representatives attached to regional Soviets is scarce, but it appears
that its powers were largely theoretical and possibly
intended as mere window dressing.  The secret police
had been involved in religious affairs from the first,
but appear to have been the major agency for the virtual suppression of religious practice from 1930-39
through massive arrests and forced closure of churches.  They were strongly assisted by the non-govern-

mental League of Militant Godless, led by Emelian
Iaroslavskii, which was closely linked with the party organizations.

## ONCE AGAIN TWO SEPARATE COUNCILS:  CROCA AND CARC

National unity became the supreme requirement in
the USSR with the outbreak of World War II, and the
Orthodox and Muslim leaders in particular were quick
to seize the initiative by calling their members to
an all out defense of the motherland.  Support of
the war effort by the religious bodies was extensive
and as a reward Stalin permitted the reestablishment
of central religious organizations, notably for the
Orthodox, Evangelical Christians-Baptist, and Muslim
confessions.  A month after the election of Patriarch
Sergei in 1943 the Soviet news agency TASS announced
that "the Council of Peoples' Commissars had established a state commission whose function would be
that of dealing with religious problems of the Russian Orthodox Church for which government permission was required."[36]  Georgi G. Karpov was named
chairman.  Another TASS announcement was printed on
July 1, 1944:

> By decision of the Council of Peoples' Com-
> missars of the USSR there has been organized
> within the USSR Sovnarkom a commission for
> affairs of religious cults for the purpose
> of establishing liaison between the govern-
> ment of the USSR and the heads of religious
> societies: Gregorian-Armenian, Old Believ-
> ers, Catholics, Greek Catholics, the Lutheran
> Church, the Muslim, Judaic, Buddhist faiths,
> and sectarian organizations for problems
> of these cults requiring the permission of
> the USSR government.  Comrade I. V. Polyan-
> sky has been named chairman of the Commis-
> sion for Affairs of Religious Cults at the
> USSR Sovnarkom.[37]

Two things were apparent. Previous administration of religious affairs had lapsed requiring the creation of new organizations. There was no clear indication that the Council for the Affairs of the Russian Orthodox Church (CROCA) and the Council for the Affairs of Religious Cults (CARC) had replaced the Permanent Commission whose duties were written into the 1932 amendments to the basic law. Secondly, it was apparent that once again Orthodox strength was sufficient and the problems apparently unique enough to warrant a separate organization. It was a tacit acknowledgement of the primacy of Orthodoxy which deserved special treatment.

The rights and duties of CROCA and CARC were not spelled out when their formation was announced. Father Leopold Braun claimed that Polianskii told him that the new organizations "represented absolutely no changes on existing laws on religion."[38] A description of their duties printed in the 1948 issue of the Soviet Encyclopedia agreed with the description given to the United Nations Commission on Human Rights.[39] First the councils were responsible for liaison between the government and the leaders of religious associations. The councils were (a) to conduct initial examinations of questions raised by religious associations which required governmental decision; (b) to draft laws and regulations on questions concerning religious cults and also to propose instructions and other directives for governmental consideration; (c) supervise full and correct realization of governmental laws and regulations concerning religious cults; (d) assist religious associations in deciding questions which required the involvement of various governmental institutions (e.g. ministries).[40]

Locally the work of the councils was to be carried out through plenipotentiaries attached to regional and provincial executive committees of Councils of Workers Deputies and also to the Councils of Ministers of union and autonomous republics.

Although outlined in the 1948 edition of the Soviet Encyclopedia, subsequently the duties and powers of CROCA and CARC have been explained most infrequently, and some observers concluded that there was a deliberate policy of secrecy. Their powers were not written into law.[41] As noted earlier, Fathers Eshliman and Yakunin charged that the functions had changed from 1957-64 making the councils much less bodies for liaison and much more agencies for extensive control of churches. Subsequent samizdat information till the present emphasizes both its controlling activity and claims that these councils and their successor, the CRA, coordinated the entire antireligious campaign.

## UNIFIED COUNCIL OF RELIGIOUS AFFAIRS AND THE LAW

On December 8, 1965, the two councils were reorganized into the Council for Religious Affairs under the USSR Council of Ministers (CRA). The new council was headed by Vladimir A. Kuroedov who had replaced Karpov as head of CROCA in 1960. Why were the two councils united and why did this take place in late 1965? No explicit reasons were given although the latest authoritative interpretation of the law presents the whole history of Soviet administration of religious affairs in a rather brief somewhat inaccurate paragraph. G. R. Gol'st remarks that in 1943-44 CROCA and CARC were set up "instead of" the Permanent Commission for Religious Matters, merely noting in passing that these two councils were "reorganized at the end of 1965 into a single organ--the Council for Religious Affairs under the USSR Council of Ministers."[42] One is, therefore, left to speculate that this reorganization came toward the end of the "Year of Drift" following Khrushchev's ouster when the state's religious policy appeared to undergo considerable scrutiny.[43] Evidence of a change in the new unified council's procedures toward a greater observance of Soviet legality or an abandonment by the CRA of its war on religious associations has been slight. Possibly A. A. Puzin, chairman of CARC, who was calling for an end to administrative abuses committed against believers at a major conference in July 1964 may have lost out in the argument over religious policy so that his opposite number, Kuroedov of CROCA, widely noted for his harsh brutal manner, was selected to coordinate overall religious policy.[44]

Although such speculation may seem plausible, recent information does not support a heavy emphasis on a change in policy beginning late in 1965 with the creation of the single CRA. In 1972 Soviet academician and mathematician Igor R. Shafarevich submitted a lengthy report to Sakharov's Human Rights Committee on the subject of "Legislation of Religion in the USSR." In it he cited a volume unknown in the West which listed twenty-one articles of the 1929 "Law on Religious Associations" as having been changed by the Supreme Soviet of the RSFSR on October 19, 1962.[45] He cited as well twelve additional articles which had undergone minor changes.[46] Fortunately, in August 1976 the secret lawbook of 1971 which Shafarevich

80

quoted was leaked to the West.[47]  This enables one to
compare the 1962 and 1975 revisions.  It is clear
that the 1975 revisions did not merely make public
what had been changed secretly in 1962.  Generally
speaking more restrictive changes were made in 1962
with slightly more conciliatory ones coming in 1975.
Since believers have been clamoring increasingly for
a copy of the "Law on Religious Associations," perhaps the 1975 amendments, closely followed by Gol'st's
interpretive commentary summarizing not only the basic law but also related ones, are a response to this
request.[48]

The most significant feature of the amended law
of 1975 is that it provides a legal foundation for
the activities of the CRA.  Taking the 1962 and 1975
changes together, the CRA is referred to in fourteen
articles[49] while an additional three articles affect
the CRA or were altered as a result of its creation.[50]
Another six articles have been dropped due to the
clarification of CRA powers.[51]  Most striking is an
apparent centralizing policy with powers formerly
held by local authorities, namely the city and district soviets, now being subordinate to the CRA.  Secondly, the changes frequently involve a simplifying
of procedures and less spelling out of detail which
is more discretionary power to the CRA.  Closely related to these trends is the fact that the references
to the local committee for religious matters, introduced in the 1932 amendments, have been dropped.  The
duties of these committees are not simply turned over
to the local plenipotentiary of the CRA, as one would
expect, but are instead left to the district or city
soviets themselves.

According to the newly revised law, the Council

for Religious Affairs takes the final decision on granting registration permission to local religious associations (articles 4 and 7) and also takes the decision to take away such registration (article 43). The CRA equivalents had already been featured in the 1962 revisions, but then it was still the Council of Ministers of autonomous republics and executive committees of district, regional and city (Moscow and Leningrad) Councils of Workers' Deputies who took the decision "with the agreement of" CROCA and CARC. The 1975 formula reversed the order so that "the CRA under the USSR Council of Ministers upon recommendation of the Councils of Ministers of autonomous republics" makes the registration and closure decisions. The law also gives the CRA the power to distinguish between registering a religious association and granting it the use of a building, the CRA taking the final decision (article 10). A great number of amended articles concern related aspects for regulating building use. The CRA now makes the final decision regarding closure of a building without right of appeal by the believers as was formerly possible (articles 36, 37, 39, 44 and 51). If a religious association wishes to build or remodel its present building the CRA must make the decision in each individual instance (article 45). The CRA also must give its permission regarding the disbursement of money collected from fire insurance in the event that a building burns and must approve the further use of a church building after the religious association using it has been dissolved. In all these matters of registration and use of building, the CRA now makes the decision formerly made by regional and city

82

soviets. The CRA, like the Permanent Commission for Religious Matters before it, grants permission for the holding of conventions, congresses and similar meetings at the all-union, republican and local levels. Formerly local and regional meetings had to be approved by local organs (article 20). Finally, local state organs are responsible for gathering systematic information about the activities of believers, their observance or violation of the law, and to forward this information to the CRA (articles 63 and 64).

It would be a mistake to think of the CRA merely as an administrative body charged with supervising observance of the "Law on Religious Association." The wording of the law itself suggests that CRA directives and legal interpretations carry the force of law. On May 10, 1966 a statute for the CRA was approved (but never made public) which stated that the CRA has the right "to introduce recommendations for changing commands, instructions, decisions, orders, resolutions and such like acts which contradict the legislation on cults, to the organ submitting the act or to the next higher ranking organ."[52] Subsequent legal commentaries of 1970, 1974, and 1975 have quoted or paraphrased this statement, but without giving their source. The latest commentary by Gol'st, in fact, includes it at the end of a short list of the fundamental legislation on religious cults.[53] So the CRA is now a legislative body as well, has been so de facto since its inception and indisputably so since 1975.

According to the secret statute of the CRA, it was "organized with the aim of consistent realization of the policies of the Soviet state in relation

83

to religion." It was assigned four main tasks: to supervise observance of the legislation, to analyze any proposed legislation affecting religion, to keep government bodies informed on the activities of religious organizations, and to "work with religious organizations in the realization of international relations, participating in the struggle for peace, for strengthening friendship among nations."[54]

The CRA has exercised these powers to a degree that makes a mockery of Soviet claims that because there is a separation of church and state, the state does not interfere in the purely internal matters of the church, an interference for which Soviet writers regularly chastise the tsarist government. At least the Soviet authorities are becoming more open on precisely what they mean by not interfering in internal affairs of the churches. Gol'st for example, states that "the Soviet State does not interfere in the internal purely religious (canonical, dogmatic, theological) activities of the church, if they do not contradict the requirements of the law."[55] Clearly church administration is not regarded as an internal purely religious matter, no recognition being given to the fundamental importance of the administrative structure for defining what is the nature of the church. The state also feels entitled to interfere in the above mentioned purely internal matters, if the state feels that they contradict legal requirements. One such interference, spelled out in a decision of the CRA of October 31, 1968 and also acknowledged in the 1975 law, is that no "servant of cult" (preacher, priest, preceptor) may carry out his duties before he has been registered by the CRA. Gol'st states explicitly that servants of cult working in an unregistered association or themselves not registered are acting illegally.[56] The basic law on religious associations requires contralized religious organizations to have their laws and regulations registered by the CRA. These religious centers are specifically forbidden to organize special children's, youth, and women's prayer meetings, circles and groups for the study of religion, etc. They may not interfere in the executive and financial-business affairs of local religious associations.[57] Several religious confessions have centralized registered organs such as the Orthodox and Baptists, while others, Gol'st notes laconically, that "Do not have religious headquarters and religious associations that are registered govern themselves by means of executive organs elected by them."[58] That is a rather euphemistic way of mentioning religious confessions which have been forbidden to establish a centralized organization. An Instruction from CROCA and CARC dated March 16, 1961 (which by the way first spelled out the changes then incorporated into the secret 1962 legal revision) stated that sects whose beliefs and character were anti-Soviet and superstitious such as "the Jehovah's Witnesses, Pentecostalists, True Orthodox Christians, the True Orthodox Church, Reform Adventists, Murashkovtsy and others" were forbidden to exist.[59]

The CRA's international activity has become increasingly important with the development of détente. The CRA coordinates the activity of religious leaders internationally in order to foster peace and international understanding among nations. All visits abroad by Soviet religious leaders require approval of the CRA which also approves religious delegations from abroad visiting the USSR.[60]

## STRUCTURE AND PERSONALITIES OF THE CRA

So the CRA is now a powerful administrative body
whose functions have been made public, but its structure is still characterized by considerable secrecy.
The central office is located in a small building at
11 Smolenskii Boulevard in Moscow.  It is headed by
a chairman, V. A. Kuroedov and three deputy chairmen, V. N. Titov, I. Iu. Bonchkovskii, and E. A. Ta-
rasov.  According to the law, CRA plenipotentiaries
are attached to union and autonomous republic, district and city Soviets of Workers' Deputies.  These
work alongside local state authorities and appear to
possess considerable independent powers, but are subordinate to the central CRA office which appoints
them.  This parallel structure calls to mind the parallel structure between party and state organizations.
It is not at all clear, however, why there should be
three deputy chairmen and how their duties are divid-
ded .

According to the secret CRA statute, the central
apparatus of the CRA is divided into seven departments:  Orthodox Church affairs; Muslim and Buddhist
affairs; Catholic, Protestant, Armenian, Jewish and
sectarian affairs; international relations; juridical
department; bookkeeping department; and a general
department.[61]  If P. V. Makartsev's statement in
1973 that there were three deputy chairmen is correct[67], then it is most likely that Kuroedov, the
chairman, administers Orthodox Affairs and his three
deputies head the next three departments leaving lower ranked officials to head the others.  The CRA also

86

has an office for handling supplies such as paper, candlewax and metal, and one for building materials and renovations. Some observers feel that the affairs of certain confessions are dealt with purely at the regional level as, for example, the Central Asian Moslems. In Armenia, Moldavia, Latvia, and Estonia, there are CRA's whose ties with Moscow are tenuous and may, in fact, function quite independently.

More detailed information has recently become available on several republican CRAs. Apparently Uzbek officials had become lax in enforcing the law. In February 1969 a new coordinating council was created for the Uzbek CRA plenipotentiary consisting of key officials from the _Znanie_ society, the procurator's office, the supreme court, the department of education, the interior ministry, finance ministry, and the deputy mayor of Tashkent.[63] In November 1974 the CRA plenipotentiary for the Ukraine was replaced with a Council for Religious Affairs for the Ukrainian SSR. This council was headed by a chairman and three deputies, employed 34 people at its headquarters and had another 91 people under it locally.[64] Obviously increased religious activity had resulted in an increased work load. Whether this will serve as a model for other republics is not yet known.

At present the structure at local levels is not at all uniform. A single individual is the CRA plenipotentiary for the Lithuanian Rupublic. Of necessity he is concerned primarily with Catholic affairs, but there is some indication that since 1965 he has also been responsible for Orthodox affairs and presumably other minority religions.[65] In the republic of Kazakhstan, in contrast, the CRA is represented by a three man committee, one of whom, named Podorigorov, usually deals with the Evangelicals. It is also interesting to note that in a major city of the republic, such as Karaganda, the CRA is represented by one man dealing with the affairs of all religious confessions. Believers appealing his decisions usually directed them to the central office of the CRA in Moscow, bypassing the republican committee based in Alma Ata.

Perhaps the most extensive criticism of the CRA by believers has centered on the abusive treatment and arbitrary actions of the local plenipotentiaries. According to the Chronicle of the Catholic Church of Lithuania the activities of Juozas Rugienis, head of Lithuanian CRA till 1973, were particularly objectionable. He openly interfered in the appointment and transfer of priests, tried to intimidate the organizers of appeals, and perhaps most objectionable was the charge that he "issues his orders mostly by phone and eschews written communication."[66] In an apparent response to complaints to Moscow, Rugienis was replaced in February 1973 by Kazimieras Tumenas, a party worker and lecturer holding the kandidat degree in history. This was an improvement, although the Lithuanian Catholics still complained that the suppressive policy had not changed. Tumenas merely used more diplomatic and sophisticated methods.[67] Other plenipotentiaries with particularly unfriendly relations with believers are: Voronichev (Tashkent); Arkhimov (Karaganda); Rakhimov (Fergana Obl. Uzbekistan) and Kalugin (Lipetsk). That breaches of the law by local officials have occurred has often been acknowledged publicly, most recently by Kuroedov on February 30, 1976 in Izvestiia. But he argued that

such incidents were becoming less and complained that
the Western press blew them up out of proportion.
This continuing problem no doubt explains why the
1975 amendment reveals such a strong centralizing
tendency, presumably centralized control will guarantee more uniform treatment of believers and a treatment, if one is to believe CRA claims, in which reason predominates over emotion.

In January 1964 Partinaia zhizn, a Communist
Party periodical, announced the formation of commissions at the local level to supervise the observance
of the legislation on cults. These commissions do
not have legal power, having to rely on the force of
moral suasion[68], but since 1964 they have become the
most active local agencies for conducting the battle
against religion. Although not a clear working arm
of the CRA, these commissions are subordinate to it.
The major function of the commissions is to verify
complaints about violations of the law and to explain
the legislation of religious cults to the public.
The commissions must meet monthly and keep minutes of
their meetings. A commission consists of representatives of various state agencies and is usually
chaired by the deputy chairman of the local Soviet of
Workers' Deputies.[69] Officially then, it is at this
level where ideology plays a major role since by being as thoroughly informed as possible about the
activities of believers and seeking to persuade believers of the superiority of scientific atheism,
the commissions hope to speed the final disintegration of religion. It is also interesting to note
that when Gol'st discussed the work of the commissions he found it necessary to warn against excesses
which might violate the civil rights of believers.[70]

By focusing on CRA powers and procedures there
is a danger of overemphasis, as if this is the only
state organ dealing with religious affairs. Gol'st
listed four other bodies directly involved in supervising the observance of the legislation of cults.
The police are a pervasive presence.

> An important role in the struggle against
> violations of the law on the separation
> of church from state and schools from the
> church is borne by the organs of internal
> affairs which act jointly with local So-
> viets in keeping oversight for the obser-
> vance of the legislation on cults. They
> prevent and suppress violations of rights,
> committed on religious soil, protect so-
> cial order and the rights of citizens.[71]

Bohdan R. Bociurkiw's remark that "an intimate involvement of the security organs in ecclesiastical
affairs has remained a permanent feature of Soviet
church-state relations"[72] is confirmed by this nearly explicit reference by Gol'st to the KGB. At certain periods state security organs were without question the crucial agency in administering religious
affairs and even at present one suspects that their
powers exceed those of the CRA. The Public Health
organs also become involved because it is their responsibility to inspect religious buildings for
health hazards and their cooperation has at times
helped the CRA in securing closure of an undesirable
church. Additionally, the Ministry of Finance and
its organs are responsible for inspecting the financial affairs of religious organizations and for enforcing the 1943 law specifying income tax rates
paid by clergy among others.[73] The procuracy, finally, is deeply involved in the prosecution of violations of the law, Gol'st noting that they take action

upon recommendations of the CRA.[74]

## CRA AS MODERNIZING AGENCY:  SOME CONCLUSIONS

In concluding his discussion of the CRA, Gol'st stated that

> carrying out checking-supervisory, informa-
> tional-consultative and similar functions,
> the council directs all its activities toward
> the firm realization of constitutional norms,
> which guarantee freedom of conscience to citi-
> zens of the USSR.[75]

Can one really expect the CRA to guarantee freedom of conscience to Soviet citizens?  Has Soviet admin-istration of religion advanced beyond that of the provisional Government, or even beyond that of Golitsyn or Peter the Great?  In other words, has the modernizing ideology originating with Peter finally become generally acceptable?

The goal of separation of church from state was intended to free each from the other's control and to allow the state to follow a common policy toward all confessions.  Separation of church and state was generally affirmed by the sectarian organizations for whom it was, after all, a fundamental theologi-cal emphasis.  By and large the main line Protestant bodies and the Roman Catholic Church have not been permitted to enunciate a church-state position.  If Orthodoxy still demanded primacy and special treat-ment in 1943, this changed when Metropolitan Nikodim replaced Nikolai in 1960 as chief negotiator with CROCA.  He appeared to be more ready to follow Soviet demands and thanks, perhaps, to his wide ecumenical experience he how seems to be personally committed to ecumenism not only abroad, but also in the USSR.  He is noted for maintaining warm personal relations with

Baptist and Lutheran leaders. Possibly the attitude
is more widespread although the Orthodox hierarchy
in general is not noted for its liberal outlook.[76]
Mr. Kuroedov of the CRA certainly expressed his doubt
as late as 1973 when in a major article he rehearsed
the story of Orthodox opposition to the state and
argued that not only the Orthodox capitulation, but
also that of the other religious confessions was due
to expediency and did not represent an inner change
of heart that might permit a relationship of trust
to be built up between the state and the religious
communities.[77] In his most recent article the tone
is more friendly. Perhaps, he has changed his mind.

Without question the Russian intelligentsia
strongly affirms the notion of separation of church
from state and favors the fostering of ecumenism.
Shafarevich was merely repeating other Orthodox dissenters when he stressed that "the principle of the
separation of church from state and their non-inter-
ference in each other's affairs provides the basis
for building a healthy relationship between believers
and the state."[78] The Regelson-Yakunin letter to the
World Council of Churches (WCC) Assembly at Nairobi
in November 1975 is perhaps the latest in a series
of affirmations for closer relations between believers
of diverse confessions. It is reminiscent of some
of the best writing along these lines during the period that Golitsyn was trying to create a universal
Christian church in the Russian empire.

Although the principles are affirmed, there
still remain fundamental disagreements between church
and state representatives on the nature of the relationship desired. The Soviet concept of freedom of
conscience is more restrictive than the classic lib-

eral theory of freedom of conscience. Gol'st, for
example, quotes once again Marx's claim that

> bourgeois freedom of conscience repre-
> sents nothing more than tolerance toward
> all possible views on religious freedom
> of conscience, but the workers' party on
> the contrary, strives to free conscience
> from the narcotic of religion.[79]

State interference in internal church life is still
growing as the new 1975 amendments indicate, while
even the 1929 law, in fact even the 1918 decree, limit the sphere of legitimate religious activity to a
degree generally considered unacceptable. Very recently Russian Orthodox dissenters have moved beyond
their emphasis on urging the state to obey its own
laws on freedom of conscience to call for thoroughgoing revision of the law. The 1975 revisions are
unacceptable, they argue. In a major letter dated
March 6, 1976 and addressed to Dr. Potter of the WCC,
Yakunin and Regelson detail four major areas of religious discrimination sanctioned by Soviet law:
Making the registration of religious societies into
a sanctioning act; denying religious societies personal rights to prayer houses and cult objects; pro-
hibiting missionary and cultural-social activity by
religious societies; and discrimination in education.[80] Solzhenitsyn summed up the dilemma aptly
when he remarked: "When Caesar, having exacted what
is Caesar's, demands still more insistently that we
render unto him what is God's - that is a sacrifice
we dare not make!"[81]

Actually recent legislation and commentary indicate that new problems now call for a somewhat
different religious policy. The limited breathing
space secured from Stalin in 1943-44 has been

acknowledged and made permanent by law. Churches
are still denied the right of a juridical person,
but other articles of the law permit nearly all the
activities which had been prohibited by denying the
right of legal entity. Another sign that a modus
vivendi has been reached is the report of a reception, held by Soviet leaders in the Kremlin during
the 1975 celebrations of the October Revolution,
where Soviet churchmen were able to hold a conversation with Brezhnev, Kosygin and Podgorny.[82]   No
doubt the continuing concern of the CRA in this regard will be to try to maintain the delicate balance
in its own interest.

   One of the basic reasons for the failure of the
Dual Ministry under Golitsyn in 1824 was the fact
that Golitsyn was using his extensive powers to foster a specific religious viewpoint, namely Pietism.
He believed very deeply that this was necessary for
Russia to progress. Without question Soviet militant atheism today accounts for a similar difficulty
in achieving a generally acceptable church-state
relationship. Cardinal Koenig in a well-reasoned
article in 1975 was not the first to accuse the Soviet government of backwardness in church-state relations, of being a confessional state in which the
state acted as protector of one established faith,
namely atheism, and thereby reduced citizens belonging to other faiths to a second class status.[83]
The charge apparently stung sufficiently for Kuroedov
to protest, in an article in Izvestiia, that believers were not second class citizens. His remarks
would have carried more credibility had he followed
the suggestion in Solzhenitsyn's Letter to Soviet
Leaders:

94

> . . . .deprive Marxism of its powerful
> state support and let it exist of it-
> self and stand on its own feet. . . .al-
> low competition on an equal and honor-
> able basis--not for power but for truth.
> . . .let the people breathe, let them
> think and develop![84]

Can one really expect normalization of church-state
relations properly overseen by the CRA if the dominant religion, sociologically speaking (i.e. atheism)
is not made subject to the "Laws on Religious Associations"?

Even putting such contradictions aside, the
Council for Religious Affairs with its interventionist policies and outlook may well be out of date
as far as further modernization is concerned. Till
now we have been using the definition of religion employed by Soviet writers in which "religion" is syn-
onymous with "church," "mosque," "synagogue," and
the institutional accoutrements that go with them.
Soviet sociologists then see secularization as the
declining influence of religious institutions in social life and project, logically, the eventual disappearance of religion. While it may be true "that
certain forms of religion are of declining influence
and can thus be regarded as implicated in the process of secularization,"[85] this does not mean that
religion _qua_ religion is disappearing. The most
influential classical sociologists, Max Weber and
Emile Durkheim, drew special attention to the per-
sistence of religion in all societies. Two modern
sociologists deeply influenced by Weber and Durkheim
present religion as "lying at the very centre of
man's experience of his natural and social environment" calling religion "the human activity above

95

all."[86]  Peter Berger adds that religion is that
over-arching complex of meanings by which a human
being legitimizes social reality.[87]  In short, religion is a primary agent of social cohesion.  This
would make the Marxist concept of religion as a tool
of the bourgeois class to be used against the proletariat quite irrelevant.  What has happened in the
modern world thanks to the decreasing influence of
historic religious institutions is that religion has
become a private matter.  Using the analogy of a
free enterprise economy, Thomas Luckmann argued, for
example, that a modern individual is bombarded with
so many ideas stemming from a great variety of world
views that he finds himself fashioning his own personal religion.[88]

     This is not a uniquely Western phenomenon and is
evident in Soviet society where the process has been
accelerated, ironically, by state attempts to suppress religion.  Metropolitan Sergei thought that the
episcopacy and institutional church needed to survive at any cost and this conviction became the basis for fashioning a policy of survival.[89]  Did the
Orthodox Church really survive because Sergei submitted to the government and accepted the restrictive terms?  The Orthodox layman Boris Talantov who
died in prison answered this very forcefully in 1968
when he asserted that,

> Metropolitan Sergei's actions saved nothing
> except his own skin.  He lost all authori-
> ty in the eyes of the faithful, but ac-
> quired the good will of Stalin. . . .  The
> greater part of those churches which re-
> mained open did not recognize Metropolitan
> Sergei. . . .  The opening of the churches
> during and just after the war. . . .was done
> by the atheist authorities themselves under

pressure from ordinary people and to appease them. . . .[90]

Few observers would doubt that it was the stubborn faith of the faithful that kept the Orthodox Church alive and, in fact, allowed Sergei to demonstrate to Stalin that he represented an organization that could exert considerable pressure. It has certainly not been lost on the Soviet authorities that there has been a proliferation of sectarian activity, largely underground and exceedingly difficult to control at precisely those times when administrative attacks on the church have been the sharpest.[91]

It would be a mistake to think, however, that by mere normalization of relations with established church institutions one could once again control religion. For the privatization of religion extends beyond this and is apparent in all of Soviet society, particularly in the Soviet intelligentsia which has shown considerable creativity in the fashioning of _ersatz_ religions. Among Russians, Christianity continues to have a major influence; a striking number of the contributors to From Under the Rubble rest their hopes on it, Barabanov noting, for example, that "the energies of Christian culture, not directly through the Church perhaps, but obliquely and through mysterious channels, continue to penetrate through to our world."[92]

In light of this it is difficult to see how real freedom of conscience can be protected by the CRA unless it adopts a much less interventionist, purely liaison function. Failing that, as seems evident at present, the Soviet Union will be confronting increasing social dissonance instead of the social cohesion so intensely sought.

NOTES

1. *Vedomosti verkhovnogo soveta RSFSR*, No. 27 (873), July 3, 1975,pp. 487-91. The amendments are dated June 23.

2. V. A. Kuroedov and A. S. Pankratov, eds., *Zakonodatel'stvo o religioznykh kul'takh (sbornik materialov i dokumentov)*, 2nd ed. (Moscow, 1971).

3. G. R. Gol'st, *Religiia i zakon* (Moscow, 1975)

4. From his speech printed in *The Call of the Russian Church,* Report of the General Council of the Russian Orthodox Church January 31 to February 2, 1945 (Moscow, 1945), p. 13.

5. Trans. in Michael Bourdeaux, *Patriarch and Prophets: Persecution of the Russian Orthodox Church* (London: George Allen & Unwin Ltd, 1970; reprint ed., London: Mowbrays, 1975), pp. 189-90.

6. Document 6 cited by Michael Bourdeaux in chap. 3 of a book in progress on the Lithuanian Catholics. This and other information not yet published was generously made available for this writer's use for which he is grateful.

7. Bourdeaux, *Patriarch and Prophets*, p. 194.

8. Marc Raeff, "The Well-Ordered Police State and the Development of Modernity in Seventeenth- and Eighteenth-Century Europe: An attempt at a Comparative Approach," *American Historical Review* 80 (December 1975):1222.

9. Ibid., p. 1225.

10. James Cracraft, *The Church Reform of Peter the Great* (Stanford: Stanford University Press, 1971), p. 198.

11. Ibid. p. 208.

12. Cracraft, *Church Reform*, pp. 162, 238-89.

13. A useful survey is F. Blagovidov, *Oberprokurory Sv. Sinoda v XVIII i v pervoi polovine XIX stoletiia* (Kazan, 1900). On administration see also

T. V. Barsov, Sinodal'nyia uchrezhdeniia prezhnago vremeni (St. Petersberg, 1897).

14. Cracraft, Church Reform, p. 217.

15. Ibid., pp. 64-79, 290-302 Cf. Robert O. Crummey, The Old Believers and the World of Anti-christ (Madison: University of Wisconsin Press, 1970).

16. For a detailed analysis of Golitsyn as Ober-Prokurator and Minister of Religious Affairs and National Instruction, see this writer's "Prince Alexander N. Golitsyn (1773-1884): Tsarist Minister of Piety" (Ph.D. dissertation, University of Minnesota, 1976).

17. The standard treatment is Nicholas Riasan-ovsky, Nicholas I and Official Nationality in Russia, 1825-1855 (Berkeley: University of California Press, 1969).

18. The best overall treatment of the synodal period is Igor Smolitsch, Geschichte der Russischen Kirche 1700-1917 (Leiden: E. J. Brill, 1964).

19. At the 1901 conference of the Orthodox Missionary Society, M. A. Stakhovich, a gentry representative from Orlov guberniia closely acquain-ted with Leo Tolstoy declared: "If the Church be-lieves in its inner spiritual strength, then it does not need the cooperation of earthly powers. And if it needs it, does this not bear witness to an in-sufficiently daring faith?" Quoted in Vladimir Rozhkov, Tserkovnye voprosy v gosudarstvennoi dume (Rome: Opere Religiose Russe, 1975), pp. 23-29. This book is a significant study of the church-state ques-tion during the Duma period by a gifted member of the present Russian Orthodox hierarchy.

20 Ibid., pp. 10-12.

21. Nicholas Zernov, The Russian Religious Renaissance of the Twentieth Century (London: Darton, Longman & Todd, 1963), p. 64.

22. Ibid., p. 67.

23. Matthew Spinka, The Church and the Russian Revolution (New York: Macmillan, 1927), p. 82.

24. Ibid. pp. 70-72; cf. Zernov, Russian Renaissance, pp. 190-91.

25. Spinka, Church and Russian Revolution, pp. 73-76.

26. Ibid., p. 89-91.

27. Available in English in Richard H. Marshall et al, eds., Aspects of Religion in the Soviet Union 1917-1967 (Chicago: University of Chicago Press, 1971), pp. 437-38.

28. Ibid.

29. Ibid.

30. See for example, Joan Delaney, "The Origins of Soviet Antireligious Organizations," in Marshall, Aspects of Religion, pp. 103-29.

31. The 1930 decree was printed in Julius F. Hecker, Religion and Communism (New York: Wiley & Sons, Ltd. 1934), Appendix.

32. Bohdan R. Bociurkiw, "The Shaping of Soviet Religious Policy," Problems of Communism (May-June 1973), p. 48. Cf. Joshua Rothenburg, "The Legal Status of Religion in the Soviet Union" in Marshall, Aspects of Religion, p. 95.

33. Bohdan R. Bociurkiw, "Church-State Relations in the USSR," Survey (January 1968), p. 18.

34. The basic study for this is William C. Fletcher, A Study in Survival: The Church in Russia, 1927-1943 (New York: Macmillan, 1965).

35. Andrew Q. Blane, "Protestant Sectarians in the First Year of Soviet Rule," in Marshal, Aspects of Religion, p. 301-22.

36. As paraphrased in Leopold L. S. Braun, Religion in Russia From Lenin to Khrushchev: An Uncensored Account (Paterson, N. J.: St. Anthony Guild Press, 1959), p. 69.

37. Ibid., p. 71.

38. Ibid., P. 72. Braun was an American Assump-

tionist priest who for twelve years was chaplain in
Moscow.

39. Bol'shaia sovetskaia entsiklopediia, 1st
edition (Moscow, 1948), vol. 50, p. 1788 s.v. "Religiia
i tserkov v SSSR," by A. Kolosov. The U. N. study
paper cited by Rothenburg, "The Legal Status," p. 83
was published January 30, 1950.

40. The U. N. report adds a fifth task: "provide for the general registration of churches and
houses of worship." See Rothenburg, "The Legal
Status," p. 83.

41. Andrew Blane, "Church and State in Soviet
Russia:  The Rise of a New Era," Canadian Slavic
Studies, forthcoming; Gerhard Simon, Church, State
and Opposition in the U.S.S.R., trans. Kathleen
Matchett (London: C. Hurst & Company, 1974), pp. 81-
82.

42. Gol'st, Religiia i zakon, p. 66-67.

43. Andrew Blane, "A Year of Drift," Religion
in Communist Lands 2 (May-June 1974):9-15.

44. Only six pages of Puzin's major address are
available in the West. See Keston College, Center
for the Study of Religion and Communism Archives
(hereafter CSRC Archives) Keston, Kent.

45. I. R. Shafarevich, Zakonodatel'stvo o religii v SSSR (Paris: YMCA Press, 1973). See footnote
2 above for reference to the volume Shafarevich cited.  The twenty-one changed articles were Arts.
4, 5, 6, 8, 10, 12, 18, 20, 27, 33, 34, 39, 41, 43,
44, 45, 47, 48, 54, 59, and 63.

46. They were Arts. 25, 28, 29, 30, 38, 40, 46,
51, 52, 57, 58 and 61. See Shafarevich, Zakonodatel'-
stvo, p. 68.

47. See the summary in this author's "Secret
Soviet Lawbook on Religion," Religion in Communist
Lands 4 (Winter 1976):24-34.

48. The writer was struck with the frequency of
the request for publication of the law in speeches
by delegates to the All-Union Congress of Evangelical Christians -Baptists which he attended in December 1974. Publication of the amendments is not quite

the same as publishing the entire law. In the following discussion in addition to the Vedomosti the writer has compared the Russian version of the 1929 law with a Russian edition of the complete law incorporating the 1975 amendments: O religioznykh ob'-edineniiakh (New York: Izdatel'stvo Khronika, 1975).

49. Arts. 4, 7, 8, 10, 20, 33, 36, 39, 41, 43, 44, 45, 51, and 63.

50. Arts. 18, 52 and 64.

51. Arts. 21, 22, 24, 35, 37, and 42.

52. Kuroedov and Pankratov, p. 79.

53. Gol'st, Religiia i zakon, p. 3. See also Administrativnoe pravo (Moscow, 1970), p. 581 and A. Sediulin, Zakonodatel'stvo o religioznykh kul'-takh (Moscow, 1974), pp. 72-74.

54. Kuroedov & Pankratov, p. 79.

55. Gol'st, Religiia i zakon, p. 8.

56. Ibid., p. 61.

57. Ibid., pp. 54-55.

58. Ibid., p. 57.

59. Kuroedov and Pankratov, p. 157.

60. V. A. Kuroedov, "Iz istorii vzaimootnoshenii sovetskogo gosudarstva i tserkvi," Voprosy istorii, No. 9 (1973), p. 30.

61. Kuroedov and Pankratov, p. 83.

62. Neues Forum, April-May, 1967, p. 352.

63. Kuroedov and Pankratov, pp. 229-33.

64. Religion und Atheismus in der UdSSR, No. 3 (March 1975), pp. 9-10; the official announcement appeared in Radianskie pravo (Kiev), No. 2 (1975), p. 104.

65. V. Stanley Vardys, "Catholicism in Lithuania," in Marshall, Aspects of Religion, p. 381.

66. Ibid. See <u>The Chronicle of the Catholic Church of Lithuania</u>, English language editions (Maspeth, N. Y., 1972-73), No.2, pp. 3, 7; No. 4, p. 37; No. 6, p. 24.

67. <u>Chronicle</u>, No. 6, p. 24.

68. <u>Administrativnoe pravo</u>, p. 583.

69. Gol'st, <u>Religiia i zakon</u>, pp. 72-74.

70. Ibid., p. 72.

71. Ibid., p. 67.

72. Bociurkiw, "Shaping of Soviet Religious Policy," p. 43.

73. Gol'st in <u>Religiia i zakon</u> refers at length to but does not give the content of a decree of the Presidium of the USSR Supreme Soviet dated April 30, 1943. (see pp 68, 84-85)

74. Ibid., p. 68.

75. Ibid., p. 69.

76. Informed sympathetic observers still worry that the dream of riding on a white horse beside the ruler has not yet lost its attractiveness for a significant section of the Church leadership.

77. Kuroedov, "Iz istorii vzaimootnoshenii", pp. 15-31.

78. Ibid., p. 70.

79. Ibid., p. 7.

80. See Hans Hebly & Eugen Voss, eds. <u>Religious Liberty in the Soviet Union</u>; WCC and USSR: <u>a post-Nairobi Documentation</u> (Keston, England: Keston College, 1976), pp. 40-53.

81. Alexander Solzhenitsyn, "As Breathing and Consciousness Return," in Alexander Solzhenitsyn et al <u>From Under the Rubble</u>, with an Introduction by Max Haywood, translated under the direction of Michael Scammell (New York: Little, Brown, Bantam Books, 1975), p. 23.

82. _Bratskii vestnik_, No. 6, (1975), p. 49; cf. _Journal of the Moscow Patriarchate_, No. 12, (1975).

83. Franz Cardinal Koenig, "Die Sowjet Union — ein konfessioneller Staat," _Frandfurter Allgemeine Zeitung_, August 16, 1975.

84. _Index on Censorship_ (London) (1974), pp. 48, 56, 57.

85. Michael Hill, _A Sociology of Religion_ (London: Heinemann Educational Books, 1973), p. 260.

86. Ibid., pp. 259-60.

87. Peter Berger's major book on the sociology of religion is aptly entitled _The Sacred Canopy_ (New York: Macmillan, 1967).

88. Thomas Luckmann, _The Invisible Religion_ (New York: Macmillan, 1967).

89. Fletcher, _Study_, passim.

90. Bourdeaux, _Patriarch and Prophets_, pp. 330-31.

91. William C. Fletcher, _The Russian Orthodox Church Underground 1917-1970_ (London: Oxford University Press, 1971). See especially pp. 279-92.

92. Evgenii Barabanov, "The Schism Between the Church and the World," in _From Under the Rubble_, p. 188.

## Chapter 4
## RELIGION AND THE INTELLIGENTSIA

Sidney Monas

My subject has a vagueness that runs the risk
of becoming positively spectral.  First, I speak of
religion in general, not a particular religion, not
religion in any of its institutional forms, but rather of a certain religious framework, a religiosity,
a need for "the tie that binds," an inclination to
total commitment and to a unitary and integral world
view that embraces all aspects of life and death.
Secondly, insofar as it refers to a social formation,
the word "intelligentsia" has never been satisfactori-
ly defined.  The most conveniently used definitions
have always had about them somewhere the flavor of
religiosity that has been closely associated with
the intelligentsia from the time the term was first
used--Ivanov-Razumnik's "spiritual brotherhood," for
example.[1]

In the most famous book written about the old
Russian intelligentsia, Vekhi (Signposts) the seven
authors in each of their essays seem to be talking
about different social groupings--a contradiction
that the book's many vehement critics were not slow
to point out.[2]  The confusion prevails to our own
day.[3]

Nevertheless, the modern history of Russia is

inconceivable without the intelligentsia, by whatever
name it is called. There is an "it," for the intelligentsia identified itself (not without confusion,
to be sure) and acted as though there were an "it."
Let us therefore call "intelligentsia" those educated
persons whose identification with their education
(secular and European) was more powerful than their
sense of social origin or the professional posts that
they occupied, and who found common cause, a "brotherhood," in transmitting to (and thereby transforming) "great, unwashed Russia" the very education by
which they identified themselves. Theirs was a mission of enlightenment, of the socialization of knowledge, very like that undertaken by the French Enlightenment a century earlier. Indeed, an astute
historian, Franco Venturi, has called the period of
Russian History from 1830 to 1900 the Russian Enlightenment.[4]

Another word for "enlightenment" (or "socialization of knowledge") in this sense is, of course,
"secularization." Yet, paradoxically, Enlightenment--
especially when spelled with a big "E"--is a religious term. Many, perhaps most, of the Enlighteners
saw conventional institutional religious authority
on the one hand, and popular superstition on the
other, as the main obstacles to the fulfillment of
their mission. Part of their mission therefore became to desacralize the world of daily life, to take
away the mystery, thereby shifting authority (wheth-
this was intended or not) from its traditional, conventional embodiments to the realm of new knowledge,
especially "scientific" knowledge, to doctrines that
purported scientific knowledge, including doctrines

106

of society, and along with the sacralization of knowledge, the endowment with charisma of those who knew.

The degree to which the philosophes and ency-
clopedistes, in attacking the authority of religion,
used a religious terminology, essentially religious
conceptions, and were imbued with a religious fer-
vor and spirit, is well known. A thousand subtle
ties (both historical and ideological) link the Enlightenment to both the Reformation and the Counter-
Reformation. Robert Palmer, among others, has demonstrated something of the origins of the Enlightenment within the Jesuit order; and Carl Becker in a
witty, erudite little work of popularization has described The Heavenly City of the Eighteenth Century
Philosophers.[5]

Curiously enough, no such study has been made
of the Russian Enlightenment, where the confrontation
of presumed opposites would certainly yield equally
striking results. Nevertheless, the religious spirit
of the secularizing, modernizing intelligentsia is
sufficiently a commonplace. In his essay on "Philosophical Verity and Intelligentsia Truth," in Signposts, castigating the intelligentsia for its philosophical shallowness, Berdiaev speaks of their giving "sociological doctrines an almost theological
color"; and Bulgakov's essay in the same volume is
subtitled, "Reflections on the Religious Nature of
the Russian Intelligentsia."[6]

Among those very few liberals who at least to
some degree and in part defended the Signposters
(Vekhovtsy) from the left wing attacks and charges
of a failure of nerve, Miliukov was willing to con-
cede that the Russian intelligentsia did indeed suf-

fer from a certain irresponsibility of attitude to
the state, and a certain narrowness of culture, while
at the same time, like a true intelligent, he blamed
that irresponsibility and that narrowness on the nature of the state.  The attitude of the intelligentsia to the state had a certain characteristic irrec-
oncilability, which, without being necessarily explicitly anarchist in ideological commitment, had a
deep underlying anarchic pull.  The opposition to
autocracy and the autocratic state order, a profound
alienation from everything associated with it, was
in turn characteristic of the intelligentsia.  It is
possible that the autocracy's attempt to enhance its
authority by intensified self-sacralization in the
middle of a process of secularization that the autocracy itself had had a very important hand in ini-
tiating aroused the latent religious sensibility of
the intelligentsia.  Apart from its obscurantism,
the official church was despised by the intelligentsia primarily because it was official, an agency for
the repression of Enlightenment and the sacralization of a narrowly repressive established authority.

If I were asked to describe the most salient
features of the nineteenth century Russian intelligentsia, I would do so in the following terms:  a
mystique of science, scientism, and closely associated with it the idea of progress through the broad
dissemination of knowledge and a "correct" (i.e.,
scientific) world view; an overwhelming commitment
to at least the idea of the narod, based on a sense
of obligation (or guilt) and a sense that whatever
integrity the Russian national tradition possessed
was preserved in the forms and essence of peasant
life.  Closely associated with commitment to the

108

idea of the narod, I would call attention to the
equally characteristic hatred for meshchantsvo.  A
meshchanin was a member of the artisan-class, a petty bourgeois, and meshchanstvo was taken to mean an
absorption in the petty, parochial, selfish, quoti-
dian concerns of this class, shaped and conditioned
by poshlost', a quality difficult to render in English, but implying a kind of monumental triviality,
banality, commonplaceness accompanied by utter com-
placency and self-satisfaction.[7]  Meshchanstvo, or
Philistinism as it is sometimes (inadequately) translated, might indeed be measured by the degree of absorption in very narrowly conceived self-interest,
whether in the grotesquely poshlovatyi form assumed
by Gogol's characters (in "Ivan Shponka and his Aunt,"
or "Old-World Landowners," for instance) or even the
more poetic form poignantly articulated by Pushkin's
anti-hero Evgeny in "The Bronze Horseman":

> A bed, two chairs, a pot of cabbage soup,
> And I my own master.[8]

The history of the Russian Revolution, in the
sense of an ongoing movement, with continuity and
contiguity of organized groups, begins in the 1860s.
It consists very largely of intelligentsia attempts
to find a mass base.  A crucial chapter begins with
the industrialization of Russia in the 1890s, and effective contact between intelligentsia and industrial
proletariat, contact that has its ramifications in
the peasant village as well.  Before the 1860s, however, acute observers tended to see "religious dissent"--the large numbers of Old Believers and sectarians, legally disadvantaged and at times actively
persecuted--as the major element of unrest and dis-

turbance.  Such was the opinion of the Marquis de
Custine, who thought that religious dissent might
well bring social revolution to Russia.[9]  Such was
also the opinion of Ivan Petrovich Liprandi, a distinguished officer in the Napoleonic Wars, chief of
military police in Paris during the Russian occupation, later a military historian, and still later,
a scholar of the history of the schism and religious
dissent in Russia.  So, too, thought Count Kiselev.[10]

It is true that Liprandi later changed his mind.
When Minister of the Interior L. A. Perovsky put him
in charge of investigating the situation of the Old
Believers and dissenters, he argued for removing the
disabilities from all but the most "pernicious"
sects, asserting their potential good will and conservatism.  Kiselev and some of the slavophiles argued similarly.[11]

Among the _raznochintsy_ of the 1860s who were to
set the tone and temper of the intelligentsia for
decades to come, many were "seminarians," children
of priests or deacons, educated in church-schools
and seminaries.  Semi-educated as they were, they
formed the only _other_ even semi-educated class at
the time.[12]

They were poor, with little chance of professional advancement, and with shades of the prison-
house censorship fast falling on their newly-kindled
passion for knowledge.  In short, even within the
Orthodox clergy the conditions for the formation of
a radical revolutionary class were highly favorable,
and what is mysterious is not that so many _popovtsy_
(sons of priests) became radicals, but that the clergy as a whole was not revolutionized.[13]

Afanasy Prokop'evich Shchapov, who came from remote Siberia, whose father had been a village deacon married to a Buryat girl, whose formal education had taken place entirely in church schools, had been among the very first scholars to examine the history of the seventeenth century schism within a framework broader than the church-institutional or the technically theological.[14] In his doctoral dissertation, Shchapov as a gifted young scholar found a socio-political basis to the schism and suggested a view of the Old Believers as rebels against a state authority illegitimately usurped. Shchapov was a lecturer at Kazan Theological Academy, and he articulated all this in a very formal scholarly context, not a political one. Shortly after the publication of his dissertation, however, two events characteristic of the period served to politicize him and push him in a more radical direction.

Dobroliubov published a scathing review of Shchapov's dissertation in Sovremennik (The Contemporary) entitled "What sometimes reveals itself in liberal phrases."[15] Dobroliubov was a publicist, not a scholarly specialist. Yet his background and sensibility were very close to Shchapov's, and his style was eloquent and effective. His early death gave, in retrospect, a martyr's glow to those review articles of his of the turn of the decade. And there is no doubt Shchapov's mind had been moving in the same direction.[16]

The second event occurred two years later, when Shchapov was arrested in connection with peasant disturbances in the Kazan countryside. The government's precipitate action, as well as the plight of the peasantry, sharpened the focus of his attention

on the socio-political element in the dissenters'
resistance to the repressive power of the state.

Shchapov was a major historian. His articula-
tion of the central importance of exploration and
settlement in the history of early Russia had the
approval of Serge Soloviev and was a decisive influence on Kliuchevsky. More important, perhaps, he
saw the religious schism as the only form that resistance to an illegitimately imposed state authority
could take, a continuous breeding ground of discontent, and possible source of mass energy for the
somewhat differently focused discontent of the Intelligentsia. Nevertheless, he remained a liberal,
not really a revolutionary. After his rather quick
release by the authorities, he even accepted a post
in the Ministry of the Interior under Valuev, not
dissimilar to the one originally occupied by Libran-
di.[17]

Far less talented, but from my present point of
view not less interesting, V. I. Kelsiev, of somewhat similar origins, a bright young raznochinets,
employed by the Russian America Company because of
his facility with languages, including Chinese, tried
to explore in a more radical manner the possibilities of a link between intelligentsia discontent and
the grievances of the religious dissenters.[18] He
found his way to Herzen in England, and under Herzen's auspices, set up a series of publications designed to reach an Old Believer audience. Significantly, however, his immersion in Old Belief led not
to the enhancement of his revolutionary convictions,
but to their abandonment. Kelsiev found his way to
Constantinople, interviewed Old Believer exiles in
Turkey, and made his way illegally back into Russia,

where he was captured, confessed, and underwent a conservative conversion.[19]

Among the intelligentsia, there were of course generational differences in attitudes to religion. A man like Herzen was by his upbringing to some degree an heir of eighteenth century voltereanstvo, from which he turned, in his sense of personal isolation, to religious experience, albeit it of an unconventional unchurchly kind. Religious experience was something he had lived through, and his atheism was tempered by a sense of respect for the depths and subleties of the need for belief. He understood his intellectual antagonists, the slavophiles, who were also his friends. Belinsky was of a more fanatical temper, yet he, too, was no stranger to religious experience. His letter to Gogol, which was a kind of founding document of the intelligentsia, merely separated Christ from the Church that arose in His name.

The men of the 1860s, for often than not, came to their radical convictions, in spite of the clerical origins of many of them, without such a personal experiential crisis. Chernyshevskii seems to have remained on good terms with his father, the learned Saratov priest.[20] In tone and practice, the generation of Chernyshevskii and Dobroliubov was far less tolerant of religion and churchly practice than the intelligenty of the previous generation had been. Nevertheless, their background spoke in every phrase they wrote. Temperamentally, a churchly zeal, an ascetic discipline, and a sense of militant moral commitment show a streak of damp lime from the church walls. As for the men of the 1870s, their religion

113

of the peasant left open a gate of access to the peasant's religion, especially insofar as this could be identified (as in the case of the Old Believers) with authentic and integral Russian native tradition. For all their militancy against the church, such people were altogether unreceptive to the appeal of traditional Christianity.

The intelligentsia tended to regard the Old Believers and sectarians as victims of the state and the official church. In that sense, they shared a common enemy. In a more positive sense, the Old Believers represented the unbroken national tradition, and many of the sectarians a native form of socialism. As in the case of Kelsiev, there were also temperamental affinities. The sects and Old Believers constituted a potential mass base for revolution. Yet in spite of all this, common cause was never joined on a mass scale. For all the role that they had played in and among the cossack and peasant uprisings of the past, the sectarians and Old Believers never made common cause with intelligentsia discontent on anything like a mass scale. Intelligenty, not uncommonly, in the manner of Kelsiev, felt the pull of Christian reconversion. The cultivation of an atmosphere of guilt and heroic self-sacrifice made the intelligenty peculiarly susceptible to the "backward" tug of reconversion, as both Andrei Biely, in his novel The Silver Dove, and Vladimir Nabokov in one of his very best short stories, "A Forgotten Poet," have dramatized.[21]

At times the religious dissenters assumed the symbolic stature of "the persecuted," or, more to the point, "those persecuted for steadfastness in their

114

belief." In his diary for 1935, for instance, a
hard-bitten old atheist like Trotsky could discover
the hidden kinship between himself in exile and the
travails of the stiff-necked archpriest Avvakum,
hero of the Old Believers.

> Concerning the blows that have fallen to
> our lot, I reminded Natasha [Trotsky's
> second wife, with him in exile] the other
> day of the life of the archpriest Avvakum.
> They were stumbling on together in Si-
> beria, the rebellious priest and his
> faithful spouse. Their feet sank into the
> snow, and the poor exhausted woman kept
> falling into the snowdrifts. Avvakum re-
> lates: "And I came up, and she, poor soul,
> began to reproach me, saying: 'How long,
> archpriest, is this suffering to be?'
> And I said, 'Markovna, unto our very death.'
> And she, with a sign, answered: 'So be
> it, Petrovich, let us be getting on our
> way.'"22

The passage is of course meant to praise Natalia
Sedova, Trotsky's faithful companion. But it shows
at the same time an unmistakable sense of kinship
between "old believers."

In the year of revolution, civil war, famine,
purge, repression and exile, the old Russian intelligentsia disintegrated and disappeared. A large
proportion went into exile abroad. Others entered
a kind of inner exile the price of which at the very
least was anonymity and isolation. Countless numbers perished. What the regime officially defined
as "intelligentsia" bore no resemblance to the nineteenth century phenomenon, but consisted simply of
what we would call "white collar workers," and all
those with the equivalent of a high school education
or better--a group lacking in any kind of inner co-
herence. All the more surprising, therefore, that

after Stalin's death, in the Khrushchev era, in the
good growing weather of destalinization, a socio-
cultural phenomenon bearing a striking resemblance
to the old Russian intelligentsia emerged.

There were ties of family, friendship, and tradition with the old intelligentsia, yet somehow these
were tenuous.  One cannot see a clear and visible
continuity.  It makes more sense to think in terms
of an intelligentsia-function in the social structure that emerged from wartime recovery and destalinization.  There has emerged, since the 1950s, an increasingly self-conscious if still rather vague group
of educated people who see implicit in their education an obligatory mission, the socialization of
knowledge, not simply the knowledge conferred by
their professional education, but a sense of civilization per se, and particularly that knowledge,
whether immediately professional or not, repressed
and distorted under Stalinism.[23]

There are some striking similarities and important differences between the new intelligentsia and
the old.  The connection with Europe (by "Europe"
of course I mean America, too), for instance, the
association of modernity with the West; yet, while
this is strikingly true with regard to developments
in the arts, the practical arts, engineering and the
sciences (especially with regard to those tendencies that have been "forbidden fruit" for a long time
in the USSR) it is not true with regard to social or
political thought, and the old intelligentsia interest in Western liberalism and socialism has either
eroded away or re-emerged in the same old nineteenth
century terms without taking into account the changes that have taken place in these fields in the

116

West since 1917. Radical political developments
tend to be regarded with aversion, no matter how distant from or antithetical to Stalinism. Libertari-
anism of a sort would seem to be the prevailing spirit within the new intelligentsia, and there is much
concern with increasing the range and depth of what
can publicly be expressed, yet the few elaborations
that have been made within the "Democratic Movement"
concerning the institutional reform needed to but-
tress libertarian gains, however courageous their
authors, have shown something of the same naivete
and shallowness of understanding for which the Signposters criticized the old intelligentsia.[24]

One notes also a very different attitude to religion. The obscurantist forces to be desacralized
for the advancement of knowledge and the improvement
of the quality of life are no longer identified even
with the Church, let alone religion. There is on
the contrary a new receptivity and openness to religion and religious thought, that has strong esthetic
and moral as well as purely religious dimensions.
While there has been a certain return to institutional religion, the more general openness, friend-
liness, and receptivity to religious faith and senti-
ment in a generalized form is much more common.
Once again, the Signposter criticism of the old intelligentsia for its lack of appreciation for the
historical, institutional forms in which religion
manifests itself has a certain application to the
new intelligentsia as well.

In two very important matters, the overall attitude of the new intelligentsia differs markedly
from the old. The first involves the idealization

117

of the narod, whether conceived basically as the
peasant and the peasant way of life, as with the
narodniki, or whether in its transmogrified Marxist
form of idealization of the proletariat.  There is
scarcely any form of expression that emerges from
the milieu of the new intelligentsia that does not
express at least a certain critical weariness and
at most a complete distrust of and disillusionment
with both the peasantry and the industrial proletariat.  It is assumed that "the people" hate the intelligentsia at least as much as they hate the regime.
Common cause, or even common ground, is difficult to
find.

The second orientation point that differs markedly from the bearings taken by the old intelligentsia is that of meshchanstvo.  It is still used as a
pejorative, of course, but its meaning has shifted
rather drastically.  Sybaritic selfcenteredness, for
the true sybarite at least, is regarded with a certain indulgence, and becomes to some extent a matter
of developed taste, refinement, and knowledge.  The
development and refinement of one's taste and esthetic sensibility are no longer seen as part of the
province of meshchanstvo; nor is the yearning for a
"merely" private existence.

Narodnichestvo is of course anything but dead,
nor has meshchanstvo lost its pejorative meaning--
but the meaning of both terms has changed.  The
narod is no longer seen as the peasantry or the proletariat.  The search for a common nationhood, for a
substantial, concrete community in which to ground
a psychologically more intense and increasingly widespread nationalism, looks elsewhere.  It is also a

need for practical politics. If the intelligentsia is to turn its hatred of and alienation from the regime to any kind of political account it must seek out some kind of mass base.

From this point of view, let us examine the current situation as four very knowledgeable observers of the Soviet scene see it. The first, Grigory Pomerants, is very much a member of the intelligentsia. He is by profession an orientalist, with philosophical training. His lectures at various conferences have been far more daring and outspoken than his published works. He has also written several brilliant essays that have had a purely samizdat circulation, of which the most interesting is called "The Man from Nowhere" ("Chelovek niotkuda").[25]

First of all, Pomerants downgrades the historical importance of the narod, both in its peasant and proletarian forms. It has lost both its political and its moral significance, he claims. Peasant countries in the modern world are by definition backward countries. To the degree that a country becomes economically more advanced, the proportion of its population directly engaged in agriculture decreases, loses its traditionally "peasant" mentality, and also emerges from the economic poverty and intellectual backwardness that compounded the burden of guilt carried by the Russian intelligent. Similarly, in an industrially advanced country, a skilled worker not only performs as "educated" a task at his job as the "white collar worker," but is often better paid and politically in a far more powerful and advantageous position. Pomerants sees the immediate future as belonging to those who produce and organize tech-

nical and professional information, and the more distant future perhaps to those who "etheticise" it, who
devote themselves to refinement of the quality of
life.

These are realms in which the intelligentsia is
preeminently at home.  Not everyone devoted to them
is of course an _intelligent_, and Pomerants identifies
two other groups which he calls meshchanstvo and
cadres.  Here, meshchanstvo, while it is devoid of
the positive creative devotion to ideas, and the
critical bent of the intelligentsia, is nevertheless
educated, engaged in the same kind of professional
activity, and open and susceptible to intelligentsia
influence.  It is in short simply a middle class; no
longer, rampant philistinism.  The three groups overlap and shade into each other in Pomerants' conception.

Pomerants, as a close reader of Dostoevsky and
a literary critic of great intelligence, also knows
something about Shigalevism, by means of which an
intellectual starts from the premise of greatest
freedom and ends with the conclusion of the necessity
for absolute repression, but he tends to shrug it off
as one of those dangers inherent in the passion for
ideas.  His temperament, though liberal and receptive
to religious ideas and sentiments, is still too
closely based on his sociological-Marxist training to
prompt him to seek religious allies in the struggle
for liberty.  He tends to see the value of religion
in its esthetic creativity and psychological depth.
In short, he reads the Bible for its prose.[26]

Andrei Amalrik takes a somewhat cooler view of
Pomerants' middle professional class.  He reminds us

that, "the planned elimination from society of the most independent minded and active of its members, which has been going on for decades, has left an imprint of grayness and mediocrity on all strata of society. . . ."[27] As against the regime, the middle class is highly privileged, and by its vested interests as well as its bureaucratic mentality, it is not easily capable of translating its dissatisfactions and resentments, however intensely felt, into action of any scale; the resentment is often that of a petty clerk against his superior. For all this, however, the middle class is nevertheless the only social milieu in which the Democratic Movement, in the ideological forms that Amalrik brilliantly and concisely adumbrates, has any chance of flourishing.

One of the most striking aspects of Amalrik's essay, as I have noted elsewhere, is his devastating portrayal of the narod, of the masses of people whether peasant or industrial proletariat. He sees them as dissatisfied, and with an enormous potential for violence.[28] He sees them as needing even an ideology of opposition to the regime; yet he sees the Democratic Movement, the intelligentsia, that is, as least able to fulfill such a need. The formerly much worshipped popular demand for justice and equality is acknowledged by Amalrik as having some psychological basis--yet he places it in the most devastating light. He sees the popular conception of justice as boiling down to the demand that "no one flourish at my expense," and the related conception of equality as meaning that "nobody live better than I do," though he may well live worse. Along with justice and equality, he sees the narod requiring

121

from the regime and respecting in it its power--the sheer exercise of force, in whatever cause. In his autobiographical account of how he became a cow herd on a Siberian kolkhoz, Amalrik sometimes humorously, sometimes grimly documents this bleak portrait.[29]

As for religion, Amalrik seems detached and a little distant from it; certainly not hostile in the manner of a nineteenth century intelligent, but not exactly a "seeker." He includes the revival of "Christian ideology" among the major ideological trends of the Democratic Movement, and he sees the revival of interest in religion as of considerably broader scope than that, and of considerable moral and esthetic significance in the context of the regime's moral-esthetic bankruptcy. He also sees the inevitable confluence of traditional Russian religion and traditional Russian nationalism, a phenomenon he acknowledges with something less than pure joy. But he does not see the movement back to religion as in itself a factor of major political significance, not does he speculate on a possible juncture of religious interests among the intelligentsia with those or a more primitive nature (the increase in the number of evangelical sects like the Baptists, Jehovah's Witnesses, and others, which seem to be today's analogies to the Old Believers and sectarians) among the narod. The central core of his apocalyptic vision however is the intensification of nationalism, and, linked to that, a coming war with China.

Solzhenitsyn, in comparison with Pomerants and Amalrik, emerges as almost a slavophile.[30] It is of course relative. He is very careful to avoid any idealization of the peasantry as a class, or a way of life.

In The First Circle, Solzhenitsyn's hero Nerzhin, an authorial surrogate, describes his education and disenchantment in the process of his peculiar "khozhdenie v narod," his experience in the
labor camps:

> It turned out that the People had no home-
> spun superiority to him. . . . They did
> not endure hunger and thirst any more
> stoically. They were no more firm of spirit
> as they faced the stone wall of a ten-year
> term. They were no more far-sighted or
> adroit than he during the difficult moments
> of transports and body-searches. They were
> blinder and more trusting about informers.
> They were more prone to believe the crude
> deception of the bosses. They awaited
> amnesties - which Stalin would have rather
> died than given them. If some camp martinet
> happened to be feeling good and smiled,
> they hastened to smile back to him. And
> they were greedier for petty things. . . .[31]

Above all, what the narod lacks is "that personal
point of view": what Nerzhin and his author value
above all else, that sense of the uniqueness and supreme value of the individual personality.

And yet this passage occurs as a kind of pre-
lude to the appearance of one of the most Tolstoyan
and Karataev-like characters in Solzhenitsyn, the
peasant Spiridon, whose wisdom Solzhenitsyn quotes
in the form of a rhyming proverb, incidentally
straight out of Dal', that might well have served
as epigraph for Solzhenitsyn's Collected Works:
"Volkodav prav, a liudoed net." (The wolf hound is
right; the cannibal is wrong).[32] Along with Ivan
Denisovich and Matriona, Spiridon projects an image
of old fashioned Russian Blagoobrazie, a kind of in-
ward beauty, religious in its roots, benevolent and

wise in its relationship to fellow sufferers in the
human community, and pious and kenotic in its acceptance of fate and the universe. None of these characters are overtly religious in the sense of maintaining ritual observances in any regular churchly
way; yet a religious sense of life is part of their
decency, dignity, and humane sensitivity.[33]

Aliosha the Baptist in One Day of Ivan Denisovich is seen by the protagonist in an admiring, even
to some degree an envious light: Ivan Denisovich
appreciates the sustaining power of his barracks-
mate's rather narrow and rigid beliefs; yet there is
also an implication in this recognition of their re-
gidity of a certain coldness and distance.[34] None
of Solzhenitsyn's major fictional protagonists, except for General Samsonov (a historical rather than
a purely fictional character) in August, 1914, are
conventionally religious.[35] Yet the element of religious openness and seeking is clearly present in
all his work, as Father Alexander Schmemann acutely
noted, and as Solzhenitsyn himself later acknowledged.[36] With time, the religious element has become increasingly self-conscious. Solzhenitsyn has
exhorted intellectuals to take religious believers
in Russia, especially the sectarians, as models of
fortitude and perseverance, especially in their
choosing to "dig in" and survive rather than emigrate.[37]

In Iz-pod glyb, (From Under the Rubble) Solzhenitsyn as editor has deliberately evoked echoes
of Signposts and its lesser known (1918) sequel,
From the Depths (Iz glubiny).[38] The book in general
is addressed to the intelligentsia, and like Sign-

124

posts it urges repentance and reflection, spiritual
introspection and a deepening of respect for both
religious and national values, for a deeper spiritu-
alization.  In one of the most interesting essays in
the volume, Solzhenitsyn himself addresses what he
calls the obrazovanshchina (translated by Max Hayward as "the smatterers"--i.e., the half-educated)
and exhorts them to become a full-fledged intelligentsia by a simple but demanding moral expedient:
not to lie.  It is programmatically consistent with
Solzhenitsyn's other exhortations:  to the Writers'
Union, to be a real union, which means to look primarily to the interests of writers; to Patriarch Pimen, to be the leader of a church; and even to the
Soviet leaders, to be genuine national leaders,
which means to abandon Marxist ideology and international adventurism.[39]  In this vein, he urges the
obrazovanshchina to become an intelligentsia.

If we compare these three very gifted writers
in terms of their attitudes to the intelligentsia,
the peasantry, their view of the importance of organized, institutional religion, we see an interesting
correlation.  To the degree that the intelligentsia
is seen as the main hope for a freer Russia, broader
liberties, and a more intensive pursuit of truth,
the peasantry and the narod is viewed negatively,
and the importance of institutional religion is
either disregarded or disparaged.  All three writers,
of course, are libertarians; all three are more open
and receptive to religious sentiments and views than
official policy would allow; and all three are critical of the narod and self consciously guarded about

125

repeating the "mistakes" of narodnichestvo. In this context, however, the gradations and correlation are clear and striking.

Pomerants has very high hopes for the intelligentsia, and takes a dim view of the narod. His interest in religion is on the level of ideas; he finds religion intellectually interesting, but invests little moral hope in it. Amalrik has a stronger sympathy for religion, which he nevertheless keeps at a fair distance from his social analyses. He is an ironist by temperament, and analyzes very acutely the weaknesses of the intelligentsia as an agent for social or political change. His view of the narod is, to put it mildly, extremely critical; yet he sees the possibility of change (perhaps for the worse; but not necessarily) as more likely to emerge from a popular than from an intelligentsia milieu. Solzhenitsyn does not completely reject, but has little hope in the intelligentsia, is critical of, yet hopeful for, the narod; and along with an increasing skepticism toward Western liberalism and conservatism) shows an increasing reliance on and hope for conventional religion in alliance with a respect for national traditions.

To the observations of the three Russian writers I have summarized, I would like to add the appraisal of the current intelligentsia made by an acute and knowledgeable American observer, George Feifer.[40] He describes a post-1968 mood of passivity and despair, tempered only by a carpe diem hedonism; a disdain for the activists of the Democratic Movement exceeded only by contempt for the regime and anything that may be preceded by the adjective "Soviet." While he attributes much of this mood to an almost

126

universal tendency on the part of intellectuals
to overreact to dramatic shifts in public posture
(such as the invasion and occupation of Czechoslovakia) and much of it to a natural unwillingness to
jeopardize positions of relative privilege, while at
the same time increasingly aware of the utter dis-
honesty and ineptitude of the heavy-handed regime.
Basically, however, he sees this withdrawal into an
unhappy "late Roman" posture as caused by a growing
conviction that even a radical change in the regime
would in the long run make little difference, because basically the condition of the great mass of
the narod is backward and repressive and would sooner or later exert its pressures on any regime and
mold it into something not terribly different from
what now prevails.

"They [Feifer's intelligentsia friends] felt
that democratic movements are futile at this stage
in Russia's history because the people are not ready
for them."[41]  One of his friends asked of him:  "Are
you mad?. . . .  Are you suggesting that I should
be?  That I should sacrifice myself for 'the people'
who don't give one damn about my 'funny' ideas about
freedom and dignity?. . . .  Yes, I love my people,
for all their trusting, pitiable gullibility and en-
durance to mistreatment.  But I'm not yet demented
enough to risk my head trying to 'help' them.  Do
you understand that they feel I'm the enemy--not the
brutes who enslave them?"[42]

It may or may not be relevant to Feifer's appraisal of intelligentsia attitudes toward the Democratic Movement, the regime, the narod, self-sacrifice and hedonistic meshchantsvo, but neither in the

essay I have cited nor in his other writings that I
have read does he evince much interest in or attribute much importance to "the new religiosity."[43]

I cannot close an essay on "Religion and the
Intelligentsia" in the context of "modernization"
without pointing out that the whole conception of
"modernization," which for both the philosophes of
the eighteenth century and the intelligenty of the
Russian nineteenth century Enlightenment had such a
vastly positive meaning, has for us at least lost
much of its afflatus. Scientism, positivism, belief
in the Idea of Progress--who among us reposes much
confidence in them any longer? Industrialism, Ur-
banism, and Education--that Holy Trinity of moderni-
zation--no longer appear to us, to put it mildly, as
wholly positive terms. We see a devastated environment, a suburbanization of our cities and a determined return of whatever segments of the population
can afford to do so to a more rural-seeming environment, and with professionalization and the proliferation of the costs of education, we begin to speak
of "de-schooling" with some earnestness. We have also learned, I think rightly, to become critical of
the conception of modernization as it is applied by
Western" scholars to what used to be known as "underdeveloped societies." Modernization, Western, underdeveloped: these are all ideological terms.[44] Surely, the sheer growth of cities, the expansion of
Gross National Product, and the increasing proliferation of schools cannot in themselves any longer be
seen as key indices of 'progress' in a humanly meaningful sense. Some writers cite the simultaneous decline of death and birth rate as the true index of
"modernization." With this, it is difficult to dis-

128

agree--as difficult as it seems for them to agree on
what the necessary social pre-conditions of such a
decline might be.

In such a context, an impulse to return to a
religious view of life is by no means confined to
the Soviet Union. There, the re-emergence of something like the "spiritual brotherhood" of the old
intelligentsia has to be seen as accompanying the
worldwide discrediting of the old-fashioned, rather
shallow scientistic rationalism that the Signposters
had deplored as the most characteristic belief of
the old intelligentsia. This impulse is by no means
accompanied by a single political tendency. Insofar
as it tends to lead a large number of people back to
conventional-traditional religious systems and the
(on the whole) quite conservative institutions that
have evolved from those systems, I think the conservative implications of the new religiosity have been
underestimated. In the Soviet Union, of course, any
impulse in the direction of religion, especially of
religious practice, must for the time being at least
be to some degree libertarian, so that there is indeed a potential common ground between "believers"
and "liberals." But how broad is that field, and
for how long will it serve? At the moment, religion
and often closely connected with it, nationalism,
seem to provide the only point of contact between
the intelligentsia and the masses. Given such a
meeting ground, and given the putative nature of the
intelligentsia and the narod, the question remains:
who will transform whom?

NOTES

1. R. Ivanov-Razumnik, <u>Istoriia russkoi obshches-tvennoi mysli</u>, 2 vols. (St. Petersburg, 1911, reprint ed., The Hague: Mouton, 1969). The book is subtitled "Individualism and <u>Meshchanstvo</u> in the Russian Literature and Life of the Nineteenth Century." See also his <u>Ob intelligentsii</u> (St. Petersburg, 1910).

2. M. O. Gershenzon (editor), <u>Vehki</u>, 2nd ed. (Moscow, 1909, reprint ed., Frankfurt: Posev, 1967); for a sympathetic appraisal and an account of the book's reception see L. Shapiro, "The <u>Vekhi</u> Group and the Mystique of Revolution," <u>Slavonic and East European Review</u>, no. 34 (December 1955), pp. 55-76.

3. As, for example, in the very interesting symposium edited by Richard Pipes, <u>The Russian Intelligentsia</u> (New York: Columbia University Press, 1961).

4. Franco Venturi, <u>Roots of Revolution</u> (New York: Alfred Knopf, 1960), p. 243.

5. Robert R. Palmer, Catholics and Unbelievers in Eighteenth Century France (New York: Cooper Square, 1961); Carl Becker, <u>The Heavenly City of the Eighteenth Century Philosophers</u> (New Haven: Yale University Press, 1932).

6. <u>Vekhi</u>, pp. 1-22; p. 23

7. For an eloquent expansion on the meaning of <u>poshlost'</u> in Gogol and elsewhere, see Vladimir Nabokov, <u>Nikolai Gogol</u> (New York: New Directions, 1944), pp. 63-74.

8. Krovat', dva stula; shchei gorshok
Da sam bol'shoi. . . .

A. S. Pushkin, <u>Polnoe sobranie sochinenii v desiati tomakh</u> (Moscow, 1949), 4:539. Since "<u>Mednyi vsadnik</u>" (The Bronze Horseman) was not published in full in Pushkin's lifetime, there is still some controversy about the most authentic text. The lines quoted here are given as a "variant" in the Academy of Sciences edition.

9. Astolphe de Custine, <u>Russia</u>, translated anon. (New York: Appleton, 1854, abridgement and trans. by P. P. Kohler, <u>Journey for our Time</u>, New York: Pel-

130

legrini and Cudahy, 1951), pp. 204-208; see also the book by George Kennan, <u>The Maruqis de Custine and his Russia in 1839</u> (Princeton: Princeton University Press, 1971).

10. For a brief sketch of Liprandi, especially in connection with his role in the Petrashevsky affair, see my book, <u>The Third Section: Police and Society in Russia under Nicholas I</u> (Cambridge: Harvard University Press, 1961), pp. 248-260; see also the article by A. El'mitsky in <u>Russkii biograficheskii slovar'</u> (New York: reprinted ed., Kraus Reprint Corp.), 10:450-453, which contains a bibliography of his published works on the Old Believers; re Count Kiselev, see N. M. Druzhinin, <u>Gosudarstvennye Krest' iane i reforms P. D. Kiselev,</u> 2 vols. (Moscow, 1946-1958), passim.

11. <u>R.b.s.</u>, 10:452; Druzhinin, 2:561.

12. The education of the dvoriantsvo tended not to take place in schools, and is held together largely by its common European orientation. Venturi, pp. 129-133, suggests that our notion of the backwardness and ignorance of the church schools, stemming from common report, and such literary works as N. G. Pomialovsky's <u>Seminary Sketches</u>, trans. A. R. Kuhn (Ithaca, New York: Cornell University Press, 1973), needs seriously to be modified. Leskov was, of course, the great literary portraitist of the Russian clergy, and in one of his most interesting novels, he describes the ordeals of a village priest in apocalyptic terms--in <u>Soboriane</u> (Cathedral Folk).

14. A. O. Shchapov, <u>Sochineniia</u>, 3 vols. (St. Petersburg, 1906-08); <u>Neizdannye Sochineniia</u>, ed. E. I. Chernyshev (Kazan, 1927).

15. The review appeared in <u>Sovremennik</u>, 1859, No. 9; see also N. A. Dobroliubov, <u>Polnoe sobranie sochinenii</u>, 6 volumes (Moscow, 1937), 4:318-323, and the note on p. 527, where some disputed details of authorship are discussed.

16. For a view of the Old Believers that seems to emerge from Shchapov's though it is far more incisive and eloquent, see Michael Cherniavsky, "The Old Believers and the New Religion," in <u>The Structure of Russian History: Interpretive Essays</u>, ed. Michael Cherniavsky (New York: Random House, 1970), pp. 140-

188.

17. See N. Serbov's excellent article on Shchapov in the R.b.s., 14:1-11.

18. Venturi, pp. 187-203; V. I. Delsiev, "Ispoved'," in Literaturnoe nasledstvo, ed. E. Kingisepp, intro. M. Klevenskii, nos. 41-42 (Moscow), pp. 253 ff.

19. Herzen seems to have treated his defection with a certain manganimity. The degree and detail in which Kelsiev turned police informer is not clear. See Lit. Nasl, nos. 41-42 (1941), p. 253.

20. W. F. Woehrlin, Chernyshevskii: the Man and the Journalist (Cambridge: Harvard University Press, 1971), pp. 13-27.

21. A. Biely, The Silver Dove, trans. George Reavey (New York: Grove Press, 1974); V. Nabokov, "A Forgotten Poet," in Nabokov's Dozen (New York: Doubleday, 1958, reprint ed., Freeport, N.Y.: Books for Libraries Press, 1969) pp. 39-54.

22. Trotsky's Diary in Exile: 1935, trans. Elena Zarudnaya (Cambridge: Harvard University Press, 1958), p. 135. The entry is for June, but undated.

23. See the excellent article by Leopold Haimson, "Three Generations of the Soviet Intelligentsia," Foreign Affairs No. 37 (January 1959), pp. 235-246; also his essay, "The Solitary Hero and the Philistines: A Note on the Heritage of the Stalin Era," in Pipes, The Russian Intelligentsia.

24. See the review-article by Marc Raeff, "Iz-pod glyb and the History of Russian Social Thought," Russian Review 34 (October 1975):476-488.

25. The essay is included in G. Pomerants, Neopublikovannoe (Frandfurt: Posev), 1972.

26. At a symposium at the Dostoevsky Museum in Leningrad in late 1974, Pomerants delivered a lecture on "Dostoevsky and Zen Buddhism."

27. Andrei Amalrik, Will the Soviet Union Survive until 1984? (New York: Harper, 1970), p. 18.

28. See my "Afterword," to Amalrik, ibid.,

"Amalrik's Vision of the End."

29. Andrei Amalrik, Involuntary Journey to Siberia, trans. Manya Harari and Max Hayward (New York:
Harcourt Brace, 1970), pp. 166-177, 184-194.

30. The best collection of essays on Solzhenitsyn is John Dunlop et al., Alexander Solzhenitsyn:
Critical Essays and Documentary Materials (Belmont:
Nordland, 1973); see also the collection of critical
essays edited by Kathryn Feuer, Solzhenitsyn (Engel-
wood Cliffs, N.J.: Prentice-Hall, 1976); see also
my essay, "Enginneers or Martyrs," in In Quest of Justice, ed. A. Brumberg (New York: Praeger, 1970). The
revival of slavophilism has been written about most
trenchantly by Aleksandr Ianov (Yanov), "Slavianofi-
ly i Konstantin Leont'ev," Voprosy f ilosofii, no. 8
(1969), pp. 97-106. Yanov left the Soviet Union in
1974, and now resides in the United States, where, to
our shame, one of the most knowledgeable and insight-
ful and witty of Russian "publitsisty" has not yet
found suitable employment. At the meeting of the
American Association for the Advancement of Slavic
Studies in Atlanta in October 1975, he delivered
an excellent paper on Solzhenitsyn called "Halfway
to Leontiev," as yet unpublished. There is an excellent discussion of Yanov's work and the phenomenon he investigated in George Kline, "Religion,
National Character, and the 'Rediscovery of Russian
Roots,'" Slavic Review 32 (1973):29-40; see also
George Pomerants, Valery Chalidze, and Alexander
Esenin-Volpin, "Recent Uncensored Soviet Philosophi-
cal Writings," in Dissent in the USSR: Politics,
Ideology, and People, ed. Rudolf L. Tokes (Baltimore:
John Hopkins University Press, 1975), pp. 158-190.

31. Aleksandr Solzhenitsyn, The First Circle,
trans. Thomas Whitney (New York: Bantam Books, 1969),
p. 451.

32. Ibid., p. 466; A. Solzhenitsyn, Sobranie
sochinenii v shesti tomakh (Frankfurt: Posev, 1968-
71) 4:561.

33. A. Solzhenitsyn, One Day in the Life of Ivan
Denisovich, trans. Max Hayward and Ronald Hingley
(New York: Bantam Books, 1963); Stories and Prose
Poems, trans. Michael Glenny (New York: Farrar,
Straus and Giroux, 1971) pp. 3-52.

34. See especially, Ivan Denisovich, pp. 195-199.

35. Samsonov, although a historic figure, is genuinely "created" by Solzhenitsyn--one of his most vivid and memorable characters. A. Solzhenitsyn, August, 1914, trans. Michael Glenny (New York: Bantam Books, 1972).

36. Alexander Schmemann's essay, "On Solzhenitsyn" is included in Dunlop's Solzhenitsyn as well as Solzhenitsyn's response.

37. This has been a running motif, along with some of the responses engendered in the journal, Kontinent, edited by Vladimir Maksimov, more or less under Solzhenitsyn's aegis.

38. See the articles already cited by Marc Raeff and Leonard Schapiro; also Schapiro's Rationalism and Nationalism in Russian Nineteenth Century Political Thought (New Haven: Yale University Press, 1967); also Max Hayward's "introduction" in From Under the Rubble, pp. v-viii.

39. Solzhenitsyn's letters to the Writers' Union and to Patriarch Pimen are included in Dunlop's Solzhenitsyn; Letter to the Soviet Leaders, trans. Hilary Sternberg (New York: Harper, 1974).

40. George Feifer, "No Protest: The Case of the Passive Minority," in Tokes, pp. 418-438.

41. Ibid., p. 422

42. Ibid., p. 424

43. See for instance Russia Close-up (London: Cape, 1973); Our Motherland and Other Ventures (New York: Viking, 1974). I do not speak of his excellent study of Soviet criminal law, Justice in Moscow (New York: Simon and Schuster, 1964).

44. Recent books on the subject, exceptionally intelligent and competent, that survey the problem critically yet do not altogether escape an ideological tint: C. E. Black, The Dynamics of Modernization (New York: Harper, 1966); C. E. Black et al., The Modernization of Japan and Russia; M. J. Levy, Modernization: Latecomers and Survivors (New York: Basic Books, 1972). For a different view of moderni-

zation, see Ivan Illich, <u>Celebration of Awareness</u> (Garden City, New York: Doubleday, 1970); <u>Deschooling Society</u> (New York: Harper, 1971); <u>Tools for Conviviality</u> (New York: Harper, 1973); <u>Medical Nemesis</u> (New York: Harper, 1976).

Chapter 5
## RELIGION AND SECULARIZATION IN THE SOVIET UNION:
## THE ROLE OF ANTIRELIGIOUS CARTOONS

David E. Powell

> The whip is still underestimated as a wea-
> pon of human progress.  I know of no more
> effective means than the whip for raising
> man from all fours, for stopping man kneel-
> ing before someone or something.  I am
> speaking, of course, not of whips plaited
> from strips of leather, but of whips plaited
> from words. . . ., the whips of irony, sar-
> casm and satire.
> Evgeny Zamiatin

For almost six decades, the Communist Party of
the Soviet Union has endeavored to remold the values,
attitudes, expectations, and behaviors of the Soviet
people.  Although they have long claimed that social
and economic revolutions would themselves alter individuals' views and behavior, the political authorities have also sought, through the use of multi-
faceted propaganda programs, to hasten the attain-
ment of these objectives.  Their programs of indoctrination and education--aimed at the so-called
"communist upbringing [kommumisticheskoe vospitanie]"
of the populace--have been designed to achieve two
purposes.  They are supposed to change the views of
adults, and at the same time, to inculcate into
younger people, who have fewer and less firmly held
preconceptions and attitudes, views that the party
deems correct.  The ultimate objective is to rid

136

Soviet society of such "negative traits" as individualism, "bourgeois nationalism," chauvinism, indolence, and "religious prejudices." The citizen of the future—the New Soviet Man—will have none of these characteristics; instead, he will be imbued with feelings of collectivism, proletarian internationalism, socialist patriotism, love of labor, and militant atheism. It is this last objective—transforming a population "suffering from religious prejudices" into one which is guided by notions of "scientific atheism,"—that will be our focus here.

Except for a few brief periods of relative accommodation, the party has been insistent on undermining the influence of the church. The Soviet leaders, that is, have always viewed secularization as basic to their political program. As Marxists, they expected secularization to follow from scientific progress and socio-economic change. But as Leninists, they decided to accelerate this process by pursuing a policy of secularization. While they professed confidence that religion would eventually die out (its disappearance was said to be "demanded by history"), they sought to hasten this supposedly inevitable process.

The linking of an ultimate goal that is allegedly inevitable with conscious, purposive activity to achieve it is a basic feature of Soviet political life, just as it was for the Bolsheviks before they assumed power. Impatience with the slow pace of history is fundamental to the Leninist version of Marxism; it is considered expedient and just to accelerate the pace of history. To be sure, there is a logical contradiction between a determinist philosophy of history and aggressive political action.

137

But, as Robert V. Daniels has pointed out, this contradiction makes a great deal of sense in psychological terms. The man who is convinced of the inevitability of his cause "strives all the more vigorously to make sure it succeeds."[1] Thus, while man cannot alter the laws of nature or social development, he can act as an agent of the historical process, and thus bring about the results that the laws of history themselves require. Current Soviet antireligious efforts make sense only in the context of this official logic.

According to the official rhetoric, as the Soviet Union draws closer to the ultimate communist society, defects in the system become matters of increasing concern and the target of more intense and energetic measures.[2] Thus, the very fact that religious belief has been partially eroded over the half-century of communist rule is said to have made the task of fully eradicating it more difficult. It is sometimes argued, much as Stalin did with respect to other class enemies, that the religious "enemy" becomes more and more resourceful with each victory on the atheist front. As one newspaper editorial put it, "Religion is on the run, but its adherents try all the harder to maintain their influence on young minds."[3]

Precisely how to combat the forces of religion has been and remains the subject of considerable controversy in official circles in the USSR. In fact, there is a great deal of confusion among party officials, including those responsible for ideological matters, on the very nature and purpose of atheist work. There is substantial disagreement on the most basic of questions, including the crucial mat-

ter of how much emphasis should be placed on persuasive techniques, and how much on coercion.

While policy toward the church has always involved a mixture of persuasion, coercion, and the
threat of coercion, the period since Stalin's death
has been marked by increased reliance on propaganda
and educational measures. As Nancy Heer has pointed
out, "the rejection of terror as the central instrument of control requires a much heavier reliance
upon internalized or subjective norms."[4] The central element in the current phase of the war on religion, then involves the use of limited means to
erode the strength of the enemy. Outright terror
has been essentially discarded as an instrument of
policy, and atheist propaganda has come to play the
dominant role in the struggle against religion.

## PROPAGANDA AND SATIRE IN THE USSR

One of the most interesting and least studied
methods of antireligious propaganda in the mass media is political satire, especially the use of cartoons. The themes that are featured, as well as the
characters, language and other symbols utilized,
tell us a great deal about the regime's values and
concerns. An observation once made about political
cartooning in the USA--"Graphic satire is a kind of
journalistic totem pole of our attitudes and feelings
. . . ."[5]--can be applied with even greater force to
the USSR. There, political satire has had a long
and fascinating history, and it would seem today to
provide a splendid opportunity for lampooning religion.

According to Soviet literary critics, over the
years satire "has played a great role in combatting

139

everything that has impeded the formation of the man of the new, socialist society." The party, it is said, "has directed the blows of satire at whatever most impeded the successful construction of social-ism."[6] But the evidence suggests a far more complex and contradictory policy. The regime has almost always been wary of satirical art as a medium of political communication, and at times official reservations have been transformed into outright repression of satire and satirists.

From the party's point of view, satire can aid in the process of ushering in the communist millenium. In particular, artists can help to show that the negative features of present day society--including religious beliefs and behaviors--are merely "vestiges of the past." These "atypical traits," which allegedly are being replaced by others more appropriate to the ultimate communist future, are viewed as a proper subject for ridicule. By lampooning inappropriate views and conduct, the satirist is supposed to contribute to their disappearance.

But the regime's enthusiasm for satirical art has generally been muted by a fear that public discussion of various "vestiges of the past" would exaggerate their significance in Soviet society. During the first decade of the Soviet regime, for example, leading members of the creative intelligentsia, as well as the authorities, seriously questioned the artistic and political value of laughter. During the 1920s some analysts even suggested that satire was outmoded or dangerous, inasmuch as the Revolution "had undermined the roots of social evil in the country." Thus, V. Blum wrote, "We do not need satire. It is harmful to the nature of the workers' and pea-

sants' state."[7]  N. Krynetskii was even more outspoken on this issue.  He argued that satire was an
inappropriate medium--even a logical impossibility--
since "we no longer have any major enemy."  He went
on to argue strenuously that the country's recent
history made any effort at humor an act bordering on
indecency.  To quote Krynetskii, "war, revolution,
famine and struggle. . . .in no way dispose people
toward laughter."  "There is," he claimed, "no one
to laugh at," and therefore "laughter has, for the
time being, died."[8]

The expression of such views soon subsided, and
"idealistic notions of laughter as a purely biological phenomenon"[9] eventually disappeared.  They were
replaced during the Stalin years by official demands
that satire be harnessed to the regime's massive
programs of "social transformation."  As a recent
Soviet study has described this shift, the discussions which took place during the 1920s "put an end
to the false conception of satire as a phenomenon
allegedly having nothing in common with politics, and
with the refusal of some writers to recognize satire
as an effective means of building socialism and
rearing the new man."[10]

After Stalin assumed control of the Soviet political system in the late 1920s, he brought cultural
life increasingly under the control of the regime.
The standards by which cultural activities were
judged soon ceased to revolve around the notion of
"art for art's sake"; instead, writers, artists, cartoonists and others active in the sphere of culture
had to devote themselves to party-defined and party-
supervised "educational work" (vospitatel'naia ra-

141

bota) among the masses. As the boundaries separating culture from politics were effaced and "cultural workers" became more and more responsive to the
the demands of official policy, political satire in
the USSR grew increasingly didactic. For a time,
the remarkable doctrine of beskonfliktnost' (non-
conflict) set the limits on acceptable satirical
themes and techniques. According to this theory,
there was no antagonism between "good" and "bad" in
Soviet society--only between "good" and "better."[11]
A number of literary figures and official spokesmen,
arguing that the Soviet system was without essential
flaws or contradictions, even called for the development of a "positive" satire, one which would draw
the appropriate political conclusions in an especially simple and explicit manner.[12]

In trying to steer writers and artists in the
desired direction, regime spokesmen emphasized the
instrumental role assigned to satire. As A. V. Lunacharsky put it in a 1931 speech, "Laughter has always
been an important dimension of social progress. The
role of laughter is great in our struggle, the final
struggle for the liberation of mankind."[13] Several
years later, in an address to the First Congress of
Writers, M. Kol'tsov was even more outspoken in
pressing for greater political and social militancy
among satirists. "Satire is the most aggressive,
the most attack-oriented [atakuiushchii], the most
powerful [vredonosimyi] kind of literary weapon,"
he declared. "Indeed," he reminded his listeners,
"it was said long ago that laughter kills."[14]

Thus, while satirical words were published during the Stalin years, and while satirists were encouraged to bring forth more works, the emphasis was

142

always on satire as a political weapon. Mirra Ginsburg has pointed out that during this era,

> . . . .the cry was raised repeatedly: 'We
> need laughter!' This was invariably quali-
> fied: 'We need healthy, positive, life-
> affirming laughter, clearing the way to a
> Communist future.' The makers of a grimly
> humorless society demanded humor--but made
> to their own specifications and serving
> their own ends.[15]

Political satire was rigidly bound by the official value system, and it was invariably used to support official policies at home and abroad.

In the years since the dictator's death in 1953, the official conception of satirical art has not changed significantly. Major developments in belles lettres, drama and poetry, as well as serious efforts to enliven the mass media, have not been accompanied by equivalent changes in the quality of Soviet satire--especially political cartooning. To be sure, the regime now considers itself to be essentially free from "domestic enemies," which means that it can afford the luxury of--and even seek to derive political profit from--satirical works. Lunacharsky's famous aphorism, "Laughter is a sign of strength," is once again being quoted frequently, after having been consigned to oblivion for almost half a century.[16] One literary analyst has even urged both readers and writers to laugh at "existing contradictions," suggesting that satirists focus on "the absurd, the pitiful, the repulsive, and the comical."[17]

But today, no less than in Stalin's time, the purpose of satire is to identify, "unmask" and root out defects in the socio-economic order, and to criticize individuals and groups whose behavior does not

143

conform to official prescriptions. The 1961 party program sets as one of the principal tasks of Soviet literature the "exposing [oblichenie] of everything that opposes society's movement forward."[18] Citing the party line, leading literary critics continue to link satire with the regime's political objectives. For example, E. K. Ozimitel' has called upon satirists "to create works which will inculcate into the Soviet people the features of the new socialist morality."[19] Similarly, A. Makarian has spoken of satire as "a special weapon in the class struggle," an instrument for "organizing the backward masses" to abandon certain customs and notions and adopt others in their stead.[20] Satirical art, Makarian has written,

> . . . .must have a sobering effect; it must move forward those who lag behind; it must combat harmful customs and attitudes that linger on from the past; and it must liberate people from vestiges of the past.
> . . . . In exposing shortcomings and defects, in waging war with obstacles which impede our progressive movement, Soviet satire reveals the truth, affirms what is new and progressive, and helps in the task of building communism.[21]

The conclusion seems inescapable, then, that the satirist remains little more than a handmaiden of the regime. His targets are those that the agitprop apparatus deems suitable, and the methods he employs must conform to the familiar standards of partiinost' (party-mindedness), ideinost' (high ideological level) and narodnost' (intelligibility to the masses).[22]

## POLITICAL CARTOONING AND SATIRE

An American professor of journalism has aptly

noted that the political cartoon "is a caricature--
an exaggeration." In a very real sense, he goes on,
it is an "inaccuracy which should have no place in
responsible journalism." By their very nature, cartoons lend themselves to over-simplification and
stereotyped imagery. "The cartoonist must tell his
story in black and white, literally and figuratively.
He cannot qualify without weakening impact, and impact is everything to a cartoonist."[23] The need for
striking visual images and the requirement that only
a few phrases or sentences accompany the picture impose severe limits on the cartoonist's ability to
genuinely explore any complex issue. In fact, of
course, political cartoonists deliberately avoid
balanced treatment of their subjects: the cartoon is
a classic form of visual agitation, not a careful
examination of the various sides of an issue. "Tem-
perance and compromise" are incompatible with the
basic requirements of political cartooning. The cartoon "is strictly an offensive weapon. . . . Asking
a cartoonist to attack deliberately is like arguing
with a cannon to do its work without so much
noise."[24]

The distortion inevitable in political cartooning is reinforced under Soviet conditons by the ten-
ets of the official ideology and the fact of political control over all forms of cultural expression.
Soviet satirists, especially political cartoonists,
are even less constrained than their "bourgeois"
counterparts by demands for accuracy, even-handed-
ness, and representativeness. They are urged to be
highly selective, to focus their attention only on
those aspects of Soviet life or conditions abroad
which the regime wishes them to highlight. Cherny-

shevskii pointed out a century ago that satire is an extreme form of criticism. "The satirical mood," he wrote, "is distinguished from the critical by its extreme character, by not being concerned with the objectivity of the pictures, and with the exaggeration it permits."[25] Today, the Soviet authorities do not merely permit exaggeration; they strongly encourage it and, on occasion, require it.

More accurately, the regime places two somewhat contradictory demands on satirists. On the one hand, they are encouraged to look honestly and critically at people's behavior and attitudes. The artist is explicitly instructed to deal with what he sees-- "not with the life which is desired, but real, honest life which is not desired, which contradicts our image of the beautiful life we desire, our aesthetic, social and political ideals, or which deviates from these ideals."[26] On the other hand, the satirist is required to let himself be guided by an optimistic vision of the future, "to depict reality in its revolutionary development, to see our own future."[27] The latter formula is interpreted by those who oversee Soviet cultural policy in a way that is incompatible with the former exhortation. Indeed, it often requires cartoonists to exaggerate the traits of their characters and the content of their messages to such a degree that they cease to be humorous. As we shall see, the antireligious cartoons carried in the Soviet media are, with few exceptions, striking chiefly for their banality, heavy-handedness, and blatantly propagandistic approach to religion.

Most newspapers--from the typical factory wall newspaper to the mass-circulation Moscow dailies-- carry occasional antireligious cartoons. In addi-

146

tion, many political journals and popular magazines publish cartoons on atheist themes. The most useful source for cartoons dealing with religion, however, is the satirical magazine Krokodil. This journal, published 36 times a year in an edition of almost 6,000,000 copies, mocks a wide range of institutions and behaviors. In fact, according to an authoritative source, Krokodil's principal function is "to combat negative phenomena, which are alien to Soviet reality, and to unmask bourgeois ideology and imperialist reaction."[28] While Krokodil is not the only publication that has been given this responsibility--there have been scores of Soviet satirical publications, many of which are still in existence[29] --it is by far the most important and most widely read.

Krokodil, it should be noted, has on occasion been subjected to severe criticism by the highest party authorities. On three occasions--in 1927, 1948, and 1951--the CPSU Central Committee has rebuked the journal's editors for their "errors and shortcomings." In 1948, the Central Committee declared that the magazine was doing its job "in a completely unsatisfactory manner," and concluded that it was no longer "a militant organ of Soviet satire and humor." Three years later, the party leaders returned to the attack, reiterating the very same charges. In the words of the central committee resolution, "The journal does a poor job of fulfilling its task of combatting survivals of capitalism in the minds of the Soviet people."[30] In the period since Stalin's death, however, the party has been satisfied and even pleased with Krokodil. Indeed, on the occasion of the journal's fiftieth anniversary in

1972, it was given an honorary award for its contributions to Soviet satirical art.

During the period 1970-1975, Krokodil printed 38 cartoons that were critical of religion, or that used religious symbols to criticize other shortcomings in Soviet society. Given the wide circulation and great popularity of this periodical, it is important to see what kind of image of religion is presented on its pages.

## KROKODIL AND ANTIRELGIOUS PROPAGANDA

Krokodil's antireligious cartoons may be grouped into several basic categories, each of which emphasizes and/or ridicules some aspect of relgious doctrine or behavior.

(1) One group of cartoons ridicules religion by trivializing its significance for people in going about their everyday business. The objective here is not to criticize religious doctrines or values per se; rather, it is to show that believers cynically exploit religion in order to achieve selfish personal aims.

One cartoon, originally published in Italy and reproduced in Krokodil in 1975, shows two monks attempting to start their car, which has obviously broken down. Apparently frustrated in their efforts to use conventional automotive repair techniques, one suggests to the other, "What if we were to try praying?" (Figure 1) A second cartoon, published in 1973, also touches on the theme of automobiles. In this picture, an Orthodox clergyman threatens his superior with the following warning: "If you don't give me a garage, I'll give up religion!" (Figure 2)

Not only is the younger priest a relatively pros-
perous individual (simply by virtue of owning an
automobile), but his car is obviously more important
to him than are his religious convictions.

Three other cartoons ridicule people who resort
to prayer in support of their efforts to derive financial gain. In one, an elderly woman, who has
just sold an icon to someone, kneels in prayer before the now empty icon frame. Her words are: "Forgive me, holy virgin mother; I did not resist temptation." (Figure 3) The important point, of course,
is that her greed was greater than her reverence for
the icon; she seeks, through religion, justification
for her low regard for a basic symbol of religion.

In the second cartoon, a young man standing before a group of icons implores: "Oh Lord, help me
to find a rich buyer for these icons!" (Figure 4)
In the third, a woman with a lottery ticket seeks
divine intervention in her quest to win the game.
Her prayer is a simple and vulgar one: "Miracle-
Working Nikolai, hear my prayer: 3, 12, 22, 23, 37,
40." (Figure 5)

(2) A second theme favored by Soviet cartoonists concerns the role played by adults (especially
grandmothers and other elderly women) in perpetua-
ting religion. Empirical research has shown that
the overwhelming majority of those who believe in
and/or practice religion have been believers from
childhood. They receive religious training from
their parents and/or grandparents, acquiring religious habits and beliefs "almost literally with their
mother's milk."[31] Disturbed by this phenomenon, the
satirical press frequently tries to criticize or
ridicule it.

Thus, a 1972 cartoon shows one old woman proudly telling her friend, "Well, you can't say about my grandson that nothing is sacred to him!" (Figure 6) A 1970 cartoon addressed itself to the same problem, but this one featured a young boy who had not succumbed to his grandmother's blandishments. Not incidentally, the boy is wearing overalls and carrying a wrench, symbols linking him to the official propaganda image of the advanced Soviet worker—someone who is, by definition, an atheist. The boy is complaining that his grandmother has been giving his toy robot religious instruction: "Grandma," he asks, "what have you done with my robot?" (Figure 7)

Other cartoons use a slightly different approach to express concern about this phenomenon. In one, an old woman, representing the stereotype of the ignorant peasant woman, is hiding behind a wall, poised with a Bible in her hand, ready to strike the unsuspecting atheist lecturer as he rounds the corner. (Figure 8) She is about to attack him in the literal, as well as the figurative, sense.

The final cartoon in this category shows a young man, wearing a mask to protect his identity, presenting his child to be baptized. One of the women standing nearby remarks to a friend, "He can't be seen in here without his mask; his face is too well-known throughout the district." (Figure 9) Her observation is testimony to the fact that members of the party and the komsomol, not just ignorant old women, sometimes utilize the church to celebrate and sanctify key events in their lives and in those of their children.

(3) A third group of cartoons uses religious symbols to criticize various defects in Soviet in-

dustry or agriculture. In these cartoons, religious
figures are only incidental to a non-religious theme;
they serve as convenient mechanisms for caricaturing
inept economic practices and officials.

For example, two cartoons deal with the chronic
problem of spare parts shortages in Soviet industry
and construction. In one, entitled "How Kizhi Was
Built," one construction worker says to the other:
"We can't keep waiting for these suppliers. Let's
build, even though we don't have any nails. . . ."
(Figure 10) (The ancient city of Kizhi was built
by fitting logs together; no nails were used in the
construction of churches, dwellings, and other buildings.) In the other a factory manager, holding a
requisition form requesting spare parts, says to
"God": "Well, Almighty, what's going on? I still
don't have those spare parts!" (Figure 11)

Figures representing religion or superstition
are used to call attention to other economic problems
as well. In a 1971 cartoon, for example, an agricultural official, apparently disturbed at the indolence
and carelessness of his farm's work force, asks a local witch for assistance. "Granny," he says, "they
say that you can prevent spoilage [of produce] by
casting a spell. Help us!" (Figure 12) Similarly,
a 1975 cartoon, published at harvest time, directed
criticism at the large-scale waste and spoilage which
occurs at agricultural collection points during the
annual harvest. The caption, "Ruined [Ugrobili]. .
. ." involves a play on words, since its root (grob)
is the Russian word for "coffin" or "grave." Instead of carrying someone to his or her grave, then,
the coffin is carrying produce that was allowed to
spoil at the food depot. (Figure 13)

Another cartoon, entitled "At the Gates of Paradise," criticizes the widespread practice of collective farmers stealing produce from the collective's land. The caption is a famous Marxist slogan (one which was first used by Terence, the Roman writer of comedies): "Nothing that is human is alien to me!" (Figure 14) Yet another cartoon calls attention to the poor workmanship so prevalent in the Soviet construction industry. The church, officially designated as a Historical Monument Protected by the State, presumably was built several centuries ago. Nonetheless, it has proved to be far more durable than the scaffolding erected around it by Soviet construction workers. The caption, "Perhaps it's time to restore the scaffolding!", emphasizes the fact that the church is in much better condition. (Figure 15)

One final cartoon also uses religious metaphors to ridicule economic irrationalities. Underscoring the irrational character of railroad freight operations--tracks and sidings heading nowhere, freight cars diverted from the rest of a train, etc.--the cartoonist uses the language of religion. The caption reads as follows: "The Ways of the Gods are Inscrutable (Railway Variant)." (Figure 16)

(4) A fourth major topic for Soviet satirists is the shortage and inadequacy of leisure time facilities in the countryside, and the implications of this for the preservation of "vestiges of religion in the minds of the people." To be sure, a great deal of effort has been invested by the regime to construct schools, and clubs, organize sports activities, raise rural standards of living, and provide outlets for the rural population's leisure time acti-

vities.  Nevertheless, as numerous opinion surveys have shown, and as the data on rural-urban migration indicate with equal clarity, the opportunities for relaxation and recreation in the Soviet countryside are distinctly limited.  In many areas of the USSR, the network of rural clubs offers less to the people (especially younsters) than the village church.

This circumstance has stimulated cartoonists to make fun of the system of clubs, as well as the individuals responsible for their operation.  For example, a 1972 cartoon contrasted the dark and empty club in one village with the large numbers of parishioners visiting the local church.  Pointing to the club's darkened windows, one young person asks another, "What is it that attracts everyone to the church, rather than to the club?"  The answer ridicules both the church and the club with one word--"Darkness." (Figure 17)  A similar cartoon, published in 1974, suggests one way of compensating for the dilapidated appearance of the local club--a giant bell to attract attention.  As the man in the picture puts it, "Now we'll see who's more powerful than whom." (Figure 18)

The final cartoon on this theme shows a priest talking to his daughter and her fiance, the director of the local club.  "My daughter marrying the director of the club--an Antichrist?", the priest asks. "Don't worry, father," his daughter reassures him. "He doesn't have anything against you." (Figure 19) The point is clear:  the club will not attempt to compete seriously with the church for the attention of the citizenry.

(5)  Another group of antireligious cartoons focuses on foreign policy themes.  Generally, they link one or another church with ultraconservative

153

political groups and ideologies. Three of them are addressed to the joint efforts of the Catholic Church and "fascist" regimes to contain "progressive" or "national liberation" movements. In one, a religious official asks a group of four soldiers to get down on their knees, presumably so that he can offer them his blessing. But the four, all of whom look like thugs and murderers, kneel only in order to assume the proper firing position, thereupon shooting the helpless, peaceful blacks. The accompanying text, providing a background and explanation for the cartoon, reads as follows: "The executions in Mozambique, recently reported in the press, have been carried out by Portuguese firing squads, with the blessing of the local bishop." (Figure 20)

A second cartoon that likens the Roman Catholic Church to an executioner, was stimulated by political developments in Spain. Captioned "Spanish Tribunal," it suggests that the church played a prominent role in General Franco's efforts to stifle the Basque separatists and other political movements he considered inimical to his regime. (Figure 21)

A third cartoon, published in 1975, shows a Roman Catholic Church official in Portugal exhorting a group of evil-looking killers to attack the local Communists. According to the accompanying text, "Portuguese Archbishop da Silva, inspiring a counterrevolutionary attack in the city of Braga, urged that Communists be opposed by the power of love." The caption, "Go with love, my children!", is designed to show the hypocrisy of the Church, its support for violence, and its hostility to the "progressive" forces in Portugal. (Figure 22)

The fourth cartoon is critical of Protestant

154

extremists in Northern Ireland. Entitled "Protestant Extremist's Prayer," it shows a minister asking
for intercession from above. "Heaven will help us,"
he declares. His prayers are answered--not by God,
but by British transport aircraft. The paratroopers
they are dropping have been called upon to stifle
the "national liberation movement" against "British
occupation" of Northern Ireland. (Figure 23)

Two more cartoons dealing with the West focus
on themes which appear at first glance to be non-
political. On further reflection, however, they can
be seen as having been designed to demonstrate that
immorality and criminal behavior are widespread in
the capitalist world. Both of these cartoons were
stimulated by acts of vandalism and theft of art
works from churches in the West. In one, a monk
tells his fellow monks who are fastening additional
nails into Christ on the cross, "Nail them in more
tightly so they can't be pulled out!" The accompanying text explains to readers that, "The theft of
works of art from Western European churches has taken
on the character of an epidemic." (Figure 24) In the
other, titled "Prayer Italian Style," the young sup-
plicant says, "Holy Madonna! Help me now, before
someone steals you. . . ." (Figure 25)

(6) Other cartoons adopt a very different
stance toward religious symbols, emphasizing that
icons, churches and other religious edifices are
monuments of Russia's past glories and artistic
creativity. We have already discussed the cartoon
which contrasted a beautiful and well-preserved
church with the ugly and dilapidated scaffolding
erected to aid workers in preserving the building.
Three other cartoons published during the 1970s

touched on related themes.

In one, a watchman angrily denounces the horde
of tourists seeking to visit and photograph a church.
As the caption indicates, the guard is seeking to
preserve the church as a historical monument--even
though the building is now being used as a ware-
house. (Figure 26)  The contrast between his "protection of the historical monument" and the transformation of the church into an overflowing storage
center underscores the fact that Soviet antireli-
giozniki have been guilty of excesses and impropie-
ties.  A second cartoon, entitled "Rafting," makes
a similar point.  It is a commentary on the resurgence of interest in the religious art of Russia's
past.  The rafters, presumably sophisticated young
urbanites, have taken the icons from a village
church.  But even as they manifest their love of religious art, they demonstrate their disrespect for
what they have collected. (Figure 27)  The final
cartoon in this category is equally critical of this
sort of vandalism.  The man, who obviously has stolen
an entire church from some remote village, says to
the woman:  "Darling, do you remember that church
that we saw?  Well, I took it as a souvenir. . . ."
(Figure 28)

(7)  The remaining cartoons are too varied to
be placed in meaningful categories.  Six of these
ten drawings explicitly attack religion, however, including the only cartoon published between 1971 and
1975 that is directed at Islam.  In this cartoon,
a Moslem religious figure points emphatically to a
copy of the Koran and demands of a young woman, "
"When did you renounce this holy book, you good-for-
nothing?"  Pointing to a volume of V. I. Lenin's

156

writings, she responds contemptuously, "Since I began reading this book!" (Figure 29)

A second cartoon is designed to ridicule the official image of the typical believer, i.e., an ignorant old woman. In this picture, entitled "A Guest of Her Daughter's," the young woman expresses amusement at her mother, who kneels in prayer before what she assumes is an icon. The caption, however, indicates that the picture is simply that of a long-haired youth. As the daughter points out, "What are you doing, mama? That's a portrait of your son-in-law." (Figure 30) A third cartoon directed at religion per se depicts the unexpected appearance of "God" at a lecture devoted to the theme, "Does God Exist?" The puzzled and disconcerted lecturer asks, "Did you really have to come to my lecture?" (Figure 31)

One other cartoon seems to suggest that God is a rather simple-minded fool, someone who is easily bewildered and manipulated, rather than someone who is all-knowing. In the cartoon, two devils in workmen's uniforms appear at the Heavenly Gates. They ask "God": "Would you like us to repair your gates? We have some imported devil's skin!" (Figure 32)

The final two cartoons explicitly mocking religion were reprinted from a West German and an Italian publication. One is aimed at the Biblical story of the Garden of Eden: two spacemen from Earth visiting another planet come across an Eden-like setting. One says to the other: "It looks like life on this planet has only just begun." (Figure 33) The other cartoon is even simpler, featuring a doctor examining a monk. The doctor says to his patient, "Just say 'Ah,' Holy Father, not 'Amen.'"

(Figure 34)

The final four cartoons concern topics which are not really religious, but which nonetheless include religious figures or structures. One of these is directed against problem drinkers, although it also shows one of the uglier examples of the appropriation of religious buildings for secular use. The two policemen are dragging an inebriated citizen to the local sobering-up station--which formerly was a church. Recognizing this fact, the drunkard objects to being brought in: "I won't go," he says. "I'm an atheist!" (Figure 35)

A second cartoon is devoted to a totally non-religious subject--cigarette smoking. To emphasize the enormity of the air pollution and health hazard caused by so much smoking, the cartoonist has shown "God" in a gas mask, declaring, "There's only one way to deal with this: we'll have to arrange for another Great Flood." (Figure 36)

A third cartoon is equally non-religious, although it does touch directly upon matters of morality. The kneeling figure, petitioning St. Peter to be allowed into Heaven, is pointing to others who have already gained entry. These people, it appears, are former employees for whom he has written critical job evaluations. "But why are they in Heaven?", the manager implores. "I wrote so many critical reports about them!" (Figure 37) The link between questions of labor-management relations and questions of religion and atheism is remote at best. But it is interesting to see how religious symbols are used to shed light on the matter of punishments and rewards in Soviet industry.

One final cartoon mocks basic religious symbols,

158

although only in order to comment on matters unrelated to religion or atheism. It shows an outdoor basketball court on which two clotheslines have been set up. Because they resemble the shape of a cross, the cartoon is entitled, "They Erected a Cross." (Figure 38) The humor here appears to be as inept as its antireligious significance.

## CONCLUSIONS

Several conclusions would appear to be inescapable. First, antireligious cartoons represent only a relatively small proportion of all cartoons printed in the Soviet satirical press. While 38 cartoons appeared on atheist themes during the period 1970-1975, several hundred drawings were devoted to such topics as alcohol abuse, bureaucracy, shabby construction practices, corruption, the shortage of consumer goods, and agricultural mismanagement.

Second, a significant proportion of Krokodil cartoons featuring religious figures or religious symbols are not, in fact, antireligious in any strict sense of the term. They use religious symbols that are familiar to Soviet readers, but seek to poke fun at matters that are only remotely connected to religion. Religious symbols, that is, are only vehicles for criticizing such phenomena as economic irrationalities in the Soviet system or reactionary politicians in the West or the Third World.

Finally, some cartoons do deal directly with religion. Most of these focus on factors promoting the continued existence of "religious vestiges" in Soviet society, such as inadequacies in the network of rural clubs or the efforts of Soviet babushki to indoctrinate youngsters with religious values and teachings.  Others refer to religious views and behaviors in a patronizing or snide manner--e.g., the cartoons which show believers cynically exploiting religion in order to obtain some sort of monetary or other reward.

Very few of the cartoons make a serious effort to come to grips with the attractive force of religion--the beauty of the ritual, the appeal of religious doctrine, the moral strength of ministers, priests and other clergymen.  The idea seems to be that religion is self-evidently an absurd "vestige of the past," a foolish and outdated dogma propagated by ignorant, disingenuous or self-indulgent charlatans.  The political cartoon, then, provides a reaffirmation of the same kinds of ideas and propositions regularly presented in the other media.  Its value in disabusing religious readers of any sort of "false consciousness" is likely to be problematical at best.  Its real value probably lies in providing entertainment and reinforcement for atheists who already reject religion.

FIGURE 1

А если попробовать молитву?

«Эпока», Италия.

"What if we were to try praying?"

Source: Krokodil, No. 22 (1975), p. 15.

FIGURE 2

"If you don't give me a garage, I'll give up
religion!"

Source: Krokodil, No. 11 (1973), p. 9.

FIGURE 3

— Прости меня, мать пресвятая богородица, не устояла перед соблазном...

Рисунок Е. ШУКАЕВА

"Forgive me, holy virgin mother; I did not resist temptation."

Source: <u>Krokodil</u>, No. 33 (1975), p. 7.

FIGURE 4

"Oh, Lord, help me to find a rich buyer for these icons!"

Source: <u>Krokodil</u>, No. 25 (1974), p. 9.

FIGURE 5

"Miracle-Working Nikolai, hear my prayer:  3, 12, 22, 23, 37, 40."

Source: <u>Krokodil</u>, No. 32 (1973), p. 11.

FIGURE 6

"Well, you can't say about my grandson that
nothing is sacred to him!"

Source: <u>Krokodil</u>, No. 1 (1972), p. 10.

FIGURE 7

— Бабушка, что это ты
натворила с моим роботом!

Рисунок
М. БИТНОГО

"Grandma, what have you done with my robot?"

Source: <u>Krokodil</u>, No. 15 (1970), p. 12.

FIGURE 8

(The old woman is holding a copy of the Bible;
according to the writing on his briefcase, the
man approaching the corner is a lecturer--pre-
sumably an antireligious specialist.)

Source: Krokodil, No. 30 (1975), p. 14.

FIGURE 9

— Ему, матушка, без маски нель-
зя: лицо всему району известное!

Рисунок
Е. ШУКАЕВА

"He can't be seen in here without his mask;
his face is too well-known throughout the
district."

Source: _Krokodil_, No, 31 (1971), p. 11.

FIGURE 10

HOW KIZHI WAS BUILT

"We can't keep waiting for these suppliers. Let's build, even though we don't have any nails. . ."

Source: Krokodil, No. 31 (1973), p. 3.

FIGURE 11

"Well, Almighty, what's going on?  I still don't have those spare parts!"

Source: <u>Krokodil</u>, No. 33 (1971), front cover.

FIGURE 12

— Ты, бабуля, говорят, от порчи         Рисунок
заговариваешь? Выручай!         Е. ВЕДЕРНИКОВА

"Granny, they say that you can prevent spoilage [of produce] by casting a spell.  Help us!"

Source: <u>Krokodil</u>, No. 25 (1971), p. 5.

FIGURE 13

УГРОБИЛИ...                    Рисунок К. НЕВЛЕРА и М. УШАЦА

RUINED . . .

Source: <u>Krokodil</u>, No. 25 (1975), p. 14.

## FIGURE 14

AT THE GATES OF PARADISE

"Nothing that is human is alien to me!"

Source: Krokodil, No. 32 (1974), p. 14.

FIGURE 15

— Пожалуй, эти леса пора реставрировать!                Рисунок В. ШКАРБАНА

"Perhaps it's time to restore the scaffolding!"

Source: <u>Krokodil</u>, No. 34 (1973), p. 11.

FIGURE 16

THE WAYS OF THE GODS ARE INSCRUTABLE
(RAILWAY VARIANT)

Source: Krokodil, No. 19 (1971), p. 4.

FIGURE 17

— Что это все вместо клуба в церковь тянутся?
— Темнота...                                Рисунок В. ЖАРИНОВА

"What is it that attracts everyone to the
church, rather than to the club?"

"Darkness."

Source: <u>Krokodil</u>, No. 2 (1973), p. 13.

FIGURE 18

— Теперь посмотрим, кто кого!

Рисунок Е. ГУРОВА

"Now we'll see who's more powerful than whom!"

Source: Krokodil, No. 4 (1974), p. 7.

FIGURE 19

"My daughter marrying the director of the club--an Antichrist?"

"Don't worry, father. He doesn't have anything against you."

Source: Krokodil, No. 10 (1972), p. 7.

FIGURE 20

"On your knees, my children!" (top)

Source: Krokodil, No. 24 (1973), back cover.

FIGURE 21

ИСПАНСКИЙ ТРИБУНАЛ

Рисунок Н. ЛИСОГОРСКОГО

SPANISH TRIBUNAL

Source: Krokodil, No. 1 (1971), p. 7.

FIGURE 22

—Идите с любовью, дети мои!

Рисунок А. КРЫЛОВА

"Go with love, my children!"   (The accompanying text reads as follows:   "Portuguese Archbishop da Silva, inspiring a counterrevolutionary attack in the city of Braga, urged
that Communists be opposed by the power of
love.")

Source: <u>Krokodil</u>, No. 27 (1975), back cover.

FIGURE 23

МОЛИТВА ПРОТЕСТАНТСКОГО ЭКСТРЕМИСТА
— Да поможет нам небо!

Рисунок Ю. ГАНФА

PROTESTANT EXTREMIST'S PRAYER

"Heaven will help us!"

Source: <u>Krokodil</u>, No. 27 (1971), p. 4.

FIGURE 24

— Крепче прибивай, чтоб не оторвали!          Рисунок А. БАЖЕНОВА

"Nail them in more tightly so they can't be
pulled out!" (The accompanying text reads as
follows: "The theft of works of art from
Western European churches has taken on the
character of an epidemic.")

Source: Krokodil, No. 32 (1972), p. 11.

FIGURE 25

—Святая мадонна! Помоги мне, пока тебя еще не украли...

Рисунок Л. САМОЙЛОВА

"Holy Madonna! Help me now, before someone steals you . . . "

Source: Krokodil, No. 8 (1974), back cover.

FIGURE 26

PRESERVING HISTORICAL MONUMENTS

Source: Krokodil, No. 1 (1970), p. 7.

FIGURE 27

СПЛАВЛЯЮТ...

Рисунок Н. СЕМЕНОВА

**RAFTING . . .**

Source: <u>Krokodil</u>, No. 18 (1974), p. 5.

FIGURE 28

"Darling, do you remember that church that
we saw?  Well, I took it as a souvenir . . . ."

Source: Krokodil, No. 24 (1971), p. 13.

## FIGURE 29

— С каких пор ты отвернулась от священной книги, негодная?
— С тех пор, как научилась читать вот эту книгу!

Рисунок Хасана РАСУЛОВА [Таджикистан]

"When did you renounce this holy book, you good-for-nothing?"

"Since I began reading this book!" (The woman is pointing to a copy of a book by V. I. Lenin.)

Source: Krokodil, No. 35 (1972), p. 10.

189

# FIGURE 30

В ГОСТЯХ У ДОЧЕРИ

— Да что ты, мама, это же портрет твоего зятя!

"What are you doing, mama?  That's a portrait
of your son-in-law."

Source: Krokodil, No. 6 (1974), p. 11.

FIGURE 31

"Did you really have to come to my lecture?"
(As the sign on the wall indicates, the title
of the lecture is, "Does God Exist?")

Source: Krokodil, No. 4 (1970), p. 12.

# FIGURE 32

— Врата обивать будем? Есть импортная чертова кожа!

Рисунок
Ю. ФЕДОРОВА

"Would you like us to repair your gates?  We have some imported devil's skin!"

Source: <u>Krokodil</u>, No. 25 (1972), p. 12.

# FIGURE 33

— Видимо, на этой планете жизнь только начинается.

«Квик», ФРГ.

"It looks like life on this planet has only just begun."

Source: <u>Krokodil</u>, No. 21 (1974), p. 15.

FIGURE 34

— Говорите только «а», святой
отец, а не «аминь»!

«Эспрессо», Италия.

"Just say 'Ah,' Holy Father, not 'Amen.'"

Source: Krokodil, No. 21 (1974), p. 15.

FIGURE 35

— Не пойду! Я атеист!                    Рисунок Г. и В. КАРАВАЕВЫХ

"I won't go!  I'm an atheist!"  (The church,
which supposedly has been set aside as "An
18th Century Monument Protected by the State,"
has been transformed into a sobering-up sta-
tion.)

Source: Krokodil, No. 28 (1974), p. 13.

195

FIGURE 36

"There's only one way to deal with this: we'll have to arrange for another Great Flood."

Source: <u>Krokodil</u>, No. 29 (1974), p. 12.

FIGURE 37

"But why are they in Heaven?  I wrote so many
critical reports about them!"

Source: Krokodil, No. 4 (1972), p. 14.

FIGURE 38

THEY ERECTED A CROSS

Source: <u>Krokodil</u>, No. 28 (1973), p. 5.

NOTES

1. Robert V. Daniels, "Fate and Will in the Marxist Philosophy of History," Journal of the History of Ideas 21 (1960):545.

2. See, e.g., "Atheist--vsegda v nastuplenii," Kommunist Tadzhikistana, January 19, 1971, p. 1.

3. "Razum--oruzhie!", Komsomol'skaia pravda, December 26, 1970, p. 2.

4. Nancy Whittier Heer, Politics and History in the Soviet Union (Cambridge, Mass.: MIT Press, 1971), p. 112.

5. Henry Ladd Smith, "The Rise and Fall of the Political Cartoon," The Saturday Review, May 29, 1954, p. 7.

6. E. K. Ozimitel', Sovetskaia satira (Moscow-Leningrad, 1964), pp. 5, 12.

7. Literaturnaia gazeta, May 27, 1929.

8. Quoted in Ozimitel', Satira, p. 8.

9. Ibid.

10. Ibid., p. 12.

11. See Peter Henry, Classics of Soviet Satire (London: Collett's, 1972), Vol. 1, p. xiv.

12. Ozimitel', Satira, p. 16.

13. Quoted in ibid., p. 14.

14. Literaturnaia gazeta, August 24, 1934.

15. Mirra Ginsburg, The Fatal Eggs and Other Soviet Satire (New York: The Macmillan Company, 1965), p. ix.

16. See I. Eventov, Lirika i satira (Leningrad, 1968), pp. 247-269. See also L. Ershov, Sovetskaia satiricheskaia proza (Moscow-Leningrad, 1966), p. 4. Lunacharsky's article, "Budem smeiat'sia," originally

published in 1920, is reproduced in <u>Klub 12 stul'ev</u> (Moscow, 1973), pp. 5-6.

17. Eventov, <u>Lirika</u>, p. 269.

18. <u>Materialy XXII s'ezda KPSS</u> (Moscow, 1969), p. 420.

19. Ozimitel', <u>Satira</u>, p. 12.

20. A. Madarian, <u>O satire</u> (Moscow, 1967), p. 13.

21. Ibid., p. 4.

22. According to a leading Soviet commentator, "The chief principle by which the satirist, as well as each worker in literature and art, must be guided is the principle of communist party-mindedness." Ozimitel', p. 23. Another analyst has written in a similar vein that "Soviet satire, like the rest of our art, is party-oriented. The satirist's creation and his ideals rest on the firm scientific foundation of Marxist-Leninist ethics." Ershov, <u>Proza</u>, p. 22.

23. Smith, p. 28.

24. Ibid.

25. N.G. Chernyshevskii, <u>Estetika i litera-turnaia kritika</u> (Moscow-Leningrad, 1951), p. 183.

26. Makarian, <u>O satire</u>, p. 273.

27. Ibid., p. 20.

28. <u>Bol'shaia sovetskaia entsiklopediia</u>, third edition (Moscow, 1973), volume 13, p. 473, s.v. "Krokodil."

29. See S. Stykalin and I. Kremenskaia, <u>Sovet-skaia satiricheskaia pechat'</u> (Moscow, 1963) for a discussion of each of these satirical magazines and newspapers.

30. For the texts of these decrees, see <u>Sovet-skaia pechat' v dokumentakh</u> (Moscow, 1961), pp. 101-102 and 107-108.

31. V. I. Evdokimov, "Ateisticheskoe vospitanie

trudiashchikhsia v protsesse stroitel'stva kommuniz-
ma," in Voprosy nauchnogo ateizma, ed. A. F. Okulov
et al., 4 (Moscow, 1967):107.   See also N. I. Boldy-
rev et al., Pedagogika (Moscow, 1968), p. 274.

# PART II

## RELIGIOUS GROUPS IN THE SOVIET UNION

Chapter 6
## BACKWARDS FROM REACTIONISM: THE DE-MODERNIZATION OF THE RUSSIAN ORTHODOX CHURCH

### William C. Fletcher

In the highly structured society of the USSR
the churches are in a difficult situation. For more
than a half century the political leadership has
been committed to the most rapid possible development of Soviet society. Modernization, while not so
advanced as in some Western nations, is progressing
at a steeper rate. In fifty years changes have been
introduced which required one and even two centuries
for their development in other countries. The chur-
ches--and Russian Orthodoxy in particular as Russia's
dominant Church--have been hard pressed to cope with
this rapid change in the environment.

The problem has been immensely complicated, however, by a government which is hostile to all religions. Severe restrictions have been placed on the
permissible activity of the churches, at times
threatening their very existence as institutions in
society. So critical is the pressure applied by the
state that the single problem of church-state relations is the overwhelming challenge which the church
must resolve--indeed, this problem has overshadowed
every area of church life. In particular, church-
state relations have defined within very narrow
limits the means which the church may employ in

seeking to adapt to the rapidly changing society.
The modernization of the Russian Orthodox Church has,
in effect, been a function of its approach to church-
state relations.

At first glance, it would appear that Russian
Orthodoxy's answer to the modernization of society
has been a conscious attempt to go the opposite direction.  So far from attempting the modifications
and innovations normally associated with modernization, the Russian Orthodox Church has moved further
and further away from innovation and experimentation.
In 1917 Russian Orthodoxy was one of the world's
more reactionary churches:  it reacted against
change, innovation and modernization in society.
Today, however, the Church is not even reactionary:
it does not react at all to change in society, much
less attempt to adapt its practice, doctrine or mission to the modernizing society.

This retreat from reactionism, suprisingly
enough, is defensible on very pragmatic grounds, as
this article will demonstrate.  However, it should
be noted that the church did not choose this particular approach to modernization on pragmatic, theoretical or any other grounds.  The position was
forced upon it by the Soviet state.  The modernization (or, in this case, anti-modernization) of the
Russian Orthodox Church is a side effect of the primary, overwhelming problem facing all forms of institutionalized religion in the USSR:  church-state relations.

Several different approaches to church-state
relations were available to the Russian Orthodox
Church.  None of them worked.

The first of these alternatives, theocracy, is
easy enough to dispose of. Theoretically, the church
could have claimed preeminence over the government.
Throughout the history of the Christian church, from
time to time this approach has been advocated. It
has never worked well or long. Aspirations to theocratic rule on the part of the Russian Orthodox
Church have usually ended in disaster, and at least
since the time of Patriarch Nikon this approach has
not represented an especially live option. Certainly
since the subordination of the church by Peter the
Great, theocracy has not been championed in Russia.

Until 1968, that is. In 1968 the curious episode of the "Union for the Liberation of the Russian
People" came to light. A secret, illegal, political
discussion group was uncovered in Leningrad which was
said to have links in several cities of the USSR.
Basing their studies, inter alia, on works by the
philosopher, Nikolai Berdiaev, these conspirators
advocated a form of government in which the Russian
Orthodox Church would have ultimate authority.[1] It
is highly questionable whether such an approach to
governing the Russian people would work and, if it
did, whether it would be at all desirable from any
point of view whatsoever. Not even the adepts of
the "Union for the Liberation of the Russian People"
could suggest this ancient theocratic innovation
without the overthrow of the present government and
hence, despite their advocacy, theocracy remains a
closed option to the church in the USSR.

Caesaropapism, or Erastianism, is an option
which is not quite so remote. This doctrine postulates that the head of the state is also the head of

the church, with the church fully subordinated to
him.  Indeed, from the time of Peter the Great this
represented the official doctrine of church-state
relations in the Russian Orthodox Church.  As a doctrine, it was eminently defensible so long as there
was an Orthodox tsar.  But can an Erastian doctrine
be defended when the head of state is an avowed atheist?  The question, of course, is rendered nugatory
by the Soviet government, which certainly does not
seek recognition as the head of the church and would
not accept a caesaropapist position if it were offered.

Nevertheless, the doctrine has attracted some
few adherents.  For a while the Russian emigration
cherished fond hopes of a restoration of the monarchy,
and the Karlovtsy Synod of the émigré church agitated
vigorously for a return to caesaropapism in Russia
under an Orthodox tsar.[2]  But this advocacy and agitation was of no particular help to the church the
émigrés left behind.  Despite more recent attempts by
some western observers to discern a revived caesaropapism in the post World War II relations of church
and state, Erastianism is not a live option for the
Russian Orthodox Church and, as will become apparent
below, the actual pattern of contemporary church-
state relations is something else entirely despite
the apparent subordination of church to state.

The church's own preference for church-state
relations was to act as society's conscience.  While
not directly participating in the governmental process, the church would be able to review the government's actions and admonish or commend in order to
influence those actions into a proper path.  Indeed,
Patriarch Tikhon's first public proclamation fol-

lowing the Bolshevik coup resounds with the thunder of outraged conscience:

> Recall yoursleves, ye senseless, and cease your bloody deeds.  For what you are doing is not only a cruel deed; it is in truth a satanic act, for which you shall suffer the fire of Gehenna in the life to come, beyond the grave, and the terrible curses of posterity in this present, earthly life.[3]

Not only did the church arrogate to itself the right to admonish and instruct the government, it also protested most bitterly against infringements against its rights:  "The enemies of the church have seized power over the church and its good property through the force of fire."[4]  The church's preferred role, then, at least during the first year or more following the Revolution, was to be the government's conscience.

Unfortunately, the new government felt no need of this particular form of a conscience.  By mid-1919 (and perhaps a year earlier) it was apparent first that the state would not accept the approach to church-state relations which the church had selected and second, the church did not possess sufficient resources to survive a head-on confrontation with an armed and hostile state.  The riots over the state's confiscation of church valuables during the famine of 1921-1922 quickly demonstrated that pitch-forks are no match for automatic weapons.[5]

Yet the idea of the church as society's conscience has continued to exert an appeal in Russia despite the fact that history has proven most convincingly that this is not a viable approach to relations with the Soviet state.  Patriarch Tikhon became a legendary figure, a patron saint for Orthodox

who went underground, and his initial approach of a
moral confrontation with the evils of communism has
been revered in the illegal Orthodox groups right
down to the present.[6]  Nor has the appeal been confined to those Orthodox who have alienated themselves from society.  In the Orthodox dissent which
arose in the middle sixties, there were many overtones of this approach to church-state relations
when the church's reaction to evil in society was
considered.  Even Alexander Solzhenitsyn, before
he emigrated, urged a similar attitude on the Patriarch:

> The Russian church has its indignant opinion
> on every evil in distant Asia or Africa, yet
> on internal ills--it has none--ever.  Why are
> the messages which we receive from the church
> hierarchy traditionally tranquil?  Why are all
> church documents so complacent, as if they were
> issued among the most Christian of peoples?
> One serene message follows another, in the
> course of the same inclement year.  Will not
> the need for these messages soon cease alto-
> gether?  There will no longer be anyone left
> to whom they should be addressed; the flock
> will disappear, with the exception of the pa-
> triarchal chancellery office.[7]

Perhaps Solzhenitsyn is right.  But the early history of the Soviet regime demonstrated fairly conclusively that if the partiarchate should attempt
to revert to being society's conscience, the institutional church would certainly soon cease altogether.

The approach to church-state relations which
has caused the Russian Orthodox Church the most
difficulty is officially promulgated by the Soviet
government:  the separation of church and state.
This doctrine was announced by the fledgling regime

in its first official statement on religion: the decree of January 23, 1918 declared the separation of church and state. This position remains the official position of the government on church-state relations. According to article 124 of the 1936 Constitution of the USSR, which remains in force, "In order to ensure to citizens freedom of conscience, the church in the USSR is separated from the state and the state from the church."[8] The actions of the Soviet regime, however, have domonstrated fairly conclusively that that state does not in fact accept the doctrine of church-state separation.

The Russian Orthodox Church was quick to comply with the state's official demand of separation of church and state. As has been noted, by 1919 it had become evident that the church's initial approach to church-state relations, whereby the church would attempt to function as society's conscience, would not serve. The church abandoned this position in favor of a position of political neutrality which would ensure that church and state would remain separate. Patriarch Tikhon officially endorsed this position with his confession that "I am henceforth not an enemy of the Soviet government" on June 16, 1923.[9] For a time, indeed, the state appeared to be satisfied with this approach to church-state relations. The church scrupulously refrained from interfering in the affairs of the state and, at least until the death of Tikhon in 1925, the state by and large permitted the church to conduct its own affairs without severe interference. However, almost immediately after the death of Tikhon it became apparent that the state would no longer accept the church's political neutrality. The doctrine of

211

separation of church and state became a dead letter.

In retrospect, it is obvious that the Soviet regime could not accept the separation of church and state as a valid approach to institutional religion. The Communist Party remains committed to a totalitarian ideal, in the sense that no area of life is outside the purview of the political authority. Church-state separation implies a pluralistic view of society: certain areas are properly the sphere of the secular leadership, while other areas belong to the church. It would be as improper for the church to interfere in political matters as it would be for the state to interfere in religious affairs. Marxism-Leninism, however, maintains a monolithic, rather than a pluralistic, view of society: the Party cannot disclaim responsiblility for any area of human endeavor. To admit the separation of church and state, with its implication that there is an area of life for which the party need not assume responsibility, is to contradict the entire theory on which the Soviet ideology is based. For this reason, separation of church and state is not a viable approach in the Soviet Union, either in theory or in practice. It cannot be.

The Russian Orthodox Church quickly learned this, and after 1927 never again did it attempt to apply this approach to church-state relations. The separation of church and state, despite its continued promulgation in the laws and statutes of the country, has not been a live option for the church. However, not all the Christians in Russia are convinced of this theory's impotence, despite the overwhelmingly persuasive evidence of the past fifty years that the church cannot apply this theory and survive. Despite the pressure of the state against religion, which at times has been very severe indeed, advocates of church-state separation continue to appear. In the thirties there were many attempts, universally unsuccessful, to claim rights which should accrue to the church according to the official doctrine of separation of church and state.[10] This doctrine became especially prominent in the dissent which arose within Orthodoxy from the mid-sixties onward.[11]

The essential argument of the dissenters was two-fold: the church was remiss in failing to insist on its rights according to the laws of the country, and the state was guilty of itself transgressing those laws. Both of these complaints assumed that the approach to church-state relations in the Soviet Union is indeed the separation of church and state. The letters of Eshliman and Yakunin, which first brought the dissent into the open in 1966, obviously were based on the pluralistic idea of separation as the proper foundation for church-state relations. The letter to the government insisted,

> It is well known that on January 23, 1918 the Soviet government published the decree, "On Separation of Church and State, and Schools from the Church" in which the fact that the independent existence of the Orthodox Church in our country is recognized. It is also well known that article 124 of the Constitution of the USSR grants all citizens of the Soviet Union freedom to practice religion.[12]

The companion letter to Patriarch Aleksei was even more explicit:

> The unconditional non-intervention of the state
> in the internal life of the church on the one
> hand, and the free cooperation of the church
> with the state in civil affairs, if the state
> so desires, on the other hand, such is the
> principle of the free relationship between
> church and state.
>
> The basic legislative documents of the So-
> viet state concerning the church--the decree,
> "On the Separation of the Church from the
> State," and article 124 of the Constitution of
> the USSR, which proclaims freedom of conscience
> and separation, and recognized the right of
> citizens in the USSR to freedom in religious
> rite--established definite juridical bases for
> the realization of this principle.13

The state's response to this challenge fairly quickly demonstrated that the dissenters were mistaken in
their assumption that the laws and statutes in fact
defined the regime's approach to church-state relations. The patriarchate, by ignoring the suggestions concerning how it should conduct the church's
public life in society, clearly indicated that it
did not agree that separation of church and state
was a viable alternative in the latter sixties, any
more than it had been in the latter twenties. The
events of the past decade have proven that the
church was correct:  separation of church and state
is not a live option in the contemporary USSR.

All of these theories of church-state relations
have proven unworkable. The Soviet state will not
accept an approach to church-state relations which
is really no approach at all:  viz., that there can
be no relations between church and state. To maintain his integrity the Christian must sever all relations with society. embracing the traditional,
eremitic doctrine of flight to the wilderness:

By all appearances it is evident that I will

> not again be brought out of the wilderness;
> yea, and I myself hasten thither, to be hidden
> there while the wrath of God passes by.  I
> grieve only that among the archpastors of the
> Russian Church there are not a few followers
> of the Sergiite theology, which is offensive in
> practice.  Forgive me and pray for me, and re-
> pent before it is too late.  Later on you will
> not be able to break free--you youself know
> why.[14]

The problem with this approach is that the state has
ample physical power to eradicate the church as an
institution in society.  Should the church embrace
this Draconian answer to the problem of church-
state relations, it must soon cease to exist, and
its ministry to the Russian people must terminate.
Even Milhail Pol'shii, one of the most ardent early
advocates of this uncompromising approach, recognized the problem in reporting a conversation with
an Orthodox bishop before he emigrated:

> I showed him the necessity of separating him-
> self from Metropolitan Sergei, and, of course,
> going to prison again.  He said to me that that
> would not correct the situation.  Nothing in
> the created order would be changed by that.  To
> deny one's chair is impossible:  he pitied the
> people, the people remain, and these people
> knew not whither to go; only the Sergiite tem-
> ples remained under the sign of Orthodoxy.[15]

Obviously, this is no solution at all.  It amounts
to a simple admission that there can be no relations
between church and state and the church must cease
to exist as an institution in society.  Society must
be abandoned.

The Russian Orthodox Church has accepted another
approach to church-state relations:  total subservience.  In 1927, Metropolitan Sergei recognized that
no other option was available.

It is the more needful for our church and the
more imperative for us all, to whom her interests are dear, who wish to lead her out into
the path of legal and peaceful existence, the
more imperative for us now to show that we, the
church functionaries, are not with the enemies
of our Soviet state, and not with the senseless
tools of their intrigues, but are with our people and our government. . . .

We must show, not in words, but in deeds,
that not only people indifferent to Orthodoxy,
or those who reject it, can be faithful citizens of the Soviet Union, loyal to the Soviet
government, but also the most fervent adherents
of Orthodoxy, to whom it is as dear with all
its canonical and liturgical treasures as truth
and life. We wish to be Orthodox and at the
same time to claim the Soviet Union as our civil
motherland, the joys and successes of which are
our joys and successes, the misfortunes of which
are our misfortunes.[16]

The church must serve the political power uncondi-
tionally. Sergei attempted to define this service
as restricted to political matters only,[17] but it
quickly became clear that the state, if it were to
accept this definition of church-state relations,
would insist that subservience must extend to all
areas in which the church interacts with society.
Early in 1928 the state, by denying a residence permit for Metropolitan Iosif to transfer to Leningrad,
forced the patriarchate to re-transfer him to Odessa,
thereby demonstrating that even on the internal matter of deployment of its clergy the church must subordinate itself to the state.[18]

This was a bitter pill to swallow. Sergei's
proclamation of 1927 very nearly tore the church
asunder. The schisms which developed following the
proclamation were massive and nationwide; at least
in terms of the number of bishops who broke relations

216

with the patriarchate, going into schism rather than accepting this subservient approach to church-state relations, the Russian Orthodox Church experienced the greatest schism of all its history in the years following 1927.[19]

However, history has proven that so far, at least, subservience is a workable approach to church-state relations in the USSR. Adhering strictly to this approach, the church managed to survive the next fifty years intact as an institution in society. Three phases may be discerned in the subsequent application of this approach.

Until 1939, Sergei's approach could be viewed as temporary. The church accepted its distasteful position as an emergency measure, a temporary expedient allowing the church to survive until conditions should change for the better.

> As it seems to us, there are grounds to affirm that broad circles of believers assimilated the proclamation of loyalty with bitterness, accepting it as a burdensome necessity, as a "gift to Caesar," but in their overwhelming majority they did not recoil from Metropolitan Sergei, but went along the same road of formal loyalty along which went the Metropolitan, and became, as before, battlers for their temples, for the preservation of divine services in them, for the saving of the lives of imprisoned priests and churchmen, for the support of the last open hearths of faith in Russia.[20]

The church did manage to survive the difficult years of the thirties, but only just. By 1939 it had been reduced to a skeletal institution, with but four bishops still in office and a mere handful of open churches (estimates range from 4,225 to 100 active churches in 1939).[21]

In 1939, conditions did change for the better,

thereby justifying the attitude that the church's political subservience was a temporary device. With the Soviet occupation of eastern Poland, a new era in church-state relations opened, in which political subservience was a price paid by the church in a bargaining situation. The church served the state politically; in return, the state gave to the church concessions sufficient for its continued functioning as an institution in society.

Subservience to the state demanded some distasteful and, from a point of view of Christian morality, highly questionable activities on the part of the church, particularly in its service during and after World War II in assisting the regime's drive for hegemony in Eastern Europe and in the subsequent peace campaigns.[22] However, the state reciprocated with a broad range of concessions, allowing the number of churches to rise to approximately 15,000,[23] limiting the harassment of believers, permitting the establishment of a system of theological education and allowing limited church publications. During these years, the bargaining situation worked fairly well and the concessions received could be claimed in justification of the price of political subservience.

In the late fifties, however, the bargaining situation broke down. In 1960 the state was committed to a vigorous anti-religious campaign, emulating and in some important respects exceeding the anti-religious campaigns of the thirties.[24] By 1964 the number of open churches had been cut in half. Theological education was reduced to a skeletal, token endeavor. A broad range of restrictions was applied against believers, rendering it virtually impossible for the church to influence society in any meaningful way. Church publications were purged of any but the most innocuous content, promulgating the political line among the churches rather than fulfilling any very significant function as religious publications. Nor did conditions change materially after the fall of Khrushchev. The antireligious campaign continued in force at the approximate level of 1964. The more brutish measures were held in abeyance, and the application of force became, not a general phenomenon, but a more focused weapon applied against dissidents. It became obvious that a new situation had developed by 1960, one which continues to the present.

Obviously, church-state relations were no longer in a bargaining situation. In effect, the state unilaterally withdrew its concessions while insisting on the continued--and in many respects increased--political service of the church. The church's approach to its relations with the state remains that of complete subordination; but it receives very little in return. The church continues to exist as an institution, but it is effectively cut off from any independent participation whatsoever in the corporate life of society. Since 1960 it has become obvious that subservience is not a temporary expedient, but a permanent position which the church must accept if it is to exist at all. Nor is it a bargaining situation: unilateral subservience is demanded of the church, while at the same time the church as an institution is forced to refrain from any interaction with society. Permanent, unrewarded subor-

dination to the state is the church's only recourse:
no other approach is viable as a solution to church-
state relations.

If this is a valid description of church-state
relations in the USSR, a number of implications
arise.  The first grows out of the question of whether, in fact, the contemporary subordination of the
church to the state is not a new phenomenon at all,
but is merely a return to the prerevolutionary
Erastian pattern.  To be sure, there is no longer an
Orthodox tsar; but the church is no less subordinate
to the secular authorities, in theory at least, than
in the Petrine age.  Is there in fact any difference?

There is one overwhelming difference, which is
sufficiently critical as to suggest that the Erastian
model is not applicable to the contemporary church.
The difference lies in the exclusion of the church
from the life of society.  In a caesaropapist situation, the church serves the monarch by organizing
certain areas of society according to his direction.
The church exercises an influence on society, even
though this influence is not independent but is
merely an executive function carrying out the ruler's
will.  In the contemporary USSR, the church is subordinated to the state, but the latter specifically
excludes the church from any significant contact
with society.  Whatever duties the regime may lay on
the church (such as providing support for foreign
propaganda or, conceivably, informing on private
citizens), it does not delegate any aspect of society's life to the church's management.  The state
attempts to supervise all areas of social life
through its own institutions; the church serves no

220

administrative arm in certain areas of life (e.g. education, registration of vital statistics, etc.).

There is a disturbing implication, however. If the church must now accept that the present pattern of church-state relations is permanent (and there are no indications as yet that it is not) then it must also accept its exclusion from the life of society as permanent. Society becomes irrelevant to the church's interests. If society is moral and good, that is all very well; if society is immoral and evil, that also is all very well. Neither condition evokes any reaction from the church and indeed, if it is to adhere to the pattern of church-state relations which it has accepted, the church should refrain from even forming (much less expressing) an opinion on either condition. At least with regard to criticism of patent evils in society, the Russian Orthodox Church has by and large adhered scrupulously to this obligation. The Moscow Patriarchate has not once criticized the elimination of kulaks as a class, the Great Puges, the Katyn Forest massacre, the Czech coup d'etat, the Korean aggression, the introduction of offensive missiles to Cuba, the invasion of Prague, or the Angola intervention. To do so would be improper. Society is irrelevant to the church's proper interests.

This seems a strange position for any church to accept, in view of the deep concern of traditional Christianity with this world's history. Such an approach to society would seem to imply that God is not in control of secular society (and hence of history), else the church should maintain a social concern as part of its total worship of God. The an-

swer to this dilemma, of course, is that according
to the logic of the church-state relations of the
Russian Orthodox Church, such a question is irrelevant. God may be directing secular life; conversely,
some satanic power may have supplanted or frustrated God's control. In neither case, however, is the
church to assist Him. If demonic forces are in control, it is not the proper function of the church to
combat them. Society is absolutely excluded from
the church's purview. It is irrelevant to the
church.[25]

Two implications follow. The first concerns
morality. Morality must be defined in exclusively
personal terms; the church, because of its position
in the Soviet state, cannot advocate any form of
collective or social morality. Morality remains a
heavy emphasis in the life of the church, but it is
an individual morality exclusively. According to a
Soviet sociologist,

> Unfortunately, the majority of the believers
> (including "traditional believers") uncriti-
> cally accept preaching that religion supports
> good morals, that faith and "the fear of God"
> preserve one from wickedness. As a rule, in
> answers believers repeat the theological asser-
> tion that religion teaches the good, that it
> defends good morals, that from it people learn
> the rules of morality (having in view some of
> the propositions of the "ten commandments")
> etc. From this also comes the conclusion about
> the beneficial influence of religion on morals.
> This for some believers constitutes the motive
> for religious propaganda among relatives and
> friends and especially among children.[26]

The individual believer, of course, can make whatever application he wishes in his own views of society, even though the church never touches upon

questions of collective good and evil in society.
The church's influence can, perhaps, have an influence on social morality, but only as it is spread
through individually moral people.

> If in 1964-1965, for example, to the question
> of what is valuable to them in religion, 94%
> of the Orthodox investigated answered that they
> see in it the hope for the preservation of the
> moral bases of society, it was established by
> the research of 1970 that already 78.5% of
> those questioned positively evaluated its sig-
> nificance for the moral education of people.[27]

As a church, however, it must be emphasized that social morality is irrelevant; only individual morality is of concern to the church.

It is the second implication which is most devastating of all. The church is exclusively otherworldly. It has no temporal mission, none. Its
only concerns are supernatural. The church serves
no function at all as an institution in society,
other than to provide a locus where individuals may
come to explore the supernatural dimension singly or
in a group. All other interests are irrelevant to
the church: its only concern is the supernatural.

The church has recognized its new situation as
"a return to its own sphere of activity--that of
concern for the salvation of the souls entrusted to
its leadership."[28] It took some time, however, for
this lesson to sink in. Prior to the new state of
affairs inaugurated by the antireligious campaign
of the sixties, there were still evidences of a no-
stalgic longing for a more social identification of
church with secular nation, even on the part of Patriarch Aleksei: "in his authoritative [1952]
speech before the Soviet people he bore witness to

223

the fact that the Russian Orthodox Church in the past had never stood aside from the national and state life of the people and that She was not doing so now."[29] In 1960, Metropolitan Nikolai again sounded this theme of identification of church and nation in what proved to be his valedictory address:

> In the name of the Holy Synod, the Episcopate, the Theological Schools, the monks, clerics, in the name of the believing people gathered here, and--I take on myself the audacity to say it--in the name of the entire believing Russian Orthodox people, of all our Russian Orthodox Church, with filial, fiery devotion and joy I greet You, Your Holiness . . . .[30]

This was the last time the church attempted to challenge the state. Since 1960, the leadership has accepted its exclusion from temporal society; aspirations to the contrary have not again been officially voiced.

The lower clergy were also quick to learn their lesson. Previously, there had been reports of priests advocating a more social, less otherworldly approach: a motorcycle priest in 1959, for example;[31] zealous younger clergy seeking a prophetic role;[32] controversial, socially oriented sermons;[33] or a priest developing a youth ministry.[34] But during the antireligious campaign of the sixties, the state was quick and competent in removing such influences from the church. Just as had been the case after 1927 in the Iosif affair, the state exercises its awesome influence to ensure that such non-conformists are removed from the life of the church, either through transfer to ever smaller and less significant parishes or through arrest, exile and imprisonment.

Changes have been introduced into the church, revising and modifying its approach to conform to this new, exclusive orientation on the otherworldly. There is a renewed emphasis on sermons, but sermons dealing with the supernatural, rather than the social, sphere.

> There is now hardly any religious service conducted without a sermon. "With their sermons, the clergy," said one believer, "are able to turn a person inside out."[35]

Sermons have become a standard part of the Orthodox worship service. "These sermons are generally brief, ten to twenty minutes, and emphasize the spiritual and moral interpretation of the gospel for the day."[36] Aspiring clergymen are specifically trained in preaching, with an emphasis "that they should on every occasion so expound the faith that every sermon might speak directly to any unconverted who might be present."[37]

Special attention has been paid to church music. As early as in 1954, Patriarch Aleksei forbade secular hymns or tunes from the liturgy. "Parish priests must take care to ensure that the singing in their churches is ecclesiastical, not merely in name but also in fact, that hymns alien to the spirit of the church are not performed."[38] The church has devoted great attention to the scholarship of music, seeking to recapture the traditions of the past to meet the peculiar challenges of the present.[39]

Finally, the liturgy has been heavily emphasized as an otherworldly event.[40]

> Religion is not philosophy; the churchgoer believes that the Holy Spirit comes down to men through the sacraments, and our Church boldly declares that that is all he

needs. In itself, the liturgy is a richly
spiritual experience which leads to a consciousness of God's Truth. The believer
steeps himself in solemnity, the language
of the service, its symbolism and tone
of its prayers; he is enveloped in an atmosphere of mysticism and his recollec-
tion leads him to God. The liturgy's influence on souls can never be sufficiently
appreciated, especially among a people as in-
tuitive as ours.[41]

Soviet observers, too, have noted the renewal of the
liturgical emphasis. "The magnificence and solemnity of the service astonished me. The choir sang
so beautifully, and people all around wept openly".[42]

Only in one regard has there been an innovation
which does not reflect a single-minded concentration
on the otherworldly. In the church's service to the
state in foreign affairs, a small number of leading
clerics have had to respond to the heavy social emphasis of Western churches. Particularly since its
entry into the World Council of Churches in 1961,
Russian Orthodoxy has become involved in the social
dimensions of modern societies (excluding the USSR).
Social action is heavily emphasized in the World
Council of Churches, to such a degree that at times
the theological dimension seems lost entirely.
Clergymen from the USSR have thus become involved in
any number of social issues arising from the modern
environment: racism, capitalism, poverty, injustice,
and the whole spectrum of problems plaguing the non-
socialist world. By and large they have reacted in-
telligently to these problems, and if service to the
interests of the Soviet state seems to take priority,
they have nevertheless responded with acute theological justification of their position.[43] However,
because the church in Russia is rigidly excluded

226

from the social dimension, the result has been the
development of a small corps of internationalists
whose concerns have no bearing whatsoever on the
church in Russia. Positions taken by Russian clergymen in international gatherings do not represent the
domestic church at all, and any new insights regarding the social role of Christianity which these internationalists may acquire are totally inapplicable
at home.

For the fact remains that the church is rigidly
proscribed by the state from playing any role whatsoever in secular affairs. Such innovations as have
been introduced into the life of the church do not
represent a response to the challenges of society.
They do not reflect new phenomena which have appeared
in the country's modernization. If modernization is
defined as adaptation to new developments in the environment, not only has the Russian Orthodox Church
failed to modernize in any respect: it has regressed
from its reactionary position at the start of this
century. The Russian Orthodox Church today does not
even react to society; it ignores it completely.
Superficially, the conclusion must be that the Russian Orthodox Church has not modernized its approach
at all. Perforce, it has had to sever its ties with
society and concentrate only on the supernatural.
If modernization is defined as an adaptation to social developments, the church has not modernized.

However, if modernization is defined as finding
an effective role in modern life, then perhaps the
Russian Orthodox Church has modernized itself very
greatly indeed. It may be that this absolute retreat, this retirement from the field of social

227

struggle, is the most effective--perhaps the only
effective--response to modern, contemporary society.

For certainly this approach seems to be working.
The Russian Orthodox Church has confounded three
generations of critics by retaining its vigor and
visibility as an institution in Soviet society. Despite the crippling restrictions imposed on it, and
regardless of the untold millions of rubles the
state has allocated to combat religion, Russian Orthodoxy retains its hold on a significant portion
of the Russian people. An inspection of sociological data gathered by Soviet researchers in a great
many studies suggests that the number of religious
believers in Soviet society has increased from 80-90
million believers in 1937 to approximately 115 million today, of whom perhaps 50 million are Orthodox.[44] Thus the concentration on the otherworldly
to the exclusion of social matters has not had an
adverse effect on the church; quite the opposite,
in fact, is the case. The church has grown rather
than diminished.

In this regard Russian Orthodoxy may be experi-
encing a widespread--perhaps universal--phenomenon
in the modern world. In Western Christianity, at
least, those denominations which have attempted most
vigorously to adapt themselves to the changes in society, seeking to exert leadership in solving the
social ills of the modern world, have fared worst,
at least insofar as membership statistics are a
criterion. On the other hand, the churches which
are growing most rapidly are precisely those denomination and sects which concentrate on the otherworldly. The evangelical movements, with their

heavy concentration on personal evangelism and the afterlife, are the despair of many socially conscious Christians; yet it is precisely these churches which are growing and which are succeeding in extending their ministry into the most rapidly changing environments (e.g., the success of Pentecostals in the inner city). It may be, therefore, that a concentration on the supernatural, even to the neglect or, indeed, exclusion of the temporal, is the only form of modernization which can succeed in the contemporary world.

Perhaps the church is simply no longer competent to meet social needs in a complex, modern society. Poverty yields, not to church philanthropy, but to a vigorous economy. Racial equality is secured, not by appeals to a brotherhood of man, but by legislation. Public immorality is corrected, not in the consistory, but in the courts. In a secular society the church simply cannot compete. Where persuasion is needed, the church is but one voice-- and a tiny one at that--in the array of competing enticements in the media. Where resources are needed, Peter's Pence can scarcely compete with the graduated income tax. Where coercion is demanded, excommunication and the ban are risible compared to the militia and modern weapons. In short, the church is ill equipped to deal with the needs of society.

Certainly in the USSR the church is incompetent in social matters. The totalitarian ideology mandates the concentration of all capabilities in the state's own institution. If the state elects to pursue the good and eradicate the evil, the church can neither help nor hinder the process. If the

229

state elects otherwise, the church is similarly
helpless. In such a society, the church's abandonment of the temporal for the eternal may be its only
practical recourse. Even if the state should cease
to prohibit social activity, the church might find
itself quite helpless to compete with the state where
social ends are in view.

The converse is also true. The Soviet state
has proven itself incompetent in matters of the
spirit. The Communist Party generally displays an
almost supernatural inability to understand religion's appeal. On rare occasions, some comprehen-
sion of religious awe will appear in the Soviet
press.

> Three figures, three angels seated at a re-
> fectory table. The conversation is un-
> hurried, quiet and loaded with meaning. One
> of those taking part in it must sacrifice
> himself in order to redeem the evil of
> the world with his death.
> And the religious content of the le-
> gend seems to fade, is concealed by the
> wonderful, humane significance of the pic-
> ture. You may not take in--indeed, you
> may be completely unaware of--the specific
> subject of the Bible legend; but you will
> inevitably appreciate, become permeated
> by, the general mood, the general tone
> of the picture, by its effulgence, its
> calm and purity. Yes, it is indeed a
> tragedy; and it would be absurd to assert
> that Rublev in one way or another was
> avoiding or simply ignoring the religious
> ideal. This very ideal was the source of
> his inspiration.[45]

Much more typical is the rank philistinism of normal antireligious propaganda:

> As for me, of the Three Persons of the Trin-
> ity I should prefer the third, that is, the
> Dove, and then only if it had been well fed.

But, after all, tastes differ, and I have
no intention of forbidding my contemporaries to partake of the Sacred Heart of
Jesus, dressed with whatever sauce they
like. In matters of religious food, everyone must enjoy complete freedom.[46]

The church creates an atmosphere of beauty and
acceptance which contrasts markedly with the harsh,
utilitarian demands of modern society. "One should
not underestimate the emotional effect of church
art, of confessions and services. . . . It is just
this emotional influence that explains why a young
man who at first goes to church because he is bored
later becomes a victim without noticing it."[47]

The liturgy now has a new and severe beauty.
Never before has it been celebrated in so
solemn and spiritual a way. The secret
of this new revelation of religious beauty is
first of all in the celebrating priest,
but it takes hold of the worshippers,
giving depth and meaning to every word
of the reader, to every exclamation of
the deacon. Even in the smallest churches
the singing is lovely, the people are
loathe to leave the temple.[48]

Particularly among the older generation, a person may
feel more at home in the timeless, traditional church
than in the kaleidoscope of change in society.
"O, Russia isn't Russia anymore; the only place you
can feel at home is in the church."[49] A Western
observer summed up this aspect of the church's appeal
succinctly:

As I went out, I said to myself: "What have
I just seen and felt here, in this little
church of Samara, that so far I have felt
nowhere else in the USSR?" I soon found
out what it was. I had, for an instant,
stepped out of the organized society of the
Soviets, built on inflexible rules. On the
faces of the old men and women praying in

231

the church, and also on the painted faces
of the icons, picturing graceful scenes
of the Annunciation or episodes in the
lives of the saints, I had found the soft-
ness of indulgence and human pity.[50]

In times of difficulty, bereavement or tragedy
the Soviet state has thus far proven itself absolutely incapable of meeting the needs of its citizens.
Not so the church:

Everything that occurred, everything that
was said or sung, was sublimely irrational;
everyday values were stood on their heads;
suffering became acceptable and easy to
bear. Outside lay the struggle for existence, fear, jealousy, lies; inside was
a peace which became all the more unreal by
contrast.[51]

Even before the war, it was recognized that converts
to atheism often relapse when they fall into difficulty.[52] The church, with its otherworldly concentration on the supernatural, is able to offer religion's balm for those bereaved or in trouble. And
the state has yet to devise any sort of substitute.

Similarly, the church is able to answer the
problem of death. Marxism's only answer to the problem of death is an appeal to the immortality of
the collective, cold comfort indeed to the individual facing bereavement or his own death. The
church, however, can meet the problems of death with
no embarrassment. To the temporal and mortal it
contrasts the eternal and immortal, to the dismay
of the secular atheist. "The preaching of death in
the midst of the Twentieth Century, a century of
man's greatest achievements, a century of mastery
over the cosmos. Is this not monstrous?"[53] The
church's ability to provide a satisfactory answer to

232

the problem of death is of immense and widespread appeal.

Ultimately, the church is able to provide answers to those seeking the meaning of life.[54] "The Soviet Press is riddled with stories of young people in search of satisfactions that materialism fails to gratify, of komsomol boys and girls and even of party members who tear up their membership cards and join the Orthodox Church or some other religious group."[55] A significant portion of believers appeal to "blessedness in the afterlife" when questioned about life's meaning.[56] Even in 1926, Metropolitan Sergei had recognized this appeal which the church possessed:

> We do not see the progress of our church in an adaptation of the church to "modern exigencies," nor in the mutilation of its ideals, nor in a modification of its doctrine or canons, but in the success of our endeavor to rekindle and conserve, under present conditions, and in all its purity, the habitual fire of faith and love of God in the hearts of our flock: so that the faithful may learn, at the zenith of material progress, to see life's true significance beyond the grave, rather than here below.[57]

This ability to provide a meaning for life which transcends the merely temporal may explain in large measure the phenomenon that the churches are filled predominantly with the elderly; a young person may be content to pursue his ambitions in secular society, but when he has reached middle age he may begin to yearn for something more.[58] "When they're older and wiser, they may find God in their hearts and come back to us completely."[59]

Thus the church retains an appeal--and it is

powerful--in contemporary Soviet society. But this appeal is premised exclusively on the otherworldly, **the supernatural, the eternal. The church** disclaims any interest in any social implications of the gospel. It concentrates solely on the sacred, leaving the profane to its own devices.

This may be a strange approach to modernization. It may well be a truncation of the church's mission. But it seems to work. Whether or not this inverse modernization, this modernization by refusing to modernize, is desirable, it is the only approach to institutional religion which the Soviet state permits. The Russian Orthodox Church has no viable alternative.

## NOTES

1. _New York Times_, April 18, 1968.

2. S. V. Troitskii, _O nepravde Karlovatskogo raskola_ (Paris: Editions do l'Exarchat Patriarcal Russe in Europe Occidentale, 1960), p. 24; W. C. Emhardt, _Religion in Soviet Russia_ (London: Morehouse, 1929), pp. 242-50.

3. Spinka, _Church and the Russian Revolution_, pp. 119-20.

4. Nikita Struve, _Christians in Contemporary Russia_ (London: Harvill, 1963), p. 344.

5. Fletcher, _Study_, pp. 16-17.

6. Fletcher, _Russian Orthodox Church Underground_, passim.

7. _New York Times_, April 9, 1972.

8. J. F. Triska, Ed., _Constitutions of the Communist Party-States_ (Palo Alto, California: Hoover Institution, 1968), p. 51.

9. _Izvestiia_, June 27, 1923.

10. Fletcher, _Study_, pp. 66-7, 74-5.

11. See Bourdeaux, _Patriarch and Prophets_.

12. _Religion in Communist Dominated Areas_ (_RCDA_) 5 (1966): 74.

13. Ibid., pp. 90-1.

14. _Delo Mitropolita Sergiia_ (unpublished type-script, np, np, nd [1930?]), No. 114, p. 133, quoted in Fletcher, _Underground_, pp. 76-7.

15. Sviashchennik Mikhail, _Polozhenie Tserkvi v Sovetskoi Rossii_ (Jerusalem: Goldberg's Press, 1939), p. 65.

16. _Izvestiia_, August 18, 1927.

17. Fletcher, _Study_, pp. 32-43.

18. Fletcher, _Underground_, pp. 62-9.

19. Ibid., pp. 43-78.

20. Gleb Rar, _Plenennaia Tserkov'_ (Frankfurt: Posev, 1954), p. 31.

21. The figure of 4,225 was given by _Religious Communities in the Soviet Union_ (London: Press Department of the Soviet Embassy, 1941), p. 2. A. Veschikov, "Etapy bol'shogo puti," _Nauka i religiia_, No. 11 (1962), p. 60, states that "in 1941 there were _nearly_ 4,000 Orthodox churches," (italics mine); Dmitrii Konstantinov, _Religious Persecution in USSR_ (London, Canada: SBONR, 1965), p. 17, estimates that there were 3,200; Kurt Hutten, _Iron Curtain Christians_ (Minneapolis, Minnesota: Augsburg, 1967), p. 13, estimates 1,500; and Michael Bourdeaux, _Opium of the People_ (London: Faber and Faber, 1965), p. 58, without specifying the basis for the estimate, places the number of operating churches on the eve of World War II at 100.

22. See W. C. Fletcher, _Religion and Soviet Foreign Policy 1945-1970_ (London: Royal Institute of International Affairs [O.U.P.], 1973), pp. 16-38.

23. For a detailed analysis of the number of Orthodox churches operating in the post-war USSR, see W. C. Fletcher, "USSR," in Western Religion: A Country by Country Sociological Inquiry, ed. Hans [J. J.] Mol (The Hague: Mouton, 1972), pp. 565-86.

24. See D. A Lowrie and W. C. Fletcher, "Khrushchev's Religious Policy, 1959-64," in Marshall, Aspects of Religion, pp. 131-55.

25. Scriptural precedent can be claimed for this subservient position, citing Romans 13. On first reading, however, it would seem that the Apostle enjoins submission on the assumption that the authorities are godly, for he states in verse 3, "For the rulers are not a terror to good works, but to evil." The difficulty can be resolved if the word "terror" (fobos; in Russian, strashny) is taken literally as referring, not to actions which the rulers indulge in, but to the effect of their actions on the individual. This reading can be paraphrased that the good man cannot be terrified by any state, thus allowing the passage to refer to any government, regardless of whether it be good or evil.

26. M. G. Pismanik, "Religioznaia kontseptsiia 'grekhovnosti' i nravstvennyi progress," in Ateizm, religiia, nravstvennost' ed. V. I. Garadzha (Moscow: "Mysl'", 1972), p. 150.

27. N. P. Andrianov, "Evoliutsiia nravstvennogo oblika sovremennogo veruiushchego," in ibid., pp. 174-75.

28. Orthodox Eastern Church, Russian, The Russian Orthodox Church, Organization, Situation, Activity (Moscow: The Patriarchate, 1959), p. 7.

29. Ibid., p. 222.

30. Zhurnal Moskovskoi Patriarkhii, April 1960; cf. W. C. Fletcher, Nikolai: Portrait of a Dilemma (New York: Macmillan, 1968), pp. 186-93.

31. Komsomol'skaia pravda, May 23, 1959.

32. T. E. Bird, "Party, the Patriarch and the World Council," Commonweal, April 13, 1962, p. 57.

33. Time, February 16, 1962, pp. 26-7.

34. *Christian Century*, September 16, 1964, p. 1143.

35. *Komsomol'skaia pravda*, June 14, 1963.

36. P. B. Anderson, "Orthodox Chruch in Soviet Russia," *Foreign Affairs* 39 (January 1961): 309.

37. M. Shaw, "Impressions of the Russian Orthodox Church," *International Review of Missions*, No. 47 (October 1958), p. 443.

38. *Zhurnal moskovskoi patriarkhii*, January, 1954, pp. 11-12.

39. Johann von Gardner, "The State of Orthodox Church Music in the USSR," *Bulletin of the Institute for the Study of the USSR* 10 (April 1963): 6-13.

40. Bird, "Party," pp. 56-7.

41. Constantin de Grunwald, *The Churches and the Soviet Union* (New York: Macmillan, 1962), p. 118, quoting a patriarchate official.

42. *Literaturnaia gazeta*, April 28, 1962.

43. See Fletcher, *Foreign Policy*, pp. 117-39.

44. W. C. Fletcher, Soviet Sociology of Religion: A Survey Assessment (Forthcoming); cf. *Ecumenical Press Service*, October 24, 1968, p. 11.

45. *Komsomol'skaia pravda*, September 20, 1960.

46. *Nauka i religiia*, No. 1 (January, 1960), quoted by Yury Marin, "The Search for New Methods in the Fight Against Religion," in *Religion in the USSR*, ed. Boris Iwanow (Munich: Institute for the Study of the USSR, 1960), p. 217.

47. V. I. Prokof'ev, "Antigumanisticheskii kharakter religioznoi morali," *Voprosy filosofii*, No. 9 (September 1959), p. 31.

48. Donald Attwater, *The Christian Churches of the East*, 2 vols. (London: Chapman, 1961), 2: 70, quoting G. P. Fedotov.

49. D. A. Lowrie, _The Light of Russia_ (Prague: YMCA Press, 1923), p. 229.

50. Eve Curie, _Journey Among Warriors_ (Garden City, New York: Doubleday, 1943), p. 144.

51. H. E. Salisbury, _To Moscow--and Beyond_ (New York: Harper, 1959), pp. 257-8.

52. "Vnimanie individual'noi propagande," _Antireligioznik_, No. 3 (March 1941), p. 1-5.

53. V. Chertikhin, "Chto propoveduet pravoslavie," _Nauka i religiia_, No. 11 (November 1961), p. 12.

54. I. N. Iablokov, "Transformatsiia religioznoi morali v soznanii veruiushchikh v usloviiakh sotsializma," in _Konkretno-sotsiologicheskoe izuchenie sostoianiia religioznosti i opyta ateisticheskogo vospitaniia_ ed. I. D. Pantskhava (Moscow 1969), p. 141.

55. M. G. Hindus, _House Without a Roof_ (Garden City, New York: Doubleday, 1961), p. 116.

56. L. T. Sytenko, "O nravstvennom oblike sovremennogo veruiushchego," in _Voprosy nauchnogo ateizma_, ed. A. F. Okulov, 3 (Moscow 1967): 121.

57. Matthew Spinka, _The Church in Soviet Russia_ (New York: Oxford University Press, 1956), p. 158.

58. Cf. W. C. Fletcher, "Protestant Influences on the Outlook of the Soviet Citizen Today," in _Religion and the Search for New Ideals in the USSR_, ed. W. C. Fletcher and A. J. Strover (New York: Praiger, 1967), pp. 75-6, 82.

59. Patricia Blake, "Alliance with the Unholy," _Life_, September 14, 1959, p. 126, quoting a Russian priest.

238

## Chapter 7
## MODERNIZATION AND CONSERVATISM IN SOVIET ISLAM

Alexandre Bennigsen

There exist but few Soviet sources for the analysis of the current evolution of Islam in the USSR.
The official organ of the Tashkent Muftiat, Musul'-
mane sovetskogo vostoka (Muslims of the Soviet East)
--the equivalent of the Zhurnal moskovskoi patriar-
chii--which appears in the Uzbek and Arabic languages (since 1968) is not to be found outside of
the USSR, at least neither in Western Europe nor in
the United States.  Additionally, the Muslim (or
rather anti-Muslim) counterparts to Nauka i religiia,
a Moscow monthly periodical, which are published in
Central Asia, the Caucasus, and the Middle Volga in
Uzbek, Azeri, Tatar, etc., come but rarely to Western Europe or the United States.

We are, therefore, reduced to reading, in large
part and often between the lines, the non-periodical
antireligious literature which is, fortunately, extremely abundant.  It is also extraordinarily dull
and naïve, but it does contain from time to time useful information.  Among the most interesting in this
respect are the two works of an Azeri specialist,
Nugman Ashirov:  Islam and the Nations (Islam i natsii) (Moscow, 1975) and The Evolution of Islam in the
USSR (Evoliutsiia islama v SSSR) (Moscow, 1973).  His

239

books are of particular importance because he uti-
lizes extracts from Muslim sources not to be found
in the West:  sermons of Soviet _imams_, reports on
proceedings of various religious conferences, edi-
torials from the _Muslims of the Soviet East_, and
legal decisions (_fetwas_) of Soviet Muftis.

## HISTORICAL BACKGROUND

It is necessary to get briefly acquainted with
the historical background of Soviet Islam in order to
understand correctly the problem of its modernization.  In tsarist Russia, before the Bolshevik revolution, Muslim communities were not, as some orien-
talists tend to believe, a "cultural backyard of the
Islam."  On the contrary, some Muslim centers, especially Baku, Kazan on the Middle Volga, Orenburg, and
Troitsk in the southern Urals were in the early twentieth century brilliant cultural centers comparable
to the greatest capitals of _Dar ul-Islam_, such as
Istanbul, Cairo, Beirut, and Aligarh in India.

The last quarter of the nineteenth century and
the early part of this century have been rightly
called the era of the "Tatar Renaissance."  While
an analysis of this phenomenon is beyond the scope of
this essay, it would be well to remember that for
various internal and external reasons, this "Renaissance" assumed from its very beginning the form of a
struggle between the "modernists" (_jadids_, from _jadid_
meaning new) and the conservatives (_kadimists_, from
_kadim_ meaning ancient), with the former rapidly gain-
ing ground almost everywhere except in Central Asia
and the north Caucasus.  These two regions remained
until 1917 the bastions of the purest traditionalism.

The modernist movement extended to all the fields of private and public life. It began as a daring religious reform, the aim of which was to conciliate religion--Islam--with modern, technical progress. This was the achievement of a group of Tatar theologians: Shihabeddin Marjani (1818-1889), Rizaeddin Fahhreddinoglu (1859-1939), and Musa-Jarullah Bigi (1875-1949). They struggled successfully against the medieval scholastics, the excessive authority of the clerics (who in Islam constitute a "parasitical class," unknown in the pure and dynamic establishment of the early Califate), for the renewal of the ijtihad (the right for every believer to interprete the Koran--the pivot issue of the Muslim reformism), and, finally, for the equality of religious and social rights between men and women. Around 1905, Kazan was certainly the world center of Islamic religious modernism. Its authority was appealed to and accepted everywhere from the Maghrib to Indonesia.

Linguistic modernism followed closely the religious reform. It was a successful, collective endeavour undertaken by Kayyum Nasyri (1824-1904) of the Volga Tatars, Ismail Gasprinsky (1851-1914) of the Crimean Tatars, Hazan Melikov-Zerdabi (1837-1907) of the Azeris, and Abay Kunanbaev (1845-1904) of the Kazakhs. Thanks to this effort, similar to the reform of the Russian language by Pushkin in the early nineteenth century, Muslims of the Russian empire could, on the eve of the October revolution, avail themselves of modern languages which were close to spoken dialects and purged of medieval Arabic or Persian endowments--comparable in this respect to the modernized Turkish of Kemal Ataturk. The corollary of this linguistic reform was the birth of a new,

241

modern, "bourgeois" literature in the Tatar, Azeri, and Kazakh languages. Once more Russian Muslims were the vanguard of the entire Dar ul-Islam. This new literature, supported and diffused by a rich, abundant, and varied press, was a "pledged" one in that its themes were inspired by problems of the modern world and by the fight for religious, social, and political reforms. Additionally it was dedicated to the new social class, the bourgeoisie, from which it drew its inspiration.

The modernization of the Muslim educational system, promoted by the Crimean Tatar, Ismail Gasprinski, followed the Russian and German models. Completed around 1905, the modernized system gave Russian Islam a leading position in the domain of Muslim education. Some of the Russian medressehs were considered the most progressive Muslim schools in the world. Particularly remarkable were Zinjirli in Bakhchisaray, Mohammediyeh in Kazan, Huseyniyeh in Orenburg, and Rasuliyeh in Troitsk. They were the first Muslim schools to include modern sciences and foreign languages in their curriculum.

Finally, between 1905 and 1917, modernizing reformism affected politics. It assumed the character of a violent struggle between the traditional leading class of a Muslim community (Ulemas, merchants, landlords, tribal chiefs) and the new candidates to leadership, generally of the same aristocratic or merchant origin, but educated in Russian or West European institutions, hence bearers of new modern political ideologies: democracy, liberalism, radicalism, and, later on, socialism. It was in Baku and in Orenburg that the first Muslim socialist organizations appeared in 1907, long before their emergence in the

Ottoman Empire, in Iran, or in the Arab world. However before 1917 even the most radical revolutionary wing of Muslim socialism refused to reject the religious basis of the society and to assimilate modernization to secularization.

Thus, because of the Russian challenge and of the possibility to imitate Russian models, Russian Islam represented on the eve of World War I a highly dynamic community, certainly one of the most progressive and modern of the entire Dar ul-Islam. In many fields, such as education, politics, language, literature, the process of modernization was already well advanced. Tatar and Azeri Jadidism was considered the lodestar by foreign Muslim modernists. The October revolution and the introduction of the Soviet regime put a stop to this process.

## SOVIET POLICY TOWARD ISLAM

Soviet policy in connection with Islam changed several times since the revolution. Grosso modo, four different stages can be specified. Between 1917-1929 during the period of the antireligious "cavalry raids," corresponding to "War Communism," the relations between the new regime and Islam were openly hostile. The Bolsheviks were convinced of their rapid world-wide victory. In the light of their ideology, Islam--as indeed any other religion-- was but an instrument in enemy hands, doomed to a necessary and quick destruction. With the exception of a few special areas, where Muslim conservative leaders were fighting on two or even three fronts (against the Reds, the Whites, and their own liberals), Islam appeared as a counterrevolutionary force.

The Bolsheviks' policies toward Islam were clumsy and
brutal and led to two important popular uprisings--
the Basmachis in Central Asia and the Naqshbanidyya
in Chechenia, Daghestan--which took on the aspect of
"holy war," jihad.

Between 1921 and 1928 relations, still tense,
became less violent. The regime was still determined to destroy religion but it was no longer con-
vinced--as during the "cavalry raids" period--that
the destruction could be achieved overnight. In
1921 the rights and privileges of Muslim institutions, canceled during the years of War Communism,
were restored. The application of the principle of
separation of state and church, laid down in 1918,
was cautious and unhurried. The wagfs (mortmain
properties), which were at the basis of the Muslim
clergy's economic power and which were suppressed
during the civil war, were set up again in Central
Asia in 1922 and survived until 1930. Muslim religious courts of justice (both the Shariyat and the
adat) passed through the same evolution. In 1917 a
decree of the Sovnarkom abolished all religious
courts of justice and replaced them by a network of
"peoples courts," but in Central Asia this decision
was never applied in practice and remained a purely
platonic declaration of principle. Religious courts
of justice were officially re-established in 1921
and in 1922 and their jurisdiction was extended to
criminal cases. Nevertheless the offensive against
Muslim courts of justice started again, though cau-
tiously, in 1923. The deathblow was finally delivered against them in 1928 with the abolishment of all
religious courts.

In contrast with what occurred in Christian ter-

ritories, the Muslim religious school network, flourishing on the eve of the revolution (in 1916 there
were some 5,000 jadid schools in Russia, not including Bukhara and Khiva) was preserved during the first
ten years of the new regime. The famous decree of
the Sovnarkom of January 23, 1918 on "Freedom of Conscience and religious societies," which prohibited
religious instruction in schools, was not applied in
Central Asia and in the Caucasus until 1928.

Though Islam fared relatively better than other
religions during the first ten years of the new regime, its position deteriorated during the period of
collectivization and industrialization. The frontal
attack began in 1928, coinciding with the liquidation
of the jadids who during the civil war years had
joined the Communist Party. The authorities made use
of all the means at their disposal: education,
stormy propaganda, and such police and administrative
measures as the shutting of mosques and the arrest
and physical liquidation of clerics--prosecuted not
only as "parasites" and "counterrevolutionaries,"
but also from 1930 on as "spies in the pay of Japan
and Germany." Out of 26,000 mosques that existed in
1912, there remained no more than 1,300 "working"
ones in 1942 in the Soviet Union.

On the eve of the war with Germany, the intensity of administrative and police pressure and of
propaganda slackened. During the war, Muslim and
other religious communities were granted the status
of legal persons. An era of relative liberalism began in 1941 and lasted throughout the hostilities.
Muslim religious authorities responded to this new
tolerance with protestations of loyalty and with support of the war effort. From 1945 on the policy of

245

the Soviet state towards Islam was rather similar to the one pursued as regards the Orthodox Church. A certain modus vivendi was established with the official Muslim establishment: the four Spiritual Directions (Muftiats) of Tashkent, Ufa, Baku and Buynaksk. It is still in force. The religious authorities are perfectly loyal to the regime, which, in turn, avoids attacking the official Muslim organization. The attitude of the Soviet Government towards official Islam is presently one of cold correctness. Direct attacks on the Muslim clerical establishment never appear in the press. However, Islam has been reduced to the performance of religious observances only; it is supposed to be a "private affair" and all institutions that formerly endowed it with prescriptive authority over its adherents have been destroyed. The Shariyat law is no longer recognized; religious courts of justice, waqfs, and religious schools (with the exception of two medressehs in Tashkent and Bukhara) no longer exist. Religious publications (except one periodical for learned clerics) and religious education are expressly prohibited. Moreover, like all other religions, Islam has been submitted since 1945 to constant and massive antireligious propaganda,[1] but in contrast to the pre-war period, this campaign is conducted on a purely ideological, "scientific" basis and not by means of administrative or police measures. Nevertheless, the effort of anti-Muslim propaganda is immense, greater in bulk than the anti-Christian effort--probably because of the deeper roots of Islam and the easy confusion between its religious and national aspects. The results of the propaganda, however, are practically nil and ever since the war the authorities have been com-

246

plaining of its dullness and inefficiency, pointing
out the waste of energy and the refusal of local intellectuals to participate in the effort.

## MODERNIZATION AND RELIGIOUS PHILOSOPHY

The powerful and promising jadid reformist movement, which had borne Russian Islam to the vanguard
of Muslim, modernist thought on the eve of the revolution, was brutally interrupted by the Soviet regime. Islam certainly managed to survive long years
of persecution and pressure of various descriptions,
but it did so by enclosing itself in a rigorous conservatism comparable to that of the Orthodox Church.
For half a century, its intellectual life was an-
nihilated. We are witnessing today the first attempts to resume that march interrupted in 1917.
These attempts are as yet cautious and modest. As
regards the field of religious philosophy, Soviet
Islam appears as one of the most conservative areas
of the Dar ul-Islam.

It is starting on its onward march from the ex-
act spot where it had left off, fifty years ago. Today, as before the revolution, the main issue of modernism remains "the reopening of the ijtihad," i.e.,
the right for the believers to study the Koran, to
understand it in a subjective way, and to find in it
answers to private and collective problems.[2] Such
an attitude implies the rejection of blind respect
for authority, the condemnation of the entire medieval scholastic philosophy, and a theoretical return
to the pure and primitive Islam of the Medina Califate, of the first "well guided" Califs, when Islam
was young, dynamic, powerful, and progressive. Noth-

247

ing is really new in this "wahhabi" type, "back to
the puritan Islam" trend.  It has been the leitmotiv
of all pre-revolutionary jadids.  Even the attempt to
reconcile Islam and socialism, to represent Mohammed
as the first revolutionary socialist, and to prove
that the best of Marxism had already been set out in
primitive Islam are not really new.  All these issues had been repeatedly discussed by radical Tatar
theologians on the eve of the revolution.

It is characteristic of the traditionalism of
Soviet Islam that Soviet Muslim authorities do not
dare to introduce any real innovations and deem it
necessary to appeal to the authority of pre-war jadid thinkers, especially to that of the nineteenth
century Tatar theologian, Shihabeddin Marjani, when
attempting to inaugurate minor change.  As a Soviet
specialist of anti-Islamic propaganda recently
wrote:  "New ideas are accepted by Muslim authorities only when they fit into the prism of traditional concept and are expressed in the classical form
of the Muslim religious dogma."[3]

In spite of the apparent modernism of the attempt to conciliate socialism and religion and to
prove that Islam can survive under any political regime, official Islamic thought, dogma, and praxis
remain perfectly orthodox and conservative.  The
"modernism" of the present day Islam is purely formal and certainly less daring and less progressive
than its predecessor of seventy or eighty years ago,
when Tatar and Azeri Ulemas were boldly discussing
the problem of the free will and advancing heretical,
almost "mutazilit" arguments.

It is impossible to discover in the USSR the
slightest evidence of the existence of an original

248

Muslim theology, and it is certainly possible to draw
a parallel between Islam and the Orthodox Russian
Church. Neither the brilliant Pleiades of Christian
thinkers of the early twentieth century (Bulgakov,
Berdiaev, and their companions) nor their remarkable
Muslim contemporaries (Musa Bigi, Abdullah Bubi, Riz-
zaeddin Fahreddin--the leading figures of the "Tatar
Renaissance") have left any heirs. Soviet Islam is
an intellectual desert, a perfect void. The Muslim
religion has not only become a "private affair," it
has also been reduced to the purely formal performance of a ritual.

In one respect only does Soviet Islam still appear in the vanguard of Muslim theology: in the matter of the relations between Sunnites and Shiites.
While in the Middle East the opposition between these
two sects of Islam is still active, in the USSR it
has practically disappeared. Even before 1917, Russian Sunni theologians considered the Shiite simply
as the fifth legal school[4] and today even the believers tend to ignore the differences between the two
rites.[5]

RELIGIOUS RIGHTS

There is nothing to say about religious rights
in Islam. It is a religion without "clergy," based
upon the belief that there is no need of intermedi-
aries between the believer and his Creator. Such
was the ideal position in the pure, primitive Islam,
to which modernists want to revert. A mosque is not
a consecrated temple, but simply a place for the performance of collective prayers, which could as well
be performed outside of it. The ritualistic, cere-

249

monial aspect of the "cult" in Islam is less important than in any other religion.  An _imam_ is only a
leader of a collective prayer, and any believer with
some knowledge of Arabic can perform the functions
of a _Mullah_.  This special situation explains why
there has never been any struggle in Soviet Islam
for the defense of religious rights.  With regards
to the five "pillars of the faith" (_arkan_) which the
believers are supposed to perform, the situation is
as follows:  the _zakat_ (legal alms) is no longer
paid because, as with all other religions, Islam is
forbidden to have a social life; the _hadj_ (pilgrimage
to Mecca) remains in theory an obligation, but since
the end of World War II only some rare selected pil-
grims have been able to travel to Arabia.  It is admitted that this pilgrimage can be performed by
proxy:  by a religious leader for the entire community, or else replaced by a pilgrimage to a local
holy place.  In the case of the latter solution what
occurs is not a modernization of the concept of pilgrimage but the opposite phenomenon:  a return to a
pre-Islamic belief.  The _salat_ or _hamaz_ (the private
prayer to be performed five times a day) is still executed in rural areas but the religious leaders tend
to minimize the obligation of this practice so as to
avoid attacks by the authorities against the believers.[6]  Fast during the month of Ramadan (_Uraza_ or
_Sawn_) has also been simplified.  Muslim authorities
now accept a fast of two weeks (the first and the
last of the month), and even of three symbolic days:
the first, middle, and last days of the lunar month.
(The same practice is observed in countries of the
Middle East.)  The leaders also stress the fact that
fasting must in no way interfere with the collective

work of Soviet citizens.[7]  However, according to recent comparisons between Soviet Central Asia and the
Muslim Middle East, it appears that the Ramadan fasting is better observed in the USSR than in the Muslim countries.

The main "pillar of faith," recognized as such
today, eludes by its nature the control of the authorities.  It is the Shahada, the profession of belief
in one God and in Mohammed His Prophet, which is made
by the believer in the secret of his heart.  The desire to be a Muslim is sufficient in itself.

Two other distinctive signs differentiate the
followers of Islam from other citizens:  circumcision
and burial in separate Muslim cemeteries.  Both are
constantly denounced as obnoxious survivals of the
past (perezhitki) by the Soviet press but seem to be
observed by the immense majority of Soviet Muslims,
even by non-believers.

## MODERNIZATION AND RELIGIOUS MORALS

The impact of modernism on religious morals in
the Soviet Islam is insignificant. Compared to other
countries of the Muslim world, Soviet Central Asia
and the Caucasus appear as bastions of moral conservatism.  Soviet press and antireligious propaganda
constantly complain of anarchronistic, moral attitudes among Soviet Muslims.  However, such attitudes
are not all based on religion.  Consciously or not
it seems that Soviet authorities confuse the purely
religious prescriptions of the koranic (Shariyat)
law and the survivals, often very strong, of the
principles of pre-modern social structure of Muslim
society, sanctified by long use into customary rules

251

(adat). The latter category includes various social customs, taboos, and rules--still very much alive-- concerning the family structure and clanic survivals: Kalym (buying of the wife), polygamy, Kaytarma, levi-rat, and various other endogamic or exogamic regu-lations.

Purely religious morals remain today much the same as before the revolution. Muslims--even those who do not observe the rites of their faith--are more sobor, more respectful of their elders (aqsaqalism-- "the exaggerated respect of white beards" is con-stantly denounced by Soviet propaganda), and more severe and rigid in their sexual morals than those of other Soviet citizens. Muslim religious authori-ties adopt an attitude toward morals comparable to that of their jadid predecessors of the early twen-tieth century: maintainance and preservation of the real religious, purely Islamic morals (alimentary taboos, sobriety, high level of sexual morals, a cer-tain sexual segregation) which are supposed to sur-vive whatever the social condition and the politi-cal regime. At the same time they dissociate them-selves from the "customary morals" originated in a clanic or patriarchal society. The result is a cer-tain modernization of the moral standard, an evolu-tion comparable to that of the recent development in the Muslim world in general but on a more modest scale. According to our somewhat limited knowledge, there is but one minor aspect of the matter on which Soviet Islam seems to have religious standards some-what different from those of their fellow co-reli-gionists of the Middle East: a more tolerant offi-cial attitude towards members of other religions, particularly towards the Ahl-al-Kitab (The People of

252

the Book--the Christians, not the Jews.  The notion
of jihad, the "holy war against the Infidels," is officially repudiated.  The official organ of the Tashkent Muftiat  declared in 1969 that "the Muslims of
our country obey the principles of Islam concerning
tolerance toward other religions, which corresponds
to the Leninist rule of freedom of confession."[7]  It
is however doubtful that the Muslim masses in USSR accept this new "ecumenical tolerance."  Judging by
the almost total absence of mixied marriages between
Muslims and Christians, the religious hostility
toward Christians (especially when they are Russians)
is still very much alive.

## MODERNIZATION AND CHURCH STRUCTURE

Since Islam lacks, as already mentioned, regular "clergy," it is impossible to talk about a "Muslim Church."  The clerics, mullahs, imam-khatibs,
imams, muezzins, muftis, etc. are not priests and the
so-called four Spiritual Directions are not spiritual
but purely administrative institutions.  Theoretically, Islam can exist without them.  At the highest
level of the Islamic administration, the four Muftiats (Spiritual Directions), nothing practically
has been modified since the re-establishment of the
Muftiat of European Russia in Ufa in the eighteenth
century by Catherine the Great, except for the fact
that before the revolution, the mufti was appointed
by the tsar, while at present he is elected--at least
in theory.  However, only clerics can participate
in the election of the muftis and, of course, the approval of the Soviet Government is necessary.  So
the situation is not really different from what it

was under the tsarist regime.  Under the circumstances, the highest religious hierarchy of the Muftiat is just as loyal and submissive to the Soviet
regime as their predecessors were to that of the
tsar.

It is at the lower level of the religious Muslim institutions--that of the parish centered around
the mosque--that the transformation of religious
structures is the most intense.  It is at this level
that the evolution towards new and original forms has
been especially bold and rapid since World War II.

A Muslim parish, compared to its pre-revolutionary predecessor is a curiously democratic body.
Before the revolution, the imam-khatib was an absolute master of his mosque and of its dependent institutions, such as the koranic school and the small
hospital; today he is only a technician, a paid em-
ployee while the main responsibility belongs to a
committee of the parishioners (Mute aliyyat) which
deals not only with the financial and administrative
business of the parish, but also, since World War II,
with the purely intellectual and spiritual problems
that might arise.  Thus, for instance, the Friday
sermons of the imam-khatib (an essential part of the
Friday religious ceremony) may be discussed on the
spot by the assembly of believers.  This is a real
novelty.  Viewed from this angle, Soviet Islam appears certainly more "democratic" than that practiced in the Middle East.  Ashirov gives many instances in which the mosque committee disagreed with
the imam on purely religious problems and dismissed
him as a consequence.  Thus, the head of the Shii
Gokchay mosque in Azerbaijan, who opposed the use of
his mosque by both Shiites and Sunnites was expelled

by his parishioners. The imam of the Leningrad
mosque, an Uzbek, trained at the very conservative
medressèh Mir-i Arab of Bukhara, forbade his Tatar
parishioners to attend concerts and theaters and was,
as a consequence, forced to leave the mosque, while
the parishioners complained to the Mufti of Ufa that
his fanatical sermons were in contradiction with the
true spirit of Islam.[9]

Soviet authorities claim that it is under the
influence of the "Soviet way of life" that Muslim believers are breaking up old traditions. In reality,
the democratic evolution of Islamic structures had
already begun--as we have seen--before the revolution
and was part of the jadid fight against medieval scho-
lasticism and the "back to the primitive Islam" movement.

It would be wrong, however, to exaggerate the
modernist evolution of Soviet Islam. In many areas,
especially in north Caucasus and in Turkestan, the
Islamic structures are still traditional, even archaic. Ashirov, our main recent source, mentions the
existence in certain regions of Central Asia of a
peculiar, "clanic religious" hierarchy.[10] As the official clerics placed under the control of the Four
Spiritual Directions do not suffice for the religious needs of the Muslim population of forty-five to
fifty million, they are supplemented by "unofficial"
mullahs, generally members of various Muslim Soufi
brotherhoods (tariqa) who escape all control of the
official hierarchy and are, as a rule, bearers of the
most conservative Islam.

MODERNIZATION, RELIGION, AND FAMILY

The fight for the "modernization" of the Muslim

255

family had started already early in the twentieth
century.  Pre-revolutionary jadids denounced polygamy, the veil, the payment of Kalym, the inferior
position of women in Muslim society, and the family.
Woman's liberation was one of the central topics of
pre-revolutionary Muslim literature.  One the eve of
the revolution a Tatar or Azeri middle class family
did not differ much from an ordinary Russian family,
but in Central Asia and in the north Caucasus the
patriarchal structure was still very alive.

   For fifty years now, the Soviet authorities
with the entire support, since World War II, of the
Muslim religious authorities, have been fighting for
the complete modernization of the family and the destruction of medieval survivals.  But in this common fight, the motives and the final goal are different for each of the partners.  Muslim religious
authorities are simply continuing in the way of their
predecessors of half a century ago.  On the other
hand, the Soviet authorities consider the Muslim
family as the real bastion of the Islamic religion.
Right or wrong, this belief of the Soviet authorities explains the intensely offensive campaign
against the perezhitki, started fifty years ago and
still going on with the same unabated violence.[11]

   Without trying to justify or to condemn the Soviet authorities on this point, it is important to
note that the Muslim family cell, even when reduced
to its most modern, conjugal structure, preserves
the moral and psychological traces of patriarchal,
extended, joint families, clans, and tribes which
are sanctified by the customary law (adat), though
not by the koranic law (Shariyat).  It is these vestiges which give to the present day Muslim family

256

its specific profile, so different from the Soviet Russian family, and which stand in the way of the biological symbiosis between Muslims and non-Muslims.[12] The originality of the Muslim family is based on two characteristics: (1) a strong sense of "collateral" solidarity, binding members of the family group in the large sense: brothers, cousins, kinsmen. . . ., and (2) the still undisputed supremacy of the elders over the younger generation and of the males over the females.

It is this original family structure that is attacked by the Soviet authorities, who have chosen women's liberation as the best means to destroy it. So far it has survived victoriously the attacks mainly because of the resistance of women themselves, and not, as Soviet propaganda claims, because of the "feudal" attitude of men.

Even in those cases where the family modernization campaign has been successful and men and women have become equal partners, the religious basis of the family has not entirely disappeared. Circumcision is still practiced, even among convinced party members and, according to the majority of Soviet sources, the proportion of religious marriages is much higher among Muslims than among Russians.[13]

The persistance of the Muslim character of the family is reflected in the use of purely Islamic names. In the 1930s those Muslims who welcomed the new regime and became communists gave their children either purely national, or Turkic names, such as Chingiz, Togrul, Arslan, etc., or simply European ones: Bella, Ernst, Rudolf. Today, there is a return to purely Muslim names, generally with an obvious religious meaning: Mohammed, Abdurrahman, Must-

257

afa. It is quite a usual paradox to find young specialists of antireligious agitprop with such names as
Abdullah ("The Slave of God"), or Nureddin ("The
light of the Faith"), etc.

## MODERNIZATION, RELIGION, AND COLLECTIVE LIFE

Islam is a collective faith, more so than any
other revealed religion. The Umma, the collectivity
of the faithful, and the ijma, the consensus of the
believers, are the foundations of the faith. But Islam is not only a faith, it is also a culture, a way
of life, and a system of human behavior. Before the
revolution, it thoroughly penetrated all spheres of
private and public life. Under the Soviet regime,
Islam, as with all other religions, has been reduced
to the state of a "private affair." As we have already stated, all social activity is strictly forbidden to the religious institutions which are supposed to deal exclusively with matters of faith. But
reality may or again may not correspond to the expectations of the authorities in this respect.

Naturally, religious authorities never challenge
openly the restrictive policy of the government.
Nevertheless it is obvious enough that the "collective character" of Islam, backed by a tradition of
thirteen centuries, could not be spirited away by a
decision of the Soviet agitprop. The inborn sense
of the Umma, of the solidarity between Muslims, even
when they do not profess their religion, remains as
strong as ever. Recent information shows that religious authorities are endeavoring to use this collective character of the Islam in order to prove that
it is better adapted to the socialist system than

any other religion, that Muslims are already prepared for socialism by their faith, and even that it is impossible to be a good socialist without being a Muslim. We find here a conscious attempt, as yet a very cautious one, to achieve a symbiosis between socialism and Islam. Such an endeavor had already been made without success in the late 1920s by certain Tatar national communists (Sultan Goliev in particular).[14]

At the other end of the religious framework, we witness a curious and little known, but nevertheless successful effort of the non-official, popular Islam (especially of the Soufi brotherhoods) to penetrate the Soviet system. Some excellent articles published in Soviet ethnographical journals (<u>Sovetskaia etnografia</u>, <u>Trudi instituta etnografii</u>) allow us to gain information on this multiform phenomenon. Generally it consists in superimposing an Islamic organization—often secret, based on traditional initiation—on the existing Soviet structures: collective farms, professional trade unions, etc.

## MODERNIZATION AND RELIGIOUS CUSTOMS

Muslim religious customs, rites, and ceremonies are simple and few. Under the Soviet regime they have been neither modified nor simplified, though some fell into disuse through neglect. There has been no attempt, for instance, to replace the sacred language, Arabic, by the local one (Turkic or Iranian) as was done in Kemalist Turkey. Islam appears in this respect as conservative as the Orthodox Church. The rites proper concerning the community of the believers, the Friday prayer, and the ceremonies

259

of the great feasts (<u>Aid al-Fitr</u>, <u>Aid al-Kebir</u>, <u>Ashra</u>) are exactly what they were before the revolution except that that they are less strictly observed. There is just one novelty in this domain and it is important: the assimilation of purely religious collective rites to "national" festivities. Ashirov gives many examples of important Muslim feasts observed even by unbelievers.[15]

Private religious rites and customs pertaining mainly to the life of Muslim families (circumcision, religious marriage, and burial) have also been preserved in their traditional form with no modifications. All the Soviet specialists of Islam admit that many more Muslims observe their religious customs than Christians. This is so not because Muslims are more religious than Christians, but because in the case of Muslims those customs are intimately intermingled with their national mode of life, integrated into its very essence. As the saying goes, "a non-circumcized cannot be an Uzbek" and consequently this essential rite is observed by practically everyone, even by the hard core, sincere communists. In 1970, over 73 percent of the young Kolkhozians of Daghestan declared that they approved of circumcision for hygienic as well as <u>national</u> reasons.[16] The same is true of other religious rites including marriage (<u>nikah</u>) and burial, observed massively even by atheists.[17]

Soviet specialists confess the failure of the official propaganda to draw up a barrier between religion and nationality. Religious authorities for their part seem to encourage this confusion between the two notions and, as a result, Soviet endeavors to replace in Muslim areas religious rites and customs by communist equivalents (such as the "komsomol marriage" or the "communist burial") meet certainly with less success than in "Christian" areas. As Nugman Ashirov writes,

> Muslim leaders accept the new European rites, with one provision: that they should be accompanied by traditional, "national" rites, inherited from our ancestors." . . . .So, the mosque makes a pretence of recognizing new Soviet rites and appears therefore as a defender of progressive novelties. . . .but at the same time it deprives them of their value of underlining the basic opposition between them and the national spirit of the Uzbeks, Tadzhiks, and Turkmens. These rites are denounced as "European," meaning that even if it is impossible to wholly reject them, they still cannot replace the true "national customs."[18]

## MODERNIZATION, RELIGION, AND URBAN LIFE

Islam has always been an urban religion, the religion of city dwellers, merchants, craftsmen, bureaucrats, and warriors rather than the religion of peasants, even less of the nomads, both groups having been traditionally considered as "bad Muslims." Before the revolution Russian Islam presented this same traditional profile with the only exception being the Tatar country of the middle Volga, where the Muslim population had been expelled from the cities as early as the sixteenth century. Muslim clerics were then obliged to move into the countryside and a new "rural" Islam was born.

Under the new regime, Islam still remains basically an urban religion with the majority of "working" mosques situated in medium size or small towns. In industrial centers the religious sense of the workers has certainly been weakened. Recent Soviet inquests show that in Turkmenistan 31.2 percent of peasants are "under the influence of religion" as against only 11.3 percent of the city dwellers.[19] In Uzbekistan the ratio is similar: 29.4 Percent peasants against 11.7 percent workers.[20] There are however many exceptions to this rule. Thus, the Azeris, who had the highest proportion of city dwellers (41.2 percent in 1970) are also the most religious of all Soviet Muslims.[21]

In rural areas, Islam is undergoing a curious evolution. Deprived of "official" religion by the paucity of <u>mullahs</u> and the absence of mosques, peasants' beliefs are tending to veer towards the archaic forms of primitive cults connected with <u>Shamanism</u>. The Soviet press provides innumerable examples of this retreat from formal pure religion towards fetishism. Thus, in the absence of mosques and of facilities to perform the pilgrimage to Mecca, the people find an outlet for their piety in frequenting the large number of local "holy places": the tombs (<u>mazar</u>) sometimes of real, but more often of mythical people. In some cases these holy places are of pre-Islamic origin, generally Avestic, Mazdaean, or even Nestorian Christian; often they are associated with the worship of totemistic ancestors. According to the Soviet press, the cult of local holy places escaping the control of the Spiritual Directorates, far from diminishing, has enjoyed an unexpected popularity during the past twenty years.

In the same way, the shortage of "official" <u>mullahs</u> under the jurisdiction of the Spiritual Directorates is largely compensated in the rural areas by the proliferation of "unofficial" <u>mullahs</u> often elected by the people. These are itinerants who know a little

Arabic and are thus able to perform the essential rites, but who elude all control and authority and are often outside the pale of orthodox Islam. Some of these itinerant <u>mullahs</u> are members of Soufi fraternities while others actually resemble the shamans, combining the functions of sorcerer, preacher, and healer, the direct descendants of the priests of the ancient, pre-Islamic animist religion.

## ISLAM AND EDUCATION

Education in all Soviet schools follows the same pattern. The curricula are the same in the RSFSR and in Muslim republics. All Soviet children, notwithstanding their national background, are supposed to acquire the same stereotyped scientific, atheistic outlook. Such at least is the theory. The reality seems somewhat different. In particular, since the end of World War II, the antireligious education in schools of the Muslim republics is regularly losing its rigor, not because the citizens of these republics are more religious or tolerant but once more because of the growing confusion between religious and national traditions.

For their part, since World War II, Muslim religious authorities have not attempted to oppose systematically the Soviet system of education. They even go so far as to accept Muslim children becoming pioneers, komsomols and communists. They believe that in the final run Islam will prove itself stronger than communism. Nugman Ashirov states that they agree. . . .

> that children should become pioneers, komsomol and communists,. . . .that they should take an active part in the social life of the

Soviet school. . . . Nothing can harm religion. . . .[because] those who learn to know themselves will inevitably, sooner or later, return to Islam.[22]

However, inspite of a slightly more neutral attitude toward Islam, the educational system in the Muslim republics remains fundamentally antireligious. The brilliant, incomparable network of pre-revolutionary jadid schools was utterly destroyed in the 1930s and never restored.

Religious education is strictly forbidden in the state schools. Purely religious schools for the training of religious functionaries are legally permitted under the control of the Spiritual Directorates. Since 1945, only two establishments of this kind have existed for the whole of the USSR: the Mir-i-Arab medresseh of Tashkent. These schools, at which the course lasts for five years, contain only about one hundred students, a few of whom are sent to the University of Al-Azhar in Cairo. By all accounts, the standard of instruction is low; the medresseh does not train either jurists versed in Muslim law (kadis and muftis) or doctors of law (Ulema), but merely readers of the Koran, preachers (khatibs), and muezzins whose duty is to summon the faithful to prayer. Both medressehs are traditional, conservative institutions, closer to pre-revolutionary kadimist than to the modern jadid schools.

The number of religious educational establishments is totally inadequate and the result is a shortage of clerics with knowledge of Arabic, the liturgical language, which is indispensable in Muslim worship. As a consequence, there exists in the Muslim territories of the USSR an important network of "non-official," illegal, underground mektebs

264

(elementary schools) where both children and adults
are taught Arabic and rudiments of religion by ultraconservative members of Soufi tariqas.

## ISLAM AND HISTORICAL TRADITION

Before the revolution, for millions of Russian
Muslims, Islam was the very essence of their ethnic
identification. Nobody was conscious of belonging
to a specific "Tatar," "Uzbek," or "Azeri" nationality. The very concept of a "nation" did not exist.
It certainly cannot be said, as imagined by some
jadid leaders, that Russian Islam was a tightly unified group; it was heterogenous linguistically, socially, and economically, but it had a strong religious-cultural unity and all Muslims had the sense of
belonging to a group with the same historical traditions. They shared the same literature, the same
art, and the same ideologies. Pre-revolutionary intellectuals, whether of the left or the right wing,
thought of themselves as "Muslims" or as "Turks" and
behaved as such. The term "Turk" was limited to the
designation of Muslim Turks only. Christian or animist Turks (Chuvash, Altayans, Yakuts) were excluded
from the Umma, the "Community of the Believers."
Since the revolution, Soviet policy aimed to
destroy this religious-cultural unity and to build
on its ruins modern nations, with their particular
literary languages, their specific national culture,
their peculiar national consciousness, and their own
limited national traditions distinct from the common
Islamic Arabo-Irano-Turkic background. It was and
still is a systematic and sophisticated endeavor,
though doomed to failure. It has pursued three main
aims: (1) To rediscover the pre-Islamic basis--the

265

ancient Buddhist, Manichean, Christian, and in some
cases Jewish(!) layers--of the local culture. This
attempt is in vain because Islam has overwhelmed all
traces of older cultures. Nothing is left except
archeological ruins and nobody, except archeologists,
is interested in their restoration. (2) To discover
and exalt antireligious trends and heretical movements in the Islamic past. This endeavor will also
meet with no success because even the most daring,
radical heresies had a solid religious basis. Their
ideology was typically reformist but certainly not
materialistic. Islam knew no "free thinker." True,
anti-clericalism had always existed in the Islamic
tradition, but it never implied atheism. (3) To discover in the past various political ideologies parallel to Islam or even opposed to it, for instance, the
Mongol imperial tradition. The success of such an
enterprise would be fraught with danger since it
would create a new basis for local nationalism. This
would be particularly true of the nationalisms of the
former Nomads, Kazakhs, Turkmens, etc. which were
based on the Mongol imperial tradition.

Thus, a double and contradictory evolution is
taking place in the Soviet Union. On the one side,
the local Tatar, Uzbek, Azeri national consciousness, artificial in the past, is tending to materi-
alize into something real. The particular economic
interests of the various Muslim republics, the increase in national trained personnel, the differentiation of languages, once closely allied to each
other, and the inevitable relaxation of the feeling
of religious solidarity all contribute to the "crys-
tallization" of the existing Muslim nations.

However, on the other hand, the ideal of the

266

Muslim _Umma_, the old dream of the _jadids_ that one
day all Muslims of the USSR would unite in one nation
is not dead. Several factors explain its survival.
Linguistic kinship is still very much alive--an Uzbek has little difficulty in understanding a Kazakh,
a Turkmen, or an Azeri. There is a community of cultural traditions and, if not an active religious solidarity, at least an identity of social customs based
on religious traditions. Finally, there is among the
intelligentsia the feeling that, faced as they are
with Russian pressure, union is strength. Additionally new factors produced by the Soviet system, for
example, the uniformity introduced into education
and production techniques, serve to draw the different Muslim peoples together.

During the last years, official and unofficial
Muslim religious leaders have tended increasingly to
play an active part in the conflict between centrifugal and centripetal tendencies among the Soviet
Muslim nations. Their _constant_ action dwells mainly
on the problem of interpretation of national history.
Claiming to speak in the name of the believers they
take positions officially on religious topics only.
But as already stressed, the realm of Islam pene-
trates every aspect of human activity. Therefore the
action of Muslim religious leaders constitutes a real
counter propaganda to the efforts of the official
_agitprop_. It tends to represent Islam not only as
the best, the most progressive, the most social and
democratic religion in world history, but also as a
"national religion" _par excellence_. "The originality of the national culture of peoples of the East can
be safeguarded only if its religious, Islamic basis
is preserved."[23] As M. G. Kurbanov, the _Mufti_ of the

north Caucasus, declared,

> The religion of the Prophet Mohammed is an
> enchanted house. Nobody can destroy it, but
> each nation can color its walls according
> to its own taste and customs. It can bring
> its own furniture and arrange it at its con-
> venience. Therefore, Islam born among Arabs
> is not a purely Arabic religion. In Turkey,
> Islam is Turkish, in Afghanistan, Afghan, in
> Iran, Persian, in the Soviet Union, it is
> Uzbek, Turkmen, Azeri, etc. . . .[24]

At the same time, by exalting the role of the
Islamic religion past and present, by promoting the
"rapprochement" between nations,[25] by emphasizing
the common, cultural, historical traditions of all
Islamic nations, Muslim leaders help to restore pan-
Islamic and pan-Turkic trends in Soviet Islam, or to
reinforce them.

The result of this conflict between centrifugal
and centripetal tendencies, between the narrow nationalism and broader panislamism is important. In
view of the fact that by the end of the century, Muslims will represent in USSR a community of some 120
million people, it is vital for the Soviet Union to
know whether these millions will constitute one cultural unit, a unique group, strong enough to challenge Russian supremacy, or be fractioned into something like 30 smaller nationalities, opposed to each
other on certain points and all in all too weak to
represent a real danger to the predominating position of the Big Brother.


RELIGIOUS LEADERSHIP

In Central Asia and in Transcaucasia, the old
pre-revolutionary leadership survived until after
World War II. As a rule, in these areas religious

268

leadership was hereditary.  It is dying out now.
The last, and probably the most typical, of these
professional, hereditary _mullahs_ was the _Mufti_ of
Tashkent, Ziauddin Baba-Khanov.  His father, whom he
succeeded in the 1950s, had been _Mufti_ of Central
Asia since the 1920s.  These clerics were authentic,
traditional _Ulemas_, with an excellent knowledge of
theology and Arabic.  Some of them were trained at
Al-Azhar.  In the Tatar country, the old pre-revolutionary _jadid_ religious leadership disappeared for
the most part during the big purges of the late 1930s.

Generally a new and very different leadership
has been taking the place of the former hereditary
_Ulemas_ since the 1960s.  As a rule, the new clerics
belong to the peasant class, but they often join the
religious establishment after graduating from Soviet
high schools, or even universities.  Some of them are
Soviet intellectuals, former engineers, doctors, etc.

Thus, in the last ten years, Soviet Islam has
passed through a new and original revolution comparable to that in the Middle East.  It is a typically modernistic phenomenon, but its importance should
not be overestimated, because the influence of these
"modernist" clerics on the masses remains negligeable.

RELIGION AND INTERNATIONAL TIES

In spite of half a century of isolation behind
the iron curtain, Soviet Muslims are deeply conscious
of belonging to the _Dar ul-Islam_, the Muslim world.
This sense of religious solidarity is reinforced by
the Soviet Muslims' close linguistic, cultural, and
ethnic kinship with Muslim nations along the Soviet
border:  Turkey or Iran.  Official propaganda has not

succeeded in persuading Soviet Muslims that the Russian "Big Brother" is closer to them than foreign coreligionists, Turks, Persians, or Afghans.

In spite, or rather because, of this sense of solidarity, Soviet authorities have always been very cautious as regards contacts between their Muslims and the world of Islam abroad.  Only the most trusted summits of the religious hierarchy, the four _Muftis_ (especially Ziauddin Baba-Khanov, the _Mufti_ of Tashkent) and their staff are employed by the Soviet Government to promote friendship between the Muslim world and the USSR.  They usually take part in the annual pilgrimage (_hadj_) to the holy cities of Arabia, visit foreign countries, and participate in various international, cultural events and also in domestic and foreign conferences organized with the object of promoting Soviet policy in the Muslim world.  Recently three such conferences have been organized by the religious authorities themselves. The first one took place in October 1970, in Tashkent, presided over by Ziauddin Baba-Khanov.  Twenty-four countries of Asia, Africa, and Europe were represented there.  The theme was "The unity of the Muslim world in the fight for peace and the struggle against imperialist aggression.." In 1973, the same Ziauddin Baba-Khanov convened a second conference with practically the same theme:  "The Zionist and American aggression in the Middle East."  In 1974, a third Muslim conference took place in Samarkand, this time on a more religious subject:  the 1,200th anniversary of the Muslim theologian Al-Bokhari.[26]

Both the Soviet and the religious authorities take care not to infringe upon the rights of Muslim leaders.  They seldom mention politics.  Their dec-

clarations are limited to vague platitudes such as
the defense of peace, democracy and liberty, the denunciation of Zionism and U.S. imperialism.  In practice, their role is limited to two issues:  They must
testify by their presence, by the beauty of their
Khalats and of their well-trimmed beards, as well as
by their excellent knowledge of Arabic that Islam is
well alive and happy.  Secondly, they must supply a
counterbalance to the anti-Sovietism still strong in
some Muslim countries, especially in Morocco, Pakis-
tan, Indonesia, Saudi Arabia, and Iran.

As a typical example of the vapidity of thought
of the Soviet Muslim leaders, we may quote the report of M. M. Agaev, the head of the mosque of Khachmas in Azerbaijan, at the October 1970 Tashkent conference:  "We may state, without any doubt, that a
capitalist regime based on unjustice and exploita-
tion will fall and be replaced by a socialist regime
founded on justice.  The laws of God are unavoidable
and truth will triumph in the end. . . ."[27]

Considered from the point of view of Central
Asia and the Caucasus, the contacts between Soviet
Islam and the Muslim world abroad may appear un-
impressive.  But since World War II, the movement is
no longer unilateral.  The frontiers of the Soviet
Islam, hermetically closed until then, have been
opening during the last ten years.  Thousands of
foreign Muslims have visited Central Asia and the
Caucasus.  What is the impact of those visits on the
evolution of Islam in USSR?  It is too early to answer this question or even to start discussing it.
It would seem, however, that though the majority of
foreign Muslims travelling in the USSR are not really
interested in religious matters, some of the most

271

distinguished among these visitors such as the Shah
of Iran, the King of Afghanistan, Colonel Nasser, and
many foreign statesmen, military leaders, etc. displayed during their visits the behavior of true believers. Some of them attended the Friday prayer,
thus giving the lie to the thesis of antireligious
propaganda according to which Islam is a primitive
creed, just good enough for illiterate peasants, but
certainly not for modern, successful, political leaders.

## RELIGION AND GEOGRAPHICAL LOCATION

At the time of the October revolution, Islam and
Orthodox Christianity were in the middle of a new
phase of competition that had been going on for centuries. The ponderous and inefficient missionary
machine supported by the tsarist establishment was
facing the Tatar jadidism, decentralized and isolated
but highly efficient and dynamic. The rival religions clashed in three main geographical regions:
In the north Caucasus and in some areas of Transcaucasia for the allegiance of former Christians who
had practically relapsed into animism or were hesita-
ting between Orthodoxy and Islam;[28] in the middle
Volga, where the rivals competed for the local Finns,
Mordvinians, Cheremisses (Maris), Votiaks (Udmurts),
the non-Muslim Turks (Chuvash), and Tatar animists
or Muslims who had been converted to Christianity,
generally by force in the sixteenth and the eighteenth centuries; and, finally, in western Siberia
for the possession of animistic Turks (Siberian Tatars, Altayans) and of the superficially Muslim nomads (Kazakhs of Semirechie). On the eve of the

272

revolution, it was still impossible to predict who would be the winner, but Islam was slowly and steadily progressing both in the Caucasus and in the middle Volga and reinforcing its hold over the Nomads of Kazakhstan.

It is almost impossible to follow the geographical evolution of the Islam under the Soviet regime. Nonetheless we may admit that its realm is more or less the same as in 1917 with only some slight changes, of which only one is historically important: Islam has lost definitely and completely--or so it seems--the Crimean peninsula, a Muslim territory since the fourteenth century. In 1943, the entire Muslim population (more than 250,000 Tatars) was deported and even after its rehabilitation was never allowed to come back to its fatherland. The Crimea of today is a purely Russian and Ukrainian territory. In Transcaucasia, the postwar deportation of Muslims from southwestern Georgia (the so-called "Meskhetian Turks") did not have the same final consequences: the territory of Akhaltzik remains for the most part Muslim. The tragically brutal destruction of Kazakh nomads of the 1930s in the steppe territory had at least one indirect "positive" result. The sedentary new comers are more receptive to the Islamic influence than the nomads.[29] In the middle Volga, which before the revolution was the main battlefield of the Islamic-Christian conflict, the positions seem to have been more or less maintained.[30]

CONCLUSION

The picture presented by the contemporary Soviet Islam is chaotic and incoherent. Since the

273

Second World War, it is torn between two contradictory trends: a modest, cautious modernism represented mainly by the "official," religious establishment and an aggressive, militant conservatism advocated by the non-official, underground Soufi brotherhood. Who will get the upper hand?

The first trend corresponds better to the general evolution of the Muslim world, but in the USSR it is handicapped by the compromise of the official religious authorities with the atheistic regime. The second, condemned at least in appearance, by the general evolutionary trend, survives in the USSR because of the constant confusion between the national and the religious traditions which tends to sanctify even the most outdated customs of Islam and also because the strict observance of the most conservative rites and traditions helps Muslim society escape Russian assimilation which is advocated and sponsored by the Soviet Government.

However, at present, especially after the publication of the 1970 census data, no one in the Soviet Union believes any more in the possibility of russification of the Muslims and there is no longer any question of the merging of nationalities (sliia-nie). One may wonder, however, whether the conservatism having accomplished its historical mission of safeguard and protection, is not ready to yield its place to the modernism.

NOTES

1. We can judge the massive character of anti-Islamic propaganda by the following data on public lectures delivered on various scientific-atheistic themes by the "Union for the diffusion of political and scientific knowledge" in the Central Asian re-

274

publics:

| | 1955 | 1959 | Total Population |
|---|---|---|---|
| Uzbekistan | 66,800 | 146,500 | 8,119,103 |
| Kirghiziia | 17,200 | 45,100 | 2,065,837 |
| Tadzhikistan | 13,800 | 40,500 | 1,980,547 |
| Turkmenistan | 13,100 | 30,400 | 1,516,375 |

According to Kratkie statisticheskie svedeniia o deiatel'nosti v sesoniuznogo obshchestva po rasprostraneniiu politicheskikh i nauchnykh znanii (Moscow, 1960), quoted by A. Kadyrov, Prichiny sushchestvovaniia i puti preodoleniia perezhithitkov islama (Leninabad, 1966), p. 73.

2. Musul'mane sovetskogo vostoka, no. 3 (Tashkent 1969), p. 17, quoted by Nugman Ashirov, Evoliutsiia islama v SSSR (Moscow 1973), p. 110.

3. Ashirov, ibid., p. 23.

4. Together with the four sunni mazhab: Hanafi, Maleki, Shafei, and Hanbali.

5. Nugman Ashirov, Islam i natsii, (Moscow, 1975), pp. 82-83, gives many examples where the same Azeri mosque serves both rites. Such was the case of the "Azarbek" mosque in Baku and of the mosques of Zakataly, Geokchay, Kuba, Khachmas, Sheki. . . .

6. Ashirov, Evoliutsiia islama, p. 139, quotes a fetwa of the imam of one of the mosques of the city of Osh in Kirghiziia, explaining that the five daily prayers are no more compulsory, when they present an obstacle to the collective work and may be prejudicial to the economy of the republic.

7. Ashirov, Evoliutsiia islama, pp. 137, 138, quotes the message of the Spiritual Direction of Central Asia and Kazakhistan of March 8, 1958, and the sermon of the imam of the mosque "Ta'bon-bavty" of Bukhara, during Ramadan 1968, exempting the believers from fast.

8. Musul'mane sovetskogo vostoka, No. 2, p. 11.

9. Ashirov, Islam i natsii, p. 83 and Ashirov,

Evoliutsiia islama, p. 10.

10. Ashirov, Islam i natsii, p. 84. It is believed in some areas that rites to be legal have to
be performed by a mullah belonging to the same tribe
and clan as his parishioners.

11. Musul'mane Sovetskogo Vostoka, No. 2, p. 9,
publishes the text of a fetwa of the Mufti of Central Asia condemning those who offer or accept the
Kalym as "impure Muslims." Ashirov, Evolutsiia
islama, p. 101, quotes another fetwa of the same mufti published in 1948 proclaiming that women must be
unveiled.

12. Such are the Kalym (payment for a bride by
the bridegroom's family), the Kaytarma (obligation
for the bridegroom to live in the bride's family),
the exogamic and endogamic taboos, etc.

13. Ashirov, Islam i natsii, p. 69, writes that
religious family rites are observed by young couples
not because they are believers but because they do
not want to hurt their elders or because they do not
distinguish between "religious" and "national" rites.

14. Nugman Ashirov gives many examples of attempts made by religious authorities to prove that
Islam can and must become the true basis of socialism:   "Contrary to Christianism and to Judaism, Islam is subtle, flexible and corresponds better to
modern (socialist) conditions."  (Vice Mufti of
Transcaucasia, Velizada Sherif, in Evoliutsiia islama, p. 61); "There is not way to God without work"
(sermon of the Imam of Hoja Alma mosque in Samarkand, March 27, 1970 in Evoliutsiia islama, p. 63).

15. Ashirov, Islam i natsii, p. 64, in particular the description of the feast of Kurban Baïram
(Aid al-Kebir), in Orenburg, observed by the atheistic students and komsomol as a "national Tatar feast."

16. Cf. Iu. Muslimov, Spetsifika proiavleniia
i preodoleniia religioznosti sel'skoi molodezhi
(Ph.d. dissertation,Makhachkla, 1970), p. 10, quoted
by Ashirov, ibid., p. 63.

17. Ashirov, ibid., p. 63.

18. Ashirov, Evoliutsiia islama, p. 149.

19. Materialy nauchnoi konferentsii, Modernizat-
siia islama i aktual'nye voprosy teorii nauchnogo ateizma, (Moscow, 1968).

20. I. Jabbarov, Obshchestvennyi progress, byt
i religiia, (Tashkent, 1973), p. 82.

21. Cf. Itogi vsesoiuznoi perepisi naseleniia
1970 goda (Moscow, 1973), G. 4, pp. 263-272(RSS of
Azerbaijan).

22. Ashirov, Islam i natsii, p. 68.

23. Quoted in ibid., p. 37.

24. Quoted by Ocherki nauchnogo ateizma, (Makha-
chkala, 1972), p. 163.

25. For instance, Musul'mane sovetskogo vostoka,
Nos. 3-4, (1972), p. 3 wrote that "the deep understanding of the Islamic religion allowed Muslims of
our land to unite themselves in one and unique State."
Ashirov, Islam i natsii, pp. 94-95, quotes the sermon of the Imam-Khatib of the Semipalatinsk mosque:
"Islam is not only a religion, a moral law and a
way of life; it is also a community, a brotherhood
of men who succeeded to overcome national differences
. . . . Under the leadership of Muhammed we find
not only the Arabs, but peoples of other nationalities and races. In our community also we find Kazakhs, Tatars, and Chechens. Nationalism endeavors
to destroy unity, while Muslim religion is a bond of
union between men. To fight for the Muslim Community is to fight against national exclusivism."

26. The proceedings of these three conferences
have never been published but the analysis appeared
in the local press (Pravda vostoka of Tashkent);
some reports have been published in the journal of
the Tashkent Spiritual Direction, Musul'mane sovetskogo vostoka.

27. Quoted by Ashirov, Islam i natsii, p. 41.
From time to time, Muslim religious leaders are carried away by their enthusiasm for the struggle of
Muslim masses against Zionist and American imperialism and exceed their attributions proclaiming broadly that "liberty is the most precious possession"
and that the "Holy Koran teaches that we must fight
for it" (Sermon of A. Isaev, Imam-Khatib of the Lenin-

grad mosque, quoted by Ashirov, Islam i natsii, p. 41). It is obvious that such generalities are double-edged and may become dangerous. Soviet authorities take care to avoid their repetition, lest their Muslims should take them too seriously.

28. In 1860, the Russian Orthodox Church created the "Society for the re-establishment of Orthodox Christianity in the Caucasus" (Obshchestvo vosstanovleniia pravoslavnogo khristianstva na Kavkaze) and placed it in 1886 under the direct control of the Holy Synod. This society was not allowed to do missionary work among Muslims, but only among Animists or crypto-Christians. Its activity was limited to eight areas:
    1) Inkilois, Shii Georgians of Eastern Kakhetia
    2) Animist Georgian tribes of Central Caucasus-Tushins, Pshavs, Khevsours
    3) Half Christian Kistin tribes (related to the Chechens)
    4) Ossetians, superficially Christian, submitted to strong Muslim pressure
    5) Svanetians of Northern Imeretia, superficially Christians
    6) Ajars, Sunni Georgians of Southwestern Georgia
    7) Abkhazians, half-Muslims and half Christians
    8) Samurzakan tribes, animist and superficially Christians
Cf. On this subject A. Bennigsen and Chantal Lemercier-Quelquejay, "Musulmans et missions orthodoxes en Russie orientale avant 1917. Essai de bibliographie critique," Cahiers du Monde russe et soviétique, 13 (janv.-mars 1972):57-113.

29) Ia. Baysenbaev, Chairman of the Muslim Spiritual Direction of Central Asia, declared at the Muslim Conference in Samarkand (1974): "We Muslim Kazakhs, formerly underdeveloped nomads, are today a modern nation, in possession of all the attributes of modern progress." Quoted in Ashirov, Islam i natsii, p. 46.

30. It is practically impossible to follow the progress of Islam among the Eastern Finns since Soviet sources practically never mention the role of the religious factor among national minorities. Moreover, as before the Revolution, the conversion of Eastern Finns to Islam is followed ipso facto by the adoption of Tatar as the first mother tongue and,

in the second stage, by a complete assimilation by the Tatars.

Chapter 8
## JUDAISM AND MODERNIZATION IN THE SOVIET UNION

Zvi Gitelman

The relationship between religion and modernization has been examined largely in the context of
Third World countries, where both religion and modernization processes are so salient to the Western
observer, or in historical analyses of the emergence
of the modern Western world. The Soviet Union, at
once an important example of modernization and of a
system which explicitly addressed the question of
religion, has not been sufficiently analyzed, either
as a case study of modernization or as a study in
the relationship of religion and modernization. One
reason for this may be the low salience of religion
as a contemporary political or even social problem
for the Soviets. Since Western analysts have always
been attracted to the study of Soviet problems, they
tend to focus on such issues as economic development,
intellectual dissent, and nationality discontents,
while treating religion, if at all, largely as a
problem for the regime. However, it would seem that
the Soviet case would hold considerable interest for
those concerned with the general issue of modernization, and the specific question of the relationship
of religion and modernization. After all, the USSR
represents a historical case wherein millions of

280

devout believers of a wide variety of faiths were intensively socialized to abandon religious practice and the religious Weltanschauung, and, at the same time, were involved in one of the most ambitious modernization undertakings in history. At least one major analytic question immediately presents itself: to what extent is the observed decline in the social power of religion in the USSR the result of coercion and indoctrination, and to what extend is it the direct and indirect consequence of modernization. This is an important case for those who would answer the question of the relative efficacy of official anti-religious efforts, on the one hand, and the seemingly unavoidable consequences of Western-type modernization, on the other. While the political limitations imposed on those who would try to answer this question in the Soviet context are formidable, it may be possible to approximate the beginnings of an answer by tracing the history of the religion-modernization relationship for various religions in the USSR, comparing it to cases wherein either the element of modernization or the element of deliberate attacks on religion is absent, and making some initial attempts to estimate the relative effectiveness of each factor. Another comparative consideration is relevant: what has been the history of the confrontation between a particular religion and modernization in non-Soviet contexts, and to what extent can we generalize about the relationship of a particular religion and modernization, irrespective of national context? Finally, to what extent is the specific nature of a religion relevant to its confrontation with modernization, and to what extent can religion be treated as a more or less uniform phenomenon, so that the relationship between religion and modernization will depend not on the nature of the particular religion, but on the nature of the particular variant of modernization--or on neither? I suspect that, in fact, the relationship between modernization and religion cannot be treated meaningfully without specifying both the characteristics of a specific religion as well as the features of a specific modernizing program and society. Therefore, this essay deals with a specific religion, Judaism, in a specific modernizing environment, the Soviet Union, while paying some attention to comparable phenomena--other religions in the USSR, and Judaism in other national settings. It also makes a very tentative attempt to assess the relative impact on Judaism of antireligious policies and of general modernizing processes, and to point to some post-modernizing phenomena affecting Judaism in the USSR.

## RELIGION AND MODERNIZATION

While "modernization" is a term used widely--and loosely--in Western social science and in more popular literature, great controversy rages as to its precise meaning. "Modernization" and "development," sometimes used synonymously, sometimes not, have become objects of scholarly dispute and even ideological contention. Nevertheless, there seems to be a general consensus, often only implicit, that religion and modernization, however defined, are not easily reconcilable, if not wholly incompatible. If modernity is counterposed to "tradition," as it often is, then religion is often assigned to the category of "tradition," and is hence assumed to be in some conflict with modernity. More sophisticated

282

views see elements of tradition being incorporated into what is labelled as "modern," and at least admit of the possibility that religion can "survive" in a modern context, if only through its own adaptability. This, too, implies a contradiction between religion and modernization, one which can be resolved through some compromise of either, or of both.

The tension perceived between religion and modernization is not, however, based on a superficial assignment of religion to the category of tradition, but arises from some serious questions. As Kalman Silvert puts it,

> Are religious beliefs and religious institutions inherently antithetical to social change over any appreciable period of time? . . . . Is a belief system based on an extended view of a complex of absolutes of a supra-worldly nature, necessarily unsusceptible to validation and just as necessarily commanding men to action, compatible with a human dedication to a constant extension of man's control over his environment, himself, and his future? Such a continuing expansion of effective interaction with environment demands an ethos of changefulness and a commitment to controlled uncertainty.[1]

Silvert points to "A very broad feeling in Western, industrialized society that religious institutions and the practices of modern life do not easily and automatically mesh."[2] He concludes that the tension between religious and political institutions in modernizing societies "is rooted in the fact that they are natural institutional competitors for the role of synthesizer amidst the growth of differentiation. . . . To the extent to which religious institutions insist on their right and duty to proclaim a truth basis for general social relations, they are in the

283

same terrain as the nation-state with its claims to overriding temporal authority."[3] We shall argue later that organized religion in the USSR, including Judaism, has survived largely by renouncing its claim to "proclaim a truth basis for general social relation," and by limiting its domain in such a way that conflicts between "church" and "state" should not arise, or should be minimized. Silvert argues that despite the claim of religion to encompass all of life, "modern societies, in their functional specificity and structural differentiation, should be able to support a sector of absolutism within the generalized social ambience of relativism."[4] But here it is necessary to differentiate among modern societies: Silvert postulates "structural differentiation" or, certainly, an "ambience of relativism." The problem in the Soviet Union is not the confrontation between modern relativism and traditional, religious dogmatism. It is, in fact, the problem of conflicting dogmas in a system which has little tolerance for relativism. When religion confronts the Soviet state there is a conflict not quite between the secular and the religious, but between a secular ideology which has the behavioral characteristics (and even some of its structural ones) of a religion, and a "traditional" religion. The parellelism between the Soviet ideological system and traditional, institutionalized religions has long been remarked upon and need not be elaborated here, except to reemphasize that even the tactics of the Soviet regime in combatting religion are very similar to the tactics some religions have used to stamp out heresy: agitation, propaganda, an inquisition, the proclamation of holy wars (campaigns), excommunica-

tion, and so forth.  Therefore, one of the specially
Soviet dimensions of the relationship between modernization and religion is this absolute and direct
confrontation, rather than indirect competition, between religion and the state.  Whereas in other societies religion is indirectly challenged by claims
which may be construed as competing, in the Soviet
case there is no room for ambiguity:  the challenge
to religion is direct; it is specifically portrayed
as the enemy of progress and modernity; and even coexistence, let alone cooperation, is very difficult
to achieve.

## JUDAISM AND MODERNIZATION

Before the emancipations of the eighteenth century, neither Jews nor others differentiated between
Judaism as a religion and Jews as an ethnic group.
The Jewish tradition itself seems to assume that Jewish religion and ethnicity are coterminous, and as
recently as the 1960s in Israel, the question has
been taken up by political and social leaders, as
well as by the Israeli Supreme Court, with the general consensus being that it is almost impossible to
divorce the religious and ethnic components of Jewishness.[5]  However, emancipation from the ghetto
meant that for the first time Jews could choose to be
Jewish, and they could enter non-Jewish society in
several ways.  As Jacob Neusner puts it,

> In the past century and a half the Jews
> have endured a lingering crisis of iden-
> tity, for they have not agreed since the
> 18th century upon the most basic proposi-
> tions of self-definition.  Some Jews have
> found it possible to exhaust the meaning
> of "Jewishness" in religion, narrowly con-

strued as the Protestant West defined it;
some in nationalism. . . .some in socialism. . . .and some in scholarship. These
are not the only options. . . . And, of
course, one cannot ignore the fact that for
many Jews, modernization signified the end
of "Jewishness" altogether.[6]

Even those who continued to define their Jewishness
largely in the religious mode found it possible to
accommodate the modernizing world around them.  In
Western Europe, and later the United States, the Reform movement sought to provide an alternative to
"modernization" through conversion and/or assimilation, the path taken by many Jews in Germany, France,
and other Western countries.  Reform claimed to preserve what it discerned as the prophetic and ethical
essence of Judaism, while adapting the forms of the
faith to modern conditions and requirements.  The ex-
ternalities would be changed to conform with the de-
mands--and ideals--of the modern period, while the
core of the religion would be preserved.  Later on,
the Conservative or Historical movement tried to do
the same thing, but argued that Rabbinic Judaism contained within itself the capacity for self-renewal
and adjustment to changing conditions, so that necessary changes could be made without abandoning as much
of the tradition as Reform had done.  Even Orthodoxy
showed tendencies to accommodation with modernization, and figures such as the German Rabbi Samson
Raphael Hirsch offered their own solutions to the
problem of reconciling tradition and European modernity on both a doctrinal-theoretical as well as
practical-communal level.

More broadly, we can discern three modal responses to the challenges of modernization:  1)  accommodation;  2)  ghettoization;  3)  compartmentaliza-

tion. Accommodation has meant either the kinds of
doctrinal and behavioral adjustments that Reform,
Conservatism, and much of Orthodoxy have made, or attempts to divorce Judaism from religion, that is,
preserving a secular Jewish identity while rejecting
its theological components. Jewish secularists, especially in the nineteenth and twentieth centuries
in Eastern Europe, sought to redefine Judaism in ethnic terms only, and to see Jews as a nation, as the
Zionists did, or at least as a separate ethnic group
with special characteristics, needs, and aspirations,
as many Jewish socialists did. While some defined
themselves as Jews by religion only, others defined
themselves as Jews by ethnicity and culture only.
The "german citizens of the Mosaic faith" were com-
plemented by Jewish atheists and agnostics.

Those who saw modernization only as a threat,
and not as an opportunity, tried to resist even min-
imal accommodation. Not only were doctrinal adjustments rejected, but even manifest behavior of no essential religious significance was strictly regulated
in order to avoid giving the slightest external indication of compromise with a changing world. Thus,
for example, certain groups, such as some Hassidim
and elements of Hungarian Orthodoxy, insisted on
maintaining traditional garb--ironically, originally
copied from non-Jews--as a symbolic rejection of the
modernizing world. General education was forbidden
or discouraged, and learning the languages of the
surrounding people was also discouraged, except insofar as it was absolutely necessary for daily commercial and official contacts. Needless to say, social
contacts with those outside the community--including
Jewish reformers, secularists, or "Enlighteners"--

were very much frowned upon.  This kind of response
to the modernizing world could be observed mostly in
Eastern Europe, and has many parallels in the more
recently modernized societies of Asia and Africa.
It could be observed among Russian Jews, but since
the challenges of reform from within, and of modernization in the surrounding society were weaker than
in parts of Poland or Hungary, this posture was often not very explicitly articulated nor was it as
rigidly adhered to.

Finally, there is the response of compartmentalization, one frequently encountered in contemporary
modernizing contexts, including the Soviet Union.
Here the claims of religion to regulate and explain
all areas of life are explicitly or implicitly denied, and there is a division of areas into those in
which religious ideas and values dominate, and those
in which modernizing values, expressed in whatever
ideological variation, are said to guide thought and
behavior.  This is, of course, a form of accommodation, but it differs from accommodation in that it
does not involve explicit doctrinal change, nor does
it necessarily mean a confrontation between religious
and modernizing values and a resolution of that conflict.  Where conflicts arise they may be resolved,
at least for the individual, by choosing to follow
the religious line or the secular line in the particular instance of conflict or by simply ignoring
them.  This response is particularly relevant to
Judaism and Islam, whose scope and demands on the
individual and the community seem to be greater than
those of Christianity, especially Protestantism
(with the exception of some of the more evangelical
sects).  In a sense, some forms of Christianity lend

themselves more easily to compartmentalization since
they have less to say about wide areas of life than
do more prescriptive and comprehensive religions,
such as Islam and Judaism, which seem more concerned
with law and practice than with belief and theology.
That is, while Judaism and Islam dictate daily human
behavior in great detail, other religions allow the
individual greater scope in his dealings with the
world around him, and so the problem of reconciling
the demands and accepted behaviors of a modernizing
society with religion is not as severe.

JUDAISM AND SOVIET MODERNIZATION

Without entering the controversy on a precise
meaning of modernization, it is sufficient for our
purposes to point to three concomitants, or perhaps
foundations, of modernization, as the ones most directly relevant to the fate of the Jewish religion
in the USSR. No doubt, more abstract considerations,
such as the philosophical premises and values of Soviet ideology, ultimately influence the situation of
religion in the USSR, but it is worth focusing on the
more concrete manifestations of Soviet modernization
and the direct and indirect impact they have had on
Judaism. These would include industrialization, urbanization, and education. I would suggest that
these secular trends--the double-entendre is deliber-
ate--have had a profound influence on Judaism, and
not only in the Soviet Union, and have done as least
as much to determine the status and fate of Judaism
as have deliberate Soviet campaigns and restrictions
against it. At present Jews are both the most urbanized as well as the most highly educated of all So-

viet nationalities, and since urbanization and education are negatively correlated in the USSR with adherence to religious institutions and practice of the faith, these demographic characteristics of the Jews are relevant to the religious condition of Jewry. Ninety-eight percent of the Jewish population is urban; in the RSFSR, 39.9 percent of the Jews had some form of higher education (1970), while the national average was only 5.5 percent. Thus, to be Jewish in the Soviet Union means almost always to be urban and, disproportionately, to be educated. To be urban and educated usually means to be a non-believer, especially in the USSR.

The relationship of modernization to Judaism is more complex than correlations between education, urbanity, and lack of religiosity. That relationship has a history which antedates the Bolshevik revolution and then has some specific features in the two crucial decades, the 1920s and the 1930s, in which the present situation was largely determined. In the first quarter of the nineteenth century, the near monolithism of the religious Jewish community began to show some cracks and fissures. The Cantonist episode of 1827-1856, wherein young Jewish boys were drafted into the army for 25 years during which time attempts were made to convert them to Christianity, drove a wedge between the elite of the Jewish community, consisting of the learned and the wealthy, and the poor, since the children of the latter were disproportionately selected by the community elders for this forced draft. This cleavage was later widened by the tensions between the Jewish bourgeoisie, the financial mainstay of the organized religious community, and the working class, some-

times forced to violate religious law by economic
necessity, as for example, by working on Saturday.
The rise of a socialist movement among the Jews in
the 1880s and 1890s exacerbated the tensions between
the religious establishment and the working class,
since the established community feared that revolutionary activity would aggravate tsarist persecution
and cause suffering to the entire Jewish community.
Though the religious community was by no means an
enthusiastic supporter of the regime, it preferred
the traditional tactic of shtadlones, or intercession, to the more radical means of the socialists,
in order to alleviate Jewish suffering.  Most of the
socialist Jewish parties, therefore, were at least
anti-clerical, and some were also explicitly antireligious, though since a substantial proportion of
the rank and file maintained the traditions, care
was taken not to offend their sensibilities.  Thus,
by the time of the revolution, there was a political
tradition in the Jewish community which was secular,
and even actively hostile to religion.  Moreover,
the Haskalah, or Enlightenment, movement of the mid-
century had created an intellectual tradition which
was largely secular, and some of the best known
writings of the movement were satirical or direct
attacks on Judaism and its practitioners.

This dual secularist tradition was built upon
by the Bolsheviks, and, specifically, the Jewish
Sections of the Communist Party.  Led largely by
former activists of the Jewish socialist parties,
the Sections launched an intensive anitreligious
campaign in 1921-22, not only in order to eradicate
religion from "the Jewish street," but in order to
destroy the Jewish religious and communal organiza-

tions which prevented them from achieving a monopoly
of power on that street. This campaign, conducted
exclusively by Jews, used three methods: agitation
and propaganda; feigned accession to the "demands of
the toiling masses"; and coercion backed by armed
forces. The campaign employed somewhat quixotic
methods at times: there were public debates, reminiscent of medieval disputations, and elaborate show
trials of religious functionaries, and even of customs and institutions, such as the kheder (religious
elementary school), various religious holidays, circumcision, etc.[7] The antireligious campaign was in
the forefront of Evsektsiia (Jewish Section) activity until 1925, but it seemed to have little immediate effect in changing people's convictions, though
it did result in the closing of many religious
schools and places of worship. In contrast to what
happened among the Russian Orthodox clergy, of about
1,000 rabbis only six can be identified as having
displayed pro-Communist sympathies, and only two attacked the Jewish religion.[8] Jewish agricultural
colonies often had their day of rest on Saturday,
and they were reluctant to engage in pig breeding.
There were numerous underground religious schools in
operation, circumcision was widely practiced, even
by members of the party, and in many towns the religious community continued to function pretty much
in the open until the early 1930s. As late as 1926
a national conference of Soviet rabbis was held, and
one publisher of religious books managed to print
100,000 books in 1927-29. In 1925 in Gomel, of 560
Jewish artisans interviewed, 431 had their day off
on Saturday, and 159 described themselves as religious, with another 104 calling themselves "semi-

religious."[9]

While the antireligious campaign did not seem
to have an immediate effect on the convictions of
religious Jews, it was to have two important consequences in the long run. First, it resulted in the
closing down of many religious institutions and it
drove religious education underground, where it
could hardly flourish. It thereby removed much of
the tangible presence of Judaism from the Soviet
scene, and it proved nearly impossible to restore
these physical manifestations of spirituality. Secondly, the antireligious campaign insured that
Judaism in the USSR would remain "frozen" at its
1917 stage. That is, because of the restrictions on
religious education, and the isolation of Soviet religious leadership from the rest of world Jewry,
Judaism was deprived of the capacity for intellectual self-renewal; because it was forced into semi-
legality, Judaism could not engage in a dialogue
with modernizing Soviet society. It became very
difficult to adapt to the new conditions, for adaptation meant compromise with an explicit and militant enemy, rather than with a sympathetic competitor, as in the West. It was also well nigh impossible to defend Judaism against the attacks on it, given the control of the media by the authorities.
Judaism was therefore suspended, as it were, in its
1917 form, and religious leaders could not easily
come to grips with the new realities, and they certainly could not interpret those realities to their
potential congregants. The kinds of adaptive responses that had been made to the modernizing challenges of the Haskalah, or later, of Zionism--the
introduction of some secular studies to the reli-

gious school curricula, the development of a religious Zionist movement, the emergence of the Mussar movement in part as a response to the Haskalah charges of moral corruption in the religious community--could not be developed under Soviet conditions. Therefore, Judaism could be convincingly portrayed as time and culture-bound, truly a "survival of capitalism" and shtetl culture, irrelevant to the brave new world of Soviet socialism. The impossibility of adaptation has meant that Judaism in the USSR today is much as it was in 1917--except shorn of its institutions, functionaries, and capacity for theological and social self-renewal. No reformist-adaptive movement of any kind has developed, in contrast to the West, and adaptation has come only in the form of necessary tactical compromises with the pressures exerted by the regime.

Explicit and direct efforts by the regime have frozen and retarded Judaism institutionally and intellectually. But perhaps an even greater influence on Judaism has been the larger process of modernization, with its social and economic consequences. These have indirectly, but effectively, influenced Judaism, and perhaps to a greater degree than official policies.

For the Jews of the Soviet Union, modernization meant migration out of the former Pale of Settlement and to the larger cities of Belorussia and the Ukraine, and, for the first time, to the larger cities of the Russian Republic. This migration influenced the size, cultural patterns, economic status, and political position of Soviet Jewry to such an extent that it would be no exaggeration to say that it represented a modernizing revolution within the Jewish

community, and not always along the lines envisioned
by those in the Jewish Sections who had proposed
various schemes for Jewish modernization. The migration of the late 1920s and 1930s resulted in the
decline, if not disappearance, of the shtetl and its
culture, in rapid urbanization and geographical dis-
persion, in linguistic assimilation and increased
intermarriage, and in a weakening of Jewish consciousness. Quite clearly, it also resulted in a
decline in Jewish religious practice and belief.

Between 1926 and 1939 the Jewish population of
the Russian, Kazakh, and Kirghiz republics, all of
which had been beyond the Pale, grew by over 60 percent, while that of Belorussia fell by nearly 8 percent and that of the Ukraine by 2.6 percent. Though
in 1939 half of Soviet Jewry was still in the Ukraine,
almost 40 percent of the Jews were outside the areas
of the old Pale, with 31.4 percent in the RSFSR. In
the Russian Republic there were far fewer Jewish
schools than in Belorussian and the Ukraine, and
there are striking data from the 1920s showing that
marriage between Jews and non-Jews was much more frequent in the Russian Republic than in Belorussia and
the Ukraine, where shtetl culture and religious traditions survived to some considerable extent, at least
until the mid-1930s.

Moving to the Russian Republic, or even to the
big cities of the Ukraine and Belorussia, was in
many ways parallel to the earlier experience of mi-
grating from Russia to the new world. Jews who moved
out of the old Pale areas tended to change their
language from Yiddish to Russian, to broaden their
social contacts to include non-Jews, to change their
jobs from the kind of petty trade, and small scale

295

artisanry typical of the shtetl to industrial and technical positions, and to see themselves as liberated from the confining and stultifying small town existence, with its conformity and cultural backwardness, that they thought characterized the shtetl. Just as many immigrants to America threw over the culture of the "Old Country," including religion, in their eagerness to become "modern" and "American," so too did a great many Soviet Jews see their migration out of the shtetl as an occasion to reject its culture, to throw over their religion, and to become "modern" and "Soviet" or even "Russian." The religiosity of many was probably situationally and environmentally based, rather than stemming from personal commitment and conviction, and once the environment was changed, religious affiliation could be dispensed with. Whereas the social pressures of the shtetl worked to promote at least formal religious affiliation, the atmosphere of the cities tended to discourage it. As Harvey Cox has written, "Urbanization means a structure of common life in which diversity and the disintegration of tradition are paramount. . . . It means that a degree of tolerance and anonymity replace traditional moral sanction."[10] Those Jews who were "sociologically," rather than theologically, religious, lost the outward appearance of religiosity when becoming urbanized; even those who had personal religious convictions found the demands of Soviet industrial life--work on Saturday, social and political pressures against maintaining the tradition, living in an environment explicitly hostile to religion--pressing hard against those convictions. Aspirations for social and educational mobility conflicted directly with any desire to main-

tain traditional religion, and painful choices had
to be made by some, while a great many others embraced the opportunities presented by modernization
with little hesitation.

Possible responses to the challenges that modernization posed to religion would include adaptation, ghettoization, compartmentalization, and, of
course, rejection of religion. Adaptation was impossible, except in a few minor cases,[11] because,
as we have argued, the Soviet authorities deliberately forclosed such an option. Rejection of religion was, in fact, a frequent response. Ghettoization, or self-isolation from the modernizing society,
was possible only to a limited extent, and became
increasingly difficult to manage. In the 1920s
groups of religious Jews migrated to Jewish agricultural colonies not only because they wanted to guarantee their economic survival, but also because they
felt that such isolated, ethnically homogeneous colonies would protect them from official scrutiny and
would allow them to practice religion in relative
tranquility. The Soviet Yiddish press of the period
is full of stories of "unmasking" such practices and
their practitioners, and by the late 1920s, when the
colonies were both collectivized and "international-
ized" (merged with non-Jewish settlements), their
ability to serve as a haven for the religious was
diminished. Still, even at present there are such
remote, small settlements where Judaism is practiced.
For example, in the Voronezh area there are reports
of a small settlement, Ilinka, where there are 130
Jewish families, most of them religiously observ-
ant.[12] In Georgia there are entire villages popu-
lated by Jews where religion is a powerful social

force (some of these have recently emigrated en masse to Israel).  In fact, it could be argued that Georgian Jewry as a whole represents this kind of response to modernization:  just as the entire republic has managed to preserve some of its unique cultural and social characteristics, often to the chagrin of the authorities in Moscow, so have Georgian Jews resisted the allure of modernization, and while they have not attained the educational and occupational levels of other Soviet Jews, they have managed, more than any other Jewish community in the USSR, to maintain religious practices and institutions, even in the absence of religious educational opportunities.[13]  Finally, here and there in the contemporary USSR there are individuals and small groups who have managed to stay apart from the rest of society, to raise their children in the religious tradition, and to withstand both the emoluments as well as the challenges of modern, secular Soviet society. These "internal emigres" have taken the recent opportunities to emigrate to Israel, but there is no doubt that some survive in the USSR.[14]  We are also aware of some Soviet Jews who have taken the road of compartmentalization, achieving conventional social success by virtue of the fact that they are engineers or even scientists, and yet maintaining their religious beliefs and practices.  Again, this is hardly typical of Soviet Jews, but the fact that the phenomenon exists at all is worthy of note.

JUDAISM IN THE POST-MODERNIZATION AGE

Lacking information on the scope and intensity of religious belief and practice in the USSR, we

cannot easily assess the relative strengths of the
different religions practiced in that country.  It
is clear that Judaism is somewhat disadvantaged relative to the other religions, since it has no central
organizing body, no facilities for training clergy
and lay leaders, very limited possibilities for producing and disseminating religious articles, and restricted contacts with co-religionists abroad.  Moreover, whereas the USSR is the main base of Russian
Orthodoxy, and whereas Islam is the religion of many
states with which the USSR maintains friendly relations, Judaism is centered in Israel and the United
States, both "enemy" states.  The motif of return to
Zion which pervades Judaism, the international connections of the religion, and the international support given to religious Jews by co-religionists all
make Judaism more suspect and less palatable to the
authorities than some of the other religions.  Whereas the recent world conference of Christian churches
meeting in Nairobi could not even pass a resolution
condemning the persecution of Christianity in the Soviet Union, Jewish and non-Jewish groups have for
several years raised public outcries about the treatment of Judaism.  Though Jews are perhaps the most
"modernized" of Soviet nationalities--in the sense
that they are most urbanized and educated--and it
can be presumed that religion is weaker among them
than among most other nationalities, Soviet efforts
against religion seem to be disproportionately focused on Judaism.  According to Mordechai Altshuler,
"Publications against the Jewish religion in 1958-67
constituted 9 percent of all words against specific
religions while the Jewish population. . . .consti-
tuted only 1.1 percent of the population. . . .  Al-

299

so, the number of copies of books against the Jewish religion was seven times as large as the number against Islam and almost twice as large as that against Christianity. This is surprising, in view of the Soviet argument that only a few Soviet Jews still observe their religion." Altshuler attributes this disproportion to attempts by the regime to "discourage feelings of national pride."[15]

It is impossible to determine how many Jews in the USSR consider themselves religious, or what is the meaning and content of Judaism to its practitioners. Though there have been more and more sociological investigations of religion in recent years, very few of them have focused on, or even included, Jews. This is in line with the general policy of either not collecting or not reporting data on Jews. (For example, we do not know how many Jews are in the Communist Party; we do not know the birth rate among Jews; data on the age structure of the Jewish population and on its educational makeup are known only for a few republics, etc.) As a Soviet author remarks, "Unfortunately, we have not used very much the scientific method, which is represented by concrete sociological investigations, of studying levels of religiosity generally and of Judaism specifically."[16] The few attempts to use "concrete investigations" have been amateurish and raise serious questions of reliability and validity. For example, we are told of a survey in several cities of Belorussia which included a sample of 200 Jews in Bobruisk. While among these Jews 98.5 percent declared themselves atheists, for the other ten samples the average was only 65 percent.[17] But we are told nothing of the method by which the sample was drawn or

300

the way in which questions were asked (one could easily imagine that the interviewers were viewed as officials or "militant atheists" and that respondents were less than candid). We are not even told the date of the study. A survey of religious Jews in Zakarpatskaia oblast' (Ukrainian SSR) "reveals" that 23 percent have an anthropomorphic conception of God, 48 percent have a "more or less abstract conception," and 29 percent respond "Don't know" in answer to "how do you conceive of God." Again, no information is supplied on the size of the sample, the way in which it was constructed, or even the period of the survey.[18]

Soviet sources are of little help in attempts to measure Jewish religiosity. While it can reasonably be argued that religious Jews would tend to be overrepresented among the over 100,000 Soviet Jews who have emigrated since 1971, it is impossible to determine to what extent this is the case, and it may be helpful to look at some data gathered from the emigres. Israeli sociologists studied over 1,500 emigres who came to Israel between 1960 and March 1971, that is, before the current wave began to arrive. It seems to me that among this earlier group there is an even greater likelihood of overrepresentation of the religious, since they were both the most likely to press for emigration as well as the most likely to be considered expendable by the authorities. Be that as it may, data were gathered on the religious practices of the émigres while they were still in the USSR. Unfortunately, the results of this aspect of the study have not yet been reported, though we are told that religious practice and education were negatively correlated.[19]

301

There are data available on the Georgian immigrants. In 1971-72, when Georgian Jews constituted 46 percent of all Soviet immigrants and 31 percent of those over eighteen, fully 77 percent of a random sample of the Georgians defined themselves as religious, while 35 percent of all Soviet immigrants defined themselves as such. Even if we subtract the Georgians from the rest of the immigrants there is still a surprisingly high proportion of self-described believers and/or practitioners among the immigrants. However, it is interesting to note the relationships between age and religiosity which are given for the Georgians and that are likely to hold true for the others.

|                  | 18-29 | 30-54 | 55+ | Total |
|------------------|-------|-------|-----|-------|
| Religious        | 63%   | 80%   | 91% | 77%   |
| Not so religious | 19    | 13    | 9   | 14    |
| Not religious    | 18    | 7     | –   | 9     |

Thus, younger Georgians are less religious than older ones, though 89 percent of all the respondents reported that they had fasted on Yom Kippur in the Soviet Union. Eighty-seven percent of all respondents said that their parents' homes had been religious. Unfortunately, the comparable data for the total Soviet emigration has not yet been reported.[20]

Finally, in a survey of 152 Soviet Jewish males I conducted as part of a study of the political socialization of Soviet and American immigrants in Israel, I found that 9 percent defined themselves as religious (in contrast to 26 percent of the Americans who did so), sixteen percent defined themselves as antireligious, and fully 36 percent defined themselves as "traditional," with another similar percentage reporting that they were neither religious nor

302

traditional--but apparently not actively hostile to religion. Upon further investigation, it turned out that "traditional" meant to most of the respondents that some Jewish customs and rituals were observed, even if out of secular national motives, or out of habit, rather than for religious reasons. Curiously, among those emigrating from the Soviet heartland rather than the western peripheries, the percentage of "religious" was slightly higher (13). This is surprising because Jewish tradition could be assumed to be stronger in those areas where traditional Jewish life flourished as late as 1939-40, in contrast to the Soviet heartland where it was driven underground more than a decade earlier. The explanation may lie in one of the most interesting phenomena of the Jewish national revival in the USSR: beginning in the 1960s, the search for Jewish identity led some young Jews, especially among the intelligentsia of Moscow and Leningrad, to the realization of the centrality of religion in Jewish history and culture. These people then adopted religious forms as an expression of their national identification, and some became genuinely religious. Moreover, whereas in the early 1960s some Jews, caught up in the search by young intellectuals for alternatives to the official materialist ideology, embraced Russian Orthodoxy and even Buddhism (just as their counterparts in the West were attracted to mystical sects and cults and to Eastern religions), by the late 1960s those looking for an alternative Weltanschauung could find it within the Jewish tradition, which had now become acceptable and respectable, if not to the regime then to the Jewish population. To continue the line of argument presented earlier, it may be that this phenomenon is parallel to the "third generation" experience among American Jews: just as the immigrant generation and their children sought to be absorbed by what they saw as the mainstream of society, and the third generation, more secure in its American identity, became curious about its non-American roots, so too did shtetl Jews and the first generation of "Soviet Jews" ignore or deliberately blot out (with many exceptions) the heritage of traditional Judaism, and the third generation, disillusioned with the vision of a meta-ethnic, purely rational and materialist society, tried to recapture its historical past and embarked on a search for its roots. Certainly, few young people, Jews or others, seem to be very much upset by the survival of religion in the USSR. The Soviet press and antireligious organs are full of complaints about the indifference of most people to the "social problem and evil" of religion. These are now generations born long after religion was identified with an oppressive regime, after the bitter struggles between church and state had been waged. Religion has become a private matter, perhaps a curiosity, but not the kind of issue which would agitate non-believers. For this reason it became possible for some people to become curious, and a few of them eventually became "converted." A fair number of those who emerged as leaders of the Jewish national revival have become practicing Jews, though sometimes in heterodox ways, and there are now well documented instances of Jewish prisoners in the labor camps insisting on wearing skullcaps, despite harsh punishment, refraining from eating non-kosher food, despite the meager rations, and trying as best they can to observe the Sabbath and reli-

gious holidays. Whereas thirty and forty years ago
they might have been ridiculed by "modern" Jews, today even those who have no personal sympathy with
religion seem to respect their attitudes and actions.

In Israel an "association of Jewish religious
professionals from the Soviet Union and Eastern
Europe" has been formed. Headed by an engineering
professor from Vilnius, this organization, know as
SHAMIR, claims a membership of about five hundred,[21]
of whom it was said by Professor Branover that only
two hundred were actually religious, with the rest
"on the way to religion and desirous of approaching
it." Of the five hundred, only 120 came from the
Soviet Union as religious Jews, and the rest turned
to religion once in Israel. SHAMIR publishes a
journal of religious thought, Vozrozhdenie, and at
least one other religious journal in the Russian
language is published in Israel.

All of this points to the conclusion that while
Judaism was stultified intellectually and institutionally as a result of the coercive modernization
process that Soviet society has experienced, in the
post-modernization era two things have changed which
alter the religious situation to a significant de-
degree. First, the ideological enthusiasm generated
by the promise of modernization and the struggle to
achieve it has faded, and among the Soviet intelligentsia, and perhaps among others as well, there
seems to be a vague dissatisfaction with official
values and the official world-view, leading some, at
least, to search for non-materialist explanations of
the universe, while others concentrate on political
and social reform--and still others do both.[22] Second, religion has been pushed into such a remote

305

corner of Soviet life that it is no longer an issue
for most non-religionists.  It has become a neutral
subject, a non-issue, which means, on the one hand,
that it is irrelevant to most people, but, on the
other hand, that those who are attracted to it for
whatever reason will not face the social opprobrium
that they would have in the period when modernization was explicitly counterposed to religion.  Secure in the belief that they are already "modernized," Soviet citizens need not feel that by interesting themselves in religion they have retreated from
modernity, despite what the regime tells them.

These two general Soviet developments, along
with the close association of Jewish ethnicity with
the Jewish religion and the reassertion of Jewish
ethnicity in the USSR, point to the prospect that
however weakened institutionally, and however much
the band of the faithful has dwindled, it would be
premature to pronounce a death sentence on Judaism--
or any other religion--in the Soviet Union.  Modernization, as many social scientists have noted, is not
necessarily a linear process, and what once were assumed to be irreversible trends now appear to be
phases in a cycle.  The relationship of modernization to religion must be examined in terms of stages
of development, and whatever it is that comes after
what we call, perhaps presumptuously, modernization,
may have consequences for religion that we do not
fully understand.  It is not at all clear what the
future of religion in a post-modernized world will
be.

NOTES

1. Kalman Silvert, "Introduction," in Churches

306

and States: The Religious Institution and Modernization, ed. Kalman Silvert(New York:  American Universities of Field Staff, 1967) p. 4.

2. Ibid., p. 5.

3. Ibid., pp. 216-217.

4. Ibid., p. 6.

5. A famous court case was that of Oswald Ru-
feisen ("Brother Daniel"), born a Jew, converted to
Catholicism, and requesting the Israeli authorities
to register him as a Jew by Nationality and a Catholic by religion.  For details see S. N. Eisenstadt,
Israeli Society (London:  Weidenfeld and Nicholson,
1967), pp. 314-316; Aharon Lichtenstein, "Brother
Daniel and the Jewish Fraternity," JUDAISM 12 (Summer 1963):260-80.

6. Jacob Neusner, "From Theology to Ideology:
The Transmutation of Judaism in Modern Times," in
Silvert, Churches and States, p. 19.

7. For details see this writer's Jewish Nationality and Soviet Politics (Princeton, N. J.:  Princeton University Press, 1972) pp. 297-314.

8. A. A. Gershuni, Yahadut Berussia Hasovietit
(Jerusalem:  Mosad Harov Kook, 1961) pp. 109-110.

9. I. Pul'ner, "Iz zhizni goroda Gomelia," in
Evreiskoe mestechko v revoliutsii, ed. B. D. Tan-
Bogoraz (Moscow-Leningrad, 1926) p. 196.

10. The Secular City, quoted in Neusner, "From
Theology to Ideology," p. 44.

11. Rabbi Samuel Alexandrov of Bobruisk, a re-
spected Jewish scholar, tried to reconcile Communism and Judaism by arguing that Communist materialism was merely a prologue to the revelation of faith
in one God.

12. Also in Kolkhoz in the Voronezh area there
are 80 Jewish families and a rabbi--who is emigrating to Israel. Insight 1 (London, November 1975):4.

13. On the ability of Georgian Jews to "compart-
mentalize" by cooperating with the regime, on one
hand, and maintaining the religion, on the other, see

Mordechai Altshuler, "Georgian Jewish Culture under the Soviet Regime," Soviet Jewish Affairs 5 (1975): 29.

14. See, for example, Sarah Honig, "Russia's Secret Jews," Jerusalem Post, January 2, 1976.

15. Mordechai Altshuler, ed., Russian Publications on Jews and Judaism in the Soviet Union 1917-1967 (Jerusalem: Society for Research on Jewish Communities, 1970), p. xii.

16. M. El'shin, "Izuchenie iudaizma Sovetskimi uchenymi," in Voprosy nauchnogo ateizma 4 (Moscow, 1967):404.

17. Prichiny sushchestvovaniia i puti preodoleniia religioznykh perezhitkov (Minsk, 1965) pp. 40 and 123.

18. A. I. Edel'man, "Iudeiskii monoteizm i ego sovremennaia interpretatsiia," Filosofskie nauki (January-February, 1968), p. 112.

19. Yehudit Shuval, Yehuda Markus, and Yehudit Dotan, Defusai histaglut shel olai Brit Hamoetsot, part 2 (Jerusalem: Israel Institute for Applied Social Research, 1974), pp. 12-14.

20. Ministry of Immigrant Absorption, "Klitat olai Gruziia tokh hashana harishone lehagiam," interanl report dated September 1973.

21. See Avraham Tirosh, "Yesh mashber rukhani beyisrael. . . .," Maariv, June 17, 1974. Shamir, No. 1 (October 1973) talked of "our more than 300 members now in Israel."

22. Alexander Voronel, one of the most perceptive of recent Soviet emigrants to Israel writes that the Soviet intelligentsia is dissatisfied with "the superficial internationalism and culture of Soviet society" and that "those who have probed more deeply have begun to recognize the fact that their culture has roots in older national, and perhaps religious, traditions. (It is not without interest that ten years ago the most sought-after and expensive books on the Russian black market were works of fiction and associated literature, whereas now it is Bibles and religious works which are most in demand.) . . . . The general renaissance of religious feeling

among the people in Russia has not been without its
impact on the Jews. . . .  The religious mood pre-
dated the national mood and identity was seen in i-
deological, and not national, terms.  While some
Jews converted, others turned towards their national
identity and some towards a combination of both."
"The Search for Jewish Identity in Russia," Soviet
Jewish Affairs 5 (1975):70.

Chapter 9

THE UKRAINIAN AUTOCEPHALOUS ORTHODOX CHURCH,
1920-1930:   A CASE STUDY IN RELIGIOUS MODERNIZATION

Bohdan R. Bociurkiw

Modernization and religion remains a largely un-
touched problem in the scholarly literature on the
post-1917 Ukraine.[1]  While Soviet writings on religion and the church in the Ukrainian SSR have on the
whole been concerned with the "unmasking" of the "reactionary" role of religion in socialist society and
with "proving" its incompatibility with science and
progress, the emphasis of the émigré and Western
writers has largely wavered between martyrology and
the politics of church-state relations in the
Ukraine.  Yet, perhaps even more so than the case of
the Renovationist movement (obnovlenchestvo) within
the Russian Church,[2] modern Ukrainian church history
offers an example of a modernizing, religious organization which attempted to restructure the Orthodox
Church in the Ukraine and reinterpret its doctrine
in such ways as to bridge the gulf separating them
from the contemporary Ukrainian political and social
aspirations.  This ecclesiastical organization which
designated itself as the Ukrainian Autocephalous
Orthodox Church (UAPTs[3]) forms the focus of this
study.  This essay will not delve into the continuing
polemics concerning the "canonicity" of this church.
Rather, we shall attempt to reconstruct briefly the

genesis and evolution of the UAPTs and analyze the
changing policy of the Soviet regime to the UAPTs
culminating in the forcible "self-dissolution" of
this church in 1930.  In conclusion the paper will
examine the principal structural and doctrinal
changes introduced within the church by the Ukrainian autocephalists, and assess their significance
from the viewpoint of the church's adaptation to political, cultural, and social change.

The revolutions of 1917--in their political,
social, and nationalist dimensions--led to the rapid
disruption of the traditional religio-political system in Russia represented by the symbiotic relationship of tsarist autocracy and Orthodoxy.  This process culminated in a revolutionary disestablishment
of the Russian Orthodox Church effected by the Bolshevik Separation Decree of February 5, 1918.

The secularization and expansion of the new
revolutionary polity, to use Donald E. Smith's con-
ceptual framework,[4] involved a total secularization
of education, law, and public life, a nationalization of the entire ecclesiastical property, and the
imposition upon the church--now deprived even of a
corporate status--of the far reaching polity domi-
nance.  The Soviet regime undertook a complete trans-
valuation of political culture with religion condemned to eventual extinction, to be replaced with a
secular "political religion" officially designated
as "Marxism-Leninsim."

In the Ukraine the secularizing impact of the
Bolshevik rule was delayed by two years, by the emer-
gence of at first autonomous and then independent
Ukrainian statehood.[5]  Until 1919, the Orthodox
Church in the Ukraine was threatened not by the loss

311

of its established status but by the rise of the
Ukrainian national church movement.  From the perspective of this movement's leaders--a small group of
the "nationally conscious" white urban priests, military chaplains, and lay intellectuals[6]--the Russian
Orthodox Church appeared to represent a major obstacle to the national and social emancipation of the
Ukrainian people; the church's past role as a legiti-
mizer of autocracy, imperial unity, and the old social order, its hostility to the "Ukrainian separa-
tism," its contempt for the Ukrainian language, its
employment of religious sanctions against "rebels"
(e.g., Mazepa) and, in recent memory, its close collaboration with the reactionary Union of the Russian
People--all these features of the old religio-political system have contributed to the alienation of the
large majority of the Ukrainian intelligentsia from
the established church prior to World War I.  More
and more of them came to dismiss religion as incompatible with modernization.  The Ukrainian church
movement which combined the renovationist objectives
of the church's post-1905 "liberals" with the Ukrainian national and social aspirations, was determined
to wrest the control of the church away from its conservative Russian episcopate, and infuse it with the
Ukrainian values, culture, and language through the
democratization of its structure.  Hence the movement's three guiding principles of "autocephaly,"
"Ukrainianization," and "conciliarism."  Perhaps more
basic was the movement's desire to bring the church
into the mainstream of the Ukrainian revolution as a
legitimizing, integrating, and nation-building force
that would bolster the fragile structure of the
Ukrainian state.

312

The Ukrainian church movement failed to realize its objectives during the shortlived Ukrainian statehood.[7] Opposed by the Russian episcopate and the conservative majority of the clergy, it was unsucessful in its attempts to secure a timely and forceful intervention on its behalf either from the socialist-dominated central Rada or from the conservative Hetman regime. When finally the directorate decreed in January 1919 the autocephaly of the Orthodox Church in the Ukraine[8] it was too late. Before it could effectively "Ukrainianize" the church, the Ukrainian state was engulfed by the successive waves of the invading Bolshevik and White armies.

Paradoxically, it was only after the Soviet takeover of the Ukraine that the autocephalist movement centered around the All-Ukrainian Orthodox Church Council (Rada) in Kiev, could successfully challenge the Russian control over the church through an ecclesiastical "revolution from below." Having "recognized" the Soviet separation decree[9] (at the time when the Moscow Patriarchate continued its confrontation with Lenin's regime), the Ukrainian autocephalists took advantage of the new legislation by promptly "registering" a number of "Ukrainianized" parishes under the All-Ukrainian Orthodox Church Council; by early 1920 the government formally recognized the "Union of Ukrainian Orthodox Parishes" as a separate ecclesiastical organization in the Ukraine under the All-Ukrainian Rada. Soon afterwards the Russian episcopate suspended all clergy of the Ukrainianized parishes to which the Rada responded in May 1920 with a formal proclamation of autocephaly for the Ukrainian Orthodox Church.[10]

The three year old struggle for control of the

church between Russian nationalism entrenched in the
hierarchy and the upper clergy and Ukrainian nationalism of the lower clergy and lay church intelligentsia thus culminated in a split of the Orthodox Church
in the Ukraine into two hostile entities:  the Russian (Patriarchal) Church headed by a Moscow-appoint-
ed Exarch, which derived its strength from its control of the entire hierarchy in an episcopate-cen-
tered church, as well as from its canonical continuity and habitual allegiance of the conservative
majority of believers; and a minority Ukrainian Autocephalous Church centered around the lay-dominated
councils (rady) which embraced the nationally conscious believers attracted by the national language
and rites of the church and its message of national
independence, ecclesiastical democratization, and
social radicalism.

Having severed its links with the Russian episcopate, the All-Ukrainian Church Rada was able at
first to secure archpastoral leadership for the
Ukrainian Autocephalous Orthodox Church (UAPTs) in
the person of a retired Ukrainian archbishop, Parfenii Levytskyi of Poltava.  However, when the Russian episcopate decided in February 1921 to unfrock
all the Autocephalist clergy and ordered under threat
of anathema an immediate dissolution of the UAPTs,
Archbishop Parfenii broke his connections with the
latter.[11]  With no bishop now willing to assume the
canonical leadership of the Ukrainian Autocephalous
Church or to ordain its episcopate,[12] the First All-
Ukrainian Sobor of the UAPTs which met on October 14-
30, 1921 took a fateful decision to create its own
episcopate by resorting to what it claimed to be the
practice of the ancient Alexandrine church.[13]  On

October 23, Archpriest Vasyl Lypkivskyi (b. 1864),
the spiritual leader of the Ukrainian church movement
and one of the organizers of the All-Ukrainian Church
Rada (in 1919 he celebrated in Kiev the first Liturgy
in the living Ukrainian language), was ordained Metropolitan of Kiev and All Ukraine through the laying-
on of hands by the clerical and lay members of the
sobor;[14] then jointly with the sobor members, Metropolitan Lypkivskyi consecrated Archpriest Nestor
Sharaivskyi as another bishop and late in October,
the two hierarchs ordained four other priests as
bishops for several Ukrainian dioceses.  This depar-
ture from the established Orthodox procedures as well
as a series of canonical reforms adopted by the 1921
sobor not only alienated some clerical supporters of
the Ukrainian church movement, but also resulted in
a virtual isolation of the UAPTs from other Orthodox
churches which refused to recognize the canonic validity of its episcopate.

Nevertheless, despite a determined opposition on
the part of the Russian church, the UAPTs rapidly expanded its following among the Ukrainian peasantry
and intelligentsia.  By early 1924 it embraced 30
bishops and approximately 1,500 priests and deacons
serving nearly 1,100 parishes in the Ukrainian SSR.[15]
At the peak of its influence, the UAPTs might have
had as many as three to six million followers.[16]
The UAPTs seriously weakened the hold of the Russian
Church over the Ukrainian peasantry, especially in
the provinces of Kiev, Podilia, Chernihiv, and Poltava, and it virtually deprived it of any following
among the Ukrainian intelligentsia.  During the
1920's the influence of the UAPTs spread beyond the
Ukraine into Ukrainian settlements in Central Asia,

among émigrés in Western Europe, and in particular
to the Ukrainians in the United States and Canada,
where a separate diocese was formed (with some 148
parishes by 1927) under Archbishop Ioan Teodorovych.[17]

After 1922, regardless of the autocephalist protestations of loyalty to the Soviet system, Soviet
authorities began to impose increasingly severe restrictions upon the Ukrainian Autocephalous Church
which they accused of nationalistic tendencies. Having failed to force a merger between the UAPTs and
the regime-supported "Living Church" in 1922-23,[18]
during the next three years, 1923-26, the authorites
attempted to split the UAPTs by manipulating internal cleavages within its leadership, offering their
support to "progressive" factions within its ranks--
in particular the so-called "Active Christian
Church."[19]  When the "Active Christian Church" failed
to seize the control of the church, the Soviet police
resorted in the summer of 1926 to repressive measures, arresting Metropolitan Lypkivskyi and a number
of autocephalist leaders and ordering a dissolution
of the church's central organ--the All-Ukrainian
Church Rada.  At the Second All-Ukrainian Sobor in
October 1927, the authorities forced the dismissal
of Metropolitan Vasyl Lypkivskyi who was replaced by
Metropolitan Mykolai Boretskyi.[20]

After a brief period of toleration during which
the UAPTs was permitted to publish its journal
Tserkva i zhyttia (Church and Life; 1927-28) as well
as several religious books, the regime undertook,
beginning in 1929, massive repressive measures
against the autocephalist episcopate and clergy,
closing most of the Ukrainian parishes.  Charging

316

the UAPTs with collaboration with the recently "un-covered" underground "league for the Liberation of Ukraine" (SVU),[21] the authorities staged in January 1930 the so-called "Extraordinary Sobor" which formally "dissolved" the Ukrainian Autocephalous Orthodox Church.[22] Metropolitan Boretskyi and a number of other autocephalist leaders, including the church's principal ideologist, Volodymyr Chekhivskyi, were imprisoned or exiled. The remnants of the church (some 300 parishes) were allowed to reconstitute themselves by the end of 1920 as a "Ukrainian Orthodox Church" under Metropolitan Ivan Pavlovskyi of Kharkiv, but only after they renounced some of the principal ideas of the UAPTs and committed themselves to a total and unconditional loyalty to the regime.[23] Closely policed by the regime, this church was progressively decimated with its last parish suppressed in 1936.[24] Most of the autocephalist bishops and clergy and thousands of its lay activists perished in the bloodbath of the great purges.[25]

In a manner characteristic of other dissident religious movements, the Ukrainian Autocephalous Church based its initial claims to legitimacy on appeals to historical right, Apostolic teachings, and practices of early Christianity. Thus the Autocephalist "declaration of independence" (the so-called "First Letter" of the All-Ukrainian Orthodox Church Rada of May 1920) argued that the proclamation of the Ukrainian ecclesiastical independence from Moscow was merely the reaffirmation of the "virtual autocephaly," conciliar constitution, and national character of the Orthodox Church in the Ukraine which the latter possessed before its unlawful annexation

317

by Moscow in 1686.  For subsequently, the "Muscovite"
church authorities, with the help of the tsars,

> used prohibitions, banishments, violence and
> terror to abolish step-by-step not only the
> independence and conciliar constitution of
> the Ukrainian church, but almost everything
> in it that contained any characteristics of
> the national creativeness peculiar to the
> Ukrainian people.[26]

The russification, centralization, and bureau-
cratization of the Orthodox Church--claimed the All-
Ukrainian Rada--had alienated the Ukrainian people,
denying them the full satisfaction of their religious needs.  Accordingly, the autocephalist movement wanted to bring the church back to the Ukrainian people and the people into the church.  But since
1917 the "Muscovite ecclesiastical authorities" have
been sabotaging all legitimate attempts to revive
the Ukrainian church and have shown themselves to be
"not a good pastor, but an enemy of the Ukrainian
people."[27]

When the fateful First All-Ukrainian Church Sobor met in October 1921 in the Kievan Cathedral of
St. Sophia, paramount in its delegates' minds were
two questions:  Was this gathering, in which no bishop participated, a canonically valid sobor, empowered
to speak for the Ukrainian Orthodox Church?  Could
the sobor itself, in the absence of bishops, ordain
the episcopate for the new church?  With reference
to the first question, the spiritual leader of the
UAPTs, Archpriest Lypkivskyi argued for the recognition of the sobor's canonical validity as its members represented the entire Ukrainian church and as
they gathered in Christ's name with firm belief in
the presence of Christ and the Holy Spirit amongst

them.[28]  Volodymyr Chekhivskyi, the church's foremost
lay ideologist, provided the answer to the second
question.  He advanced a thesis that since bishops
in the apostolic times were consecrated by presby-
ters, the exclusisve assumption of this right by the
bishops represented a violation of the apostolic
practice; since the grace of the Holy Spirit resides
in the entire church, it should have the right to
ordain its episcopate through its sobor representatives, despite the absence of the already ordained
bishops, as this would simply be a return to the ancient practice of the Alexandrine church.[29]  An overwhelming majority of the sobor members accepted the
above arguments; a small minority of delegates, however, rejected this line of thought as a "Protestant
deviation" and walked out of the sobor.[30]

Having thus declared itself the genuine "voice
of the Ukrainian church, inspired by the Holy Spirit,"
the 1921 sobor resolved that it should have the
right to change those canons of the Orthodox church
that, although established by the first seven Ecumenical Councils and justified in the past, could no
longer meet the present vital needs of the Ukrainian
church or further its organic development.[31]  This
was indeed a momentous decision, for the sobor thereby assumed the prerogatives of the ecumenical councils and thus broke away from the established canonical framework of the Orthodox church.  On this, rel-
ativistic, instrumental notion of the canonic rules
were based all the subsequent innovations in the
church rules introduced by the Kiev sobor.

The sobor proceeded to restructure the constitution of the Ukrainian church in an egalitarian,
conciliar manner.  "Episcopal autocracy" of the

traditional Orthodox church was declared a product
of historical conditions and of a monarchic state,
contrary to the spirit of Orthodoxy and the present
needs of the Ukrainian Orthodox.[32]   "Among members
of the Church there must be neither domination or
coercion."

> The constitution of the Ukrainian Ortho-
> dox Autocephalous Church. . . .shall hence-
> forth be popular and conciliar (vsenarodnio-
> sobornopravnyi).  The church itself should
> administer all ecclesiastical affairs. . . .[33]

The episcopal, organization of the church was
now to be replaced by a loose hierarchy of the lay-
dominated, self-governing church councils (rady),
from the All-Ukrainian Orthodox Church Council heading the UAPTs between the All-Ukrainian sobors, down
to the regional, district, and parish church councils.  All church offices, including episcopal ones,
were made elective.[34]  The bishops and the clergy
were to serve merely as honorary chairmen of the re-
spective rady.  Like the later "Living Church," the
Kiev sobor declared that the "white," married priests
shall have equal rights with the monastic clergy in
elevation to the episcopal rank.[35]  Rules governing
the clergy were liberalized granting them the rights
of divorce and remarriage, and allowing them to wear
civilian clothes outside the church, shave their
beards, and cut their hair.[36]

The Autocephalists had shown little sympathy for
the monastic clergy--the staunchest defenders of the
status quo:  "today's monasteries," resolved the
1921 sobor, "have departed a long way from their
ideal and should be transformed in the direction of
the ancient monastic religious-toiling communes. .
. ."[37]

The sobor confirmed the autocephaly of the
Ukrainian Orthodox Church proclaimed by the All-
Ukrainian Church Rada in May 1920, and repudiated
the seventeenth-century annexation of the Kiev met-
ropoly by the Moscow patriarchate as an "immoral,"
"anti-canonical," and illegitimate act of violence.[38]
The gathering also decreed the complete Ukrainianization of the church life, including a broad utili-
zation of folk art and folk music in church rites,
the revival of the historic Ukrainian religious customs and traditions, and a wide scope for "ecclesiastical creativity."[39] It also provided for the
broadest participation of laymen in all phases of ecclesiastical life and emphasized the further development of church brotherhoods (a traditional form of
the organized lay influence in the Ukrainian church)
and the cultivation of lay preaching (blahovistia)--
a novum for the Orthodox church.[40]

As for the church's relationship to the Soviet
state, the sobor accepted the official separation of
the church from the state as corresponding to "the
teachings of Christ"[41] and granting "freedom of confession in the Ukrainian Soviet Socialist Republic."[42] At the same time, the gathering committed
the church to an apolitical platform:

> whoever introduces elements of coercion, of
> social class, political or national oppres-
> sion into the life of the church should be
> excluded from the church until he repents.[43]

The 1921 All-Ukrainian Sobor represented a radical break with the canonical status quo, a break
which, at least as far as the mode of ordaining the
first two bishops of the church was concerned, was
less a matter of choice than the consequence of the

unfavorable circumstances attending the birth of the
UAPTs.[44] What emerged from the reforms effected by
this gathering was a new church which, while profes-
sing to be Orthodox, severed its canonical links
with other Orthodox churches. Its canons, doctrine,
and organization combined elements of Orthodoxy with
such apparently Protestant features as elected, married episcopate; abolition of rigid distinctions between priesthood and lay believers; lay preaching;
conciliar self-government at all levels of the
church; and, above all, a pragmatic approach to the
Orthodox canons.

As could be expected, the Russian Orthodox Church
(and later, the Renovationist Church) now condemned
the UAPTs as "anti-canonical," "deprived of Divine
Grace," "heretical," and "Protestant" sect. Singled
out as the sobor's chief "heresy" was its conciliar
consecration of the new episcopate--hence the derog-
atory names of samosviaty (the "self-consecrated
ones") or lipkovtsy (after the name of the first
bishop of the UAPTs) or the "Ukrainian schism."[45]
Despite some abortive attempts on the part of the
UAPTs to establish relations with other Orthodox
churches,[46] none of them has ever recognized the
canonicity of the Ukrainian Autocephalous Church. A
few of the bishops and the clergy of the UAPTs appeared to be troubled by the question of their "canonicity" as Orthodox,[47] but most seemed to have reconciled themselves to their ecclesiastical isolation.
Indeed, they probably agreed with Metropolitan Lypkivskyi's view that this isolation of the UAPTs, its
"distinct stream of grace" offered the best guarantee of the church's spiritual independence from
Moscow:

322

> As long as it remains a Ukrainian church
> based on the principles established by the
> 1921 sobor, it cannot merge with anyone,
> and must pursue its own road, perhaps the
> most difficult one, but also the most dig-
> nified one.[48]

The ecclesiastical revolution effected by the
1921 sobor could be viewed as a delayed extension of
the idelas of the Ukrainian revolution into the ecclesiastical and religious-cultural spheres.  The
Autocephalist reinterpretation of the Orthodox doctrine sought to provide religious legitimation for
the cause of the Ukrainian national and social liberation, while the structural changes within the church
clearly reflected the movement's egalitarian, popu-
list orientation.  The restructured church clearly
relied on those strata of the church which were most
sympathetic to the nationalist cause and, at least
indirectly, it aimed at "politicizing" the Ukrainian
masses, at drawing them _via_ the Ukrainian parishes
and self-governing _rady_ into the process of nation-
building, at "awakening" the Ukrainian peasantry to
the realization of their social potential.

To gain an insight into the nature of the Ukrainian Autocephalous Church, the underlying values, mo-
tiviations, and goals of its leaders, we shall examine more systematically the Autocephalist "ideology"
as it evolved during the 1920s.  It will be analyzed
especially from the viewpoint of its relationship to
the rapid political, cultural, and socio-economic
changes experienced by the Ukraine during its first
decade of the Soviet rule.  The Autocephalist writers[49] described their own ideology in terms of the
following five principles:  (1) The separation of the

church from the state; (2) autocephaly; (3) conciliarism; (4) Ukrainianization; and (5) Christianization of life.[50]

The first of the avowed principles of the UAPTs--
that of the separation of the church from the state--
undoubtedly aimed at the church's adaptation to the
new political reality:  the traditional Orthodox formula of the "symphony" of spiritual and temporal powers could not anymore be applied with regard to the
militantly atheistic state; moreover, it was this
very separation principle of the Soviet religious
legislation that enabled the Ukrainian autocephalist
movement to wrest away from the Moscow patriarchate
a number of churches in the Ukraine.  Setting forth
the pattern to be followed by other religious organizations in the USSR, the Autocephalist reformulation
of church-state relations reached back to the pre-
Constantine times, invoking Christ's distinction between "the things that are Caesar's and those that
are God's."  Only in separation from the civil power,
where there is no mutual interference on the part of
the state and the church, can the latter enjoy "true
freedom," for being built on love, the church is incompatible with coercion--the necessary attribute of
the state.

> The church should be strictly apolitical.
> The church's efforts to obtain support and
> protection from the state, the resulting
> transformation of the church into a hand-
> maiden of the state, a willing submission of
> the church to the exploitation by the state
> as a political factor, as well as hostile
> activities of the church against the state--
> [all these] are contrary to the nature of
> the church. . . .[51]

By the same token, the church must be loyal to the

state--regardless of its form or regime--as the protector of order and justice in society, in accordance
with the teachings of Christ and the Apostles.  But
should the truth of men (i.e., of the state) contradict that of God, "we shall courageously carry out
the will of God."[52]

Nevertheless, at least one of the submissions of
the Autocephalist All-Ukrainian Rada to the Soviet
Ukrainian Government[53] went beyond this prescription
in its attempt to "prove" basic compatibility of the
UAPTs and the socialist state--perhaps reflecting
the influence of some radical socialist members of
the church.[54]  Yet the very same document insisted
that "the church is not a political organization and
cannot assume any party or state functions," and it
pointedly proclaimed that "any persecution of the
Christian faith is contrary to the truth of proletarian life."[55]

Much more fundamental to the ideology of the
UAPTs was its second basic principle--that of auto-
cephaly--the ecclesiastical equivalent of the ideal
of national independence from Russia.  After the demise of the shortlived Ukrainian People's Republic,
the Ukrainian church remained the one area in which
this ideal could still be pursued; not accidentally
and, of course, not unbeknown to the Soviet authorities, it was the UAPTs that offered a haven to many
former participants in the Ukrainian liberation
struggle, including some prominent Ukrainian intellectuals turned "internal émigres" within a political system they could not accept, and which would
not accept them.[56]  In demanding the autocephaly for
the Ukrainian Orthodox Church, after the break-up of
the Russian empire the Ukrainian movement neverthe-

less stood on firm canonical and historical grounds.
Even after the collapse of the Ukrainian People's
Republic, the largely fictitious "sovereignty" of
the Ukrainian SSR was a strong enough argument for
church autocephaly (which was indirectly admitted
by the Moscow patriarchate when it offered its be-
lated recognition to the autocephaly of the Orthodox church in Georgia in 1943).[57]  Whatever arguments
they advanced for the ecclesiastical independence of
the Ukraine from Moscow, the Autocephalists firmly
believed that subordination to the Russian church
was not compatible anymore with the state of national
consciousness in the Ukraine and represented a major
obstacle to the still unfinished task of nation-
building and that autocephaly was a prerequisite for
realizing such other goals of the movement as the
Ukrainianization and democratization of the church
in the republic.

Ukrainianization--another basic principle of the
UAPTs--was based on the premise that true religious
experience can only be attained in a national church,
in one's native tongue, in the familiar context of
national culture.  "Christianization of life," too,
demands that the teachings of Christ be transmitted
to the faithful in their own language; only when the
people understand the services, rites, and teachings
of the church can they meaningfully and creatively
participate in church life.  At the same time, this
principle of the UAPTs antedated and later paralleled (and, to some extent, competed with) the official "Ukrainianization policy" of the Soviet regime,
a policy which aimed at both the sinking of the regime's roots into the Ukrainian ethno-cultural ground
and the political mobilization of the Ukrainian

masses. The Ukrainianization program of the UAPTs not only involved the replacement of Church Slavonic and Russian by the living Ukrainian language, but also included derussification of church rites, traditions, religious art, music, and other aspects of "ecclesiastical culture." The once ridiculed "market language" of the common people, viewed as "uncultured" and "unfit" for sacral purposes,[58] was--together with the peasant folk speaking this language--given a new sense of dignity and respect. According to the contemporaries, among the Ukrainian peasantry it was indeed the Ukrainian-language church services with their revived native rites and chants that offered the strongest attraction to the new church.[59]

The most characteristic feature of the Autocephalist doctrine and practice--that of conciliar self-government (sobornopravnist)--was derived from the egalitarian, participatory self-government of the ancient Christian communities. But subsequently, argued the Autocephalist writers, the church was "corrupted" by monarchic and oligarchic principles as a result of the "Christianization" of the Roman empire. As it grew in power, wealth, and privilege, the church abandoned its conciliar practices and became increasingly alienated from the people, the process which was also due to the growing influence of the monastic clergy "who generally professed contempt for the world and everything temporal. . . ."[60] In Russia, having been assimilated into the bureaucratic and police system of the empire, the Orthodox church "ceased to be apostolic and became an imperial [church]."[61] At the same time, conciliarism in the UAPTs was rationalized as a revival of the traditional democratic practices of the Ukrainian church

327

before its absorption by Moscow.[62]

"Live ecclesiastical creativity" also demands the
fullest participation of laymen in all phases of
church life. Being built on love and concord, church
life excludes coercion; hence the only legitimate
order in the church is that in which there is a conscious spiritual and moral identity between those
who make decisions and those who carry them out.[63]

In his somewhat idealized description of the
Autocephalist parishes, Metropolitan Lypkivskyi noted
that

> in the countryside, a Ukrainian parish leaves
> its peculiar imprint over the whole village,
> elevates it and unites it, gives it its aim--
> an idea to live for, . . . . Almost every
> Ukrainian parish has a composer of its own
> and sings his works in the church; in al-
> most every parish there are homegrown poets. .
> . .and chroniclers. This has already be-
> come a general feature of all Ukrainian
> parishes--beautiful choirs, both artistic
> and popular, . . . .[with] their own, self-
> taught choir directors, their own original
> songs; . . . .parish church councils meets
> every week, discuss all church matters, even
> look after the moral life of the parish like
> the ancient brotherhoods. Each Ukrainian
> parish has its own sisterhood, which looks
> after the cleanliness and the beautifying of
> of the church, . . . .aids the clergy. . . .
> [and] on holy days, together with the parish
> council, the sisterhoods provide common meals
> for the poor and the visitors, . . . .a kind
> of fraternity develops among the individual
> Ukrainian parishes. One feels that pre-
> cisely on this basis can one achieve the unity
> of our people.[64]

Closely intertwined with the principle of conciliarism was the Autocephalist belief that both the
apostolic succession and the gift of grace reside in
the whole church, including its laymen. Accordingly,

the canons of the 1921 sobor significantly narrowed
the gap between the priesthood and laity and largely
reduced distinctions between the orders of the clergy to that of function, while the ecclesiastical
potestas jurisdictionis was vested in the elected,
predominantly lay rady and sobors.

The Autocephalist attempts to combine conciliarism with the institution of the episcopate and the
insistence of the UAPTs on remaining genuinely Orth-
odox--could not but institutionalize within the
church a tension between these two principles of ecclesiastical organization.  Before long, the Soviet
authorities began to exploit and manipulate for
their own ends personality conflicts and factional
cleavages which began to surface within the UAPTs
largely as a result of difficulties experienced by
the church in reconciling the autocratic tradition
of episcopal rule with the modernized notion of ecclesiastical democracy ("radopraviie").[65]

"Christianization"--the last of the five major
prinicples of the Autocephalist doctrine--was conceived as the mission of the church to Christianize
human life, to fill in the chasm between Christian
values and actual life.  The UAPTs was to strive
towards the realization of "the kingdom of social
truth [justice] on earth," to impress upon society
and the state the hitherto neglected social ideals
of Christianity.[66]  These ideals coalesce into a single precept--"love thy neighbor"--which, in the words
of an Autocephalist bishop--calls for (1) the love
of the "lesser brother" (the neglected, oppressed
social strata); (2) love for other peoples; (3) the
equality and brotherhood of men and nations; (4) the
love of truth and, for the sake of truth, of those

329

who disagree with us; and (6) love of our enemies.[67]

Viewed as a whole, the ideology of the Ukrainian Autocephalous Church yields some striking analogies with the social and cultural ideals of the Ukrainian national movement, attesting to the interdependence of social-political and religious thought. Thus the Ukrainian intelligentsia's exaltation of the "people," or to be more precise, the peasantry as the mainstay of nationality and the repository of its cultural values and creative energies, finds its parallel in the UAPTs in the implicit recognition of the "people" as the bearer of divine grace and the locus of true piety and living faith.[68] In addition to the already noted parallel between claims to political and to ecclesiastical independence, we find an analogy between the democratic aspirations and procedures of the Ukrainian revolution and the autocephalist emphasis on conciliarism and egalitarianism. Furthermore, both political and ecclesiastical manifestations of Ukrainian nationalism reveal a markedly ethnographic, defensive notion of nationality, reflected especially in their sometimes exaggerated cult of the national language.

Some elements of the autocephalist ideology appear to be rationalizations of the frustrated aspirations of the Ukrainian church movement or justifications of the revolutionary methods, partly chosen by, and partly forced upon, the movement in the realization of its objectives. The canonical innovations of the 1921 sobor seem to be a case in point. In some ways, this can also be said of the autocephalist defense of sobornopravnist. Meeting hostile reaction on the part of the Russian episcopate, and finding little support from the clergy, the movement could

330

best promote its ends by introducing the conciliar
principle in ecclesiastical government, whereby
Ukrainian laymen could be relied upon to neutralize
the Russian influence entrenched in the hierarchy of
the church.

At the same time, allowance must be made for the
influence on autocephalist ideology of the existing
political situation in the Ukraine (i.e., the Soviet
regime), whether in terms of the church's adaptation
to the official values and norms (including the Soviet legislation on religion), or in terms of assum-
ing a "protective coloring" to ward off harassment
and persecution by the regime. This environmental
influence can be detected in the autocephalist doctrine of church-state relations and in the social
principles of the UAPTs, but it could have also
played some part in the radical interpretation of
the conciliar principle in the Autocephalous Church.

The ideology of the UAPTs, especially its ideals
of autocephaly, Ukrainization, and conciliarism (sobornopravnist'), found many adherents in the Ukraine,
as it objectified and elevated to the level of conscious action the traditional national values and aspirations. There can be no better testimony to the
vitality of the autocephalist ideology, despite the
hindering effect of the canonical reforms of 1921,
than the fact that both the patriarchal and the Renovationist branches of the Russian Orthodox Church in
the Ukraine were compelled by their flock to adopt
at least some of the autocephalist principles.[69]
The revival of the Ukrainian Autocephalous Orthodox
Church during World War II in the German-occupied
Ukraine (however with a canonically ordained episcopate) further underlines the tenacity of the ideals

331

espoused by the UAPTs.[70]

Soviet attitudes towards the Ukrainian Autocephalous Orthodox Church underwent radical changes during the decade 1920-1930, changes which in part paralleled the shifts in the party's religious and nationalities policies. During its early years, the new regime maintained a relatively benevolent position vis-á-vis the Ukrainian church movement and placed no major obstacles in the way of the formation and initial expansion of the UAPTs.[71] Underlying this official line were probably such tactical considerations as, on the one hand, the desire to undermine the Russian Orthodox Church in the Ukraine which was compromised by its collaboration with the Whites and which continued to defy Soviet religious legislation; and, on the other hand, the hope of winning the sympathies of the Ukrainian intelligentsia and the peasantry for the still unstable Bolshevik rule in the Ukraine. It also seems that the UAPTs was enjoying a degree of sympathy and support from the national communist minority within the Communist Party of the Ukraine, especially some Borotbisty and Ukapisty[72] who might have viewed this church as a useful vehicle for raising national consciousness of the peasant masses.

It seems that the regime did not expect at that time that the Autocephalist movement would soon get out of hand, develop mass following, and transform itself from a faction in the Orthodox ranks into a national church, preaching a revolutionary gospel that combined a revitalized Christian message with Ukrainian nationalism and social radicalism. The rapidly rising popularity of the UAPTs made the authorities more suspicious of the political implications

332

of the Autocephalist ideology. As Metropolitan Lypkivskyi was to observe some years later, the very
idea of autocephaly "also conceals within itself the
idea of political independence" and "educates the
people in national consciousness."[73]

Not long after the 1921 sobor, the Soviet Ukrainian press began to attack the UAPTs for the alleged
betrayal of its "revolutionary" platform  Writing in
June 1922, in the official daily of the Kharkiv government, Visty, V. Ellan (Blakytnyi) openly accused
the Autocephalists of "counterrevolutionary" tendencies:

> The first period of the Autocephalous Church's
> existence--the period of a 'revolutionary
> struggle against the monarchist church,'
> the period of 'revolutionary' phrase[ology]--
> comes to an end. A second [period] begins--
> the crystallization of the forces of the
> kulak counterrevolution under the domes of
> the conquered churches. And then, inevit-
> ably, there will come the third period--the
> attempt openly to attack our Soviet fortresses,
> riding the waves of the petty-bourgeois ele-
> ment. . . . The mask comes off the face of
> the yellow-blue[74] clericalism, and all those
> who have believed the mask and have followed
> the charlatans, will repudiate them. . . .[75]

The press attacks signalled the start of a concerted
campaign--that was to continue until 1926--at first,
to intimidate the leaders and the following of the
UAPTs, into joining the so-called "Living Church,"
and subsequently to paralyze the normal operation of
the church and to split and destroy it from within
through a succession of the so-called "progressive"
and "loyalist" schisms to which the authorities and
the OGPU were prepared to offer their open support.[76]
Even if eventually the regime had had some success in
"persuading" several Autocephalist bishops and a

group of clergy to launch a splinter "Active Christian Church," it soon discovered that it was much more difficult to break down or "re-educate" the large lay following of the UAPTs who overwhelmingly repudiated the "Active Church" faction through which the authorities hoped to win internal control of the UAPTs. The Autocephalist laymen and conciliar grassroots democracy proved to be the church's most reliable bulwark against the take-over and corruption from within by the so-called "progressives."

Its failure with the "Active Church" led the regime to adopt new tactics against the UAPTs. By 1926 the authorities resorted to direct administrative and police repressions, suppressing the activities of the All-Ukrainian Church Rada, and arresting the primate of the church, Metropolitan Lypkivskyi. The government made it now clear that the church would be allowed to function only if it would adopt a more "acceptable" policy, under such new leadership as would have the "confidence" of the authorities. By playing on the growing anxiety in the Autocephalist ranks about the future of the UAPTs and by encouraging hopes that the submission to the government's pressure might bring the church some of its long denied rights--the authorities succeeded in bringing about a change in the leadership and orientation of the UAPTs. There was a striking analogy between the line taken by the regime in the Ukraine and the tactics used to break down the remaining opposition in the Russian Orthodox Church.[77]

In return for its "confession" of political sins and the purge of Metropolitan Lypkivskyi and some other "unacceptable" Autocephalist leaders as well as the church's adoption of a more "loyalist" line

vis-à-vis the regime and its submission to the
stricter governmental control, the Soviet Ukrainian
government allowed the UAPTs to resume its activities and to hold its second sobor in 1927.  Despite
the fact that some new concessions were now offered
to the church,[78] including the dissolution of the
"Active Church," the UAPTs had to pay an additional
price for its survival in terms of the growing alienation of its grass-roots following who grew suspicious of the new Autocephalist leadership; some laymen now openly accused the new All-Ukrainian Rada
of having "sold out" to the atheist state.  Perhaps
this deepening division between leaders and followers
was one of the principal expectations motivating the
shift in the regime's tactics towards the UAPTs.

By mid-1928, the Soviet authorities began to
withdraw their recent concessions to the "reformed"
UAPTs:  its publications were suppressed and more
and more of its churches and clergy were deprived of
the official "registration" in the rising tide of
antireligious campaign.  By the summer of 1929, the
OGPU began mass arrests of the Autocephalist leaders
and clergy, without sparing even those who faithfully
collaborated with the regime in "purging" the church.
In November of that year the OGPU announced the "un-
covering" of a "counterrevolutionary" League for the
Liberation of the Ukraine and accused the UAPTs of
having served as a "branch" of this organization[79]--
an accusation which amounted to a death verdict for
the Autocephalous Church.

The end was not long in coming.  Terrorized remnants of the Autocephalist episcopate and clergy
were assembled at the so-called "extraordinary Sobor" in Kiev in January 1930 and "persuaded" to dis-

solve the UAPTs and to "confess" to all charges addressed against it by the authorities. The resolution of this "Sobor"--undoubtedly drafted with the participation of the OGPU[80]--sheds some light on the motives underlying the Soviet decision to liquidate the UAPTs:

> . . . .after liberating itself from political-monarchic oppression, the UAPTs was not destined to become a true Christian church, free and removed from the peculiar nationalistic, chauvinistic politics (politykanstvo). This is a fact, because the UAPTs was reborn during the political struggle and it was revived and later led by people who had suffered defeat on the open political front and who, having joined the church, intended to, and actually did, exploit it as an instrument for further struggle against the Soviet regime and hence also against the justice of the social revolution.
>     It was natural that the leading organs of the UAPTs. . . .revealed themselves through clearly non-ecclesiastical actions of a nationalist-political, anti-Soviet, counterrevolutionary nature. The same can also be said of the clergy of all ranks, beginning with Metropolitan Lypkivskyi. . . .
>     All this, accordingly, made the UAPTs a synonym of counterrevolution in the Ukraine . . . . Under the circumstances, it was completely logical that autocephaly should become a symbol of Petlurite independence, that Ukrainianization should be exploited as a means of inciting national enmity, and that conciliarism should transform itself into a demagogical means of political influence in order to reach the appointed end.[81]

What motivated the Soviet authorities in forcing "self-dissolution" of the Ukrainian Autocephalous Church? To supply possible answers to this question, one has to place this event in the broader context of Soviet religious, economic, and nationality policies around the turn of the decade.

The period extending from the early months of
1929 to March 1930 featured an attack on religion
unprecedented in its violence throughout the USSR,
an attack which coincided with the industrialization
drive and the forcible collectivization of agriculture. The 1929-1930 developments in the Ukraine revealed two major tendencies: on the one hand, all
religious groups were affected by the new legal and
administrative restrictions on religious activities
and the Godless campaign of church-closing and
"priest-baiting;" on the other hand, however, the
Ukrainian Autocephalous Church was singled out for
sweeping repressive measures and ultimate "self-
dissolution" as an allegedly "political organization"
engaged in "anti-Soviet," "counterrevolutionary"
activities. The complete suppression of the UAPTs,
after it had accepted the regime's terms in 1926
(analogous to those adopted earlier by the Living-
Renovationist Church and, in 1927, by the Patriarchate), as well as the nature of the official charges
against this church and the timing of its dissolution, point to considerations other than mere antireligious zeal on the part of the Soviet Ukrainian
authorities. Nor was it accidental that the Autocephalous Church was dragged into the affair of the
"League for the Liberation of the Ukraine," despite
the lack of any convincing evidence to support the
official charge that the former served as the "propaganda apparatus" and "military reserves" of the
"League;" by lumping the UAPTs together with the
"League," the All-Ukrainian Academy of Sciences, and
a number of other Ukrainian institutions, the regime
underlined the common object of its attacks--the
Ukrainian nationalism in its political, religious,

337

cultural, and other manifestations.

The events of 1930 dramatized the reversal of Soviet nationality policy, from maintaining a balance between the Russian and Ukrainian nationalisms to a growing reliance on Russian nationalism as an integrating, centralizing force in an increasingly totalitarian regime. The struggle for the ecclesiastical liberation of the Ukraine, the autocephalist "Away from Moscow," could no longer be reconciled with the official formula of the "leading role" of the Russian people, which was now projected from the political sphere onto all the other facets of Russo-Ukrainian relations, including the ecclesiastical-religious sphere.

To be sure, Stalin's "Dizziness from Success" warning in March 1930[82] brought about some abatement in the antireligious campaign. In the Ukraine, the well-purged remnants of the new "dissolved" UAPTs were allowed for the time being to organize themselves into a closely policed "Ukrainian Orthodox Church," but had to abandon the Autocephalist ideology, especially the principle of conciliar self-government.[83] Not a single Ukrainianized parish, however, was destined to survive the great terror. Though soon after, following the Nazi invasion of the USSR, Stalin would embark on a "religious NEP," never again would the Soviet authorities tolerate an independent Ukrainian Orthodox Church.

One is tempted to ascribe one more motive to the Soviet decision to suppress the UAPTs and, that is, the long standing Bolshevik hostility--once articulated by Lenin--to any "refined," "modernized" religion as much more dangerous obstacle to the realization of the party's blueprint for society, than a

338

"primitive," "obscurantist," or "corrupt" religion.
In his 1909 polemics against the so-called "bourgeois anticlericalism," Lenin accused the Octobrists
of combating "the extremes of clericalism and police
surveillance [over the church]"

> in order to strengthen the influence of
> religion on the masses, to substitute more
> subtle and more advance methods of stupefy-
> ing the people, in place of at least some
> methods which are too crude, too antiquated,
> and too played-out to achieve their purpose.
> A police religion will not suffice anymore
> to fool the masses--give us religion that is
> more cultured, renovated, more clever, one
> that would do its work in a self-governing
> parish--this is what capital[ism] demands
> from autocracy.[84]

Elsewhere, in his articles on Tolstoy (1908-11),
Lenin again voiced his hostility to modernized, refined religion.  A "renovated" religion of love,
purged of state domination, corruption, and obscurantism he considered a more dangerous enemy to the
Bolshevik cause than the petrified established
church:

> . . . .the advocacy of one of the most vile
> things existing in the world--religion--and
> the attempts to replace the official priests
> by priests of moral conviction, represents
> the cultiviation of the most subtle and,
> therefore, most loathsome kind of clerical-
> ism.[85]

It may well be that the modernizing orientation
of the Ukrainian Autocephalist Church--its attempts
to update the Orthodox Church, to make it relevant
to the rapidly changing society, to employ it as an
instrument of nation-building--were no less important reasons for the Soviet suppression of this
church than the regime's fear of Ukrainian national-

ism which, it believed, found its massive institutional expression in the UAPTs after suffering temporary defeat on the military and political fronts.

NOTES

1. For principal studies on the Orthodox Church
in the Ukraine since 1917, see: Vasyl Lypkivskyi,
Istoriia Ukrainskoi pravoslavoi tserkvy. Rozdil VII:
Vidrodzhennia Ukrainskoi tserkvy (Winnipeg, 1961);
Friedrich Heyer, Die Orthodoxe Kirche in der Ukraine
von 1917 bis 1945 (Koeln-Braunsfeld: R. Muller,
1953); Ivan Vlasovskyi, Narys istorii Ukrainskoi
Pravoslavnoi Tserkvy, vol. IV (New York-Bound Brook,
N.J., 1961); and this writer's doctoral dissertation,
"Soviet Church Policy in the Ukraine, 1919-1939,"
University of Chicago, 1961. For Soviet accounts of
the UAPTs, see Vasyl Ellan (Blakytnyi), Ukrainska
Avtokefalna Tserkva i ii poperednyky (Kharkiv, 1923);
and Iu. Samoilovich, Tserkov ukrainskogo sotsial-
fashizma (Moscow, 1932). Russian émigré interpretation of the UAPTs appears in K. V. Fotiev, Popy-
tki ukrainskoi tserkovnoi avtokefalii v XX veke
(Munich, 1955).

2. On the Renovationist Church, see Julius F.
Hecker, Religion under the Soviets (New York: Vanguard Press, 1927); B. Titlinov, Novaia tserkov
(Petrograd-Moscow, 1923); Sergius Troitsky, "The
Living Church," appended to William C. Emhardt,
Religion in Soviet Russia: Anarchy (Milwaukee: Morehouse, 1929); Heyer, Kirche; R. Stupperich, "Leben-
dige Kirche," Kirche in Osten, vol. 3 (1960); and
this writer's "The Renovationist Church in the Soviet Ukraine, 1922-1939," The Annals of the Ukrainian Academy of Arts and Sciences in the U.S., No.
1-2 (New York 1961), pp. 41-74. Of special interest
are A. Levitin and V. Shavrov, "Ocherki po istorii
russkoi tserkovnoi smuty," in Novyi zhurnal, Nos.
85-88 (New York, 1966-67); and A. Krasnov, "Zakat
obhovlenchestva," Grani, No. 86 (1972), pp. 93-116;
and Nos. 87-88(1973), pp. 235-73. For a recent Soviet treatment of the problem, see A. A. Shishkin,
Sushchnost i kriticheskaia otsenka "obnovlenchesko-
go" raskola russkoi provoslavnoi tserkvy.

3. The abbreviation stands for Ukrainska Avtokefalna Pravoslavna Tserkva.

4. See Donald Eugene Smith, <u>Religion and Political Development</u> (Boston: Little, Brown, 1970).

5. See John S. Reshetar, Jr., <u>The Ukrainian Revolution, 1917-1920</u> (Princeton: Princeton University Press, 1952).

6. Most of them attended theological seminaries, where they participated in secret Ukrainian circles.

7. The maximum offered by the Moscow Patriarchate, in response to Ukrainian demands, was a limited autonomy approved by Patriarch Tikhon in September 1918. For details, see Dmytro Doroshenko, <u>Istoriia Ukrainy 1917-1923 rr</u>. 2 (Uzhhorod, 1932): 328-30.

8. The Law on the Supreme Authority in the Ukrainian Autocephalous Orthodox Church of January 1, 1919.

9. The Soviet Ukrainian Decree on the Separation of the Church from the State and the School from the Church (adopted on January 22, 1919) significantly omitted the provision of the Russian Decree denying religious associations the rights of a juridical person (added only in 1921). See Iv. Sukhopliuev, <u>Vidokremiennia tserkvy vid derzhavy. Zbirnyk zakonopolozhen. . . .</u>(Kharkiv, 1930). Ukrainian Autocephalists were the first ecclesiastical organization to recognize this Decree in the Ukraine.

10. "Vid Vseukrainskoi Provoslavnoi Tserkovnoi Rady do udrainskoho pravoslavnoho hromadianstva. Lyst pershyi" (May 5, 1920), reproduced in <u>Tserkva i zhyttia</u>, No. 1 (1927), pp. 120-23.

11. See Ivan Shram, "Iak tvorylas Ukrainska Avtokefalna Tserkva," <u>Na varti</u> (Volodymyr Volynskyi), Nos. 7-8 (May 1925), pp. 2-5.

12. During the summer and early fall of 1921, the All-Ukrainian <u>Rada</u> desperately searched for sympathetic bishops to consecrate two of its candidates for episcopal offices in the UAPTs. Hopes that the newly autocephalous Georgian Orthodox Church would assist the UAPTs in this respect, could not be realized due to Soviet-Georgian hostilities.

13. See Volodymry Chekhivskyi, <u>Za Tserkvu, Khrys-</u>

tovu hromadu, proty tsarstva tmy (Kharkiv, 1922).

14. For description of the ceremony by a participant, see V. Chekhivskyi, "Osnovy vyzvolennia Ukrainskoi Avtokefalnoi Pravoslavnoi Tserky," Tserkva i zhyttia, Nos. 2-3 (1927), p. 189.

15. See Vlasovskyi, Narys, pp. 359-62.

16. In 1925, Archbishop Iosif (Krechetovich) of the same church, spoke of three million Autocephalists in Proiskhozhdenie i sushchnost samosviatstva lipkovtsev (Kharkiv, 1925), cited in A. Richynskyi, Problemy ukrainskoi relihiinoi svidomosty (Volodymyr Volynskyi, 1933), p. 6. Former secretary of the Renovationist Synod in the Ukraine, Archbishop Serafim (Ladde)estimated in 1929 the Autocephalist following at some six million in "Die Lage der Orthodoxen Kirche in der Ukraine," Eiche 10 [1931]:11-40.

17. In December 1923, Archbishop Teodorovych was sent by the All-Ukrainian Rada to assume leadership of a combined American-Canadian diocese of the Ukrainian Orthodox Church.

18. See Zhivaia Tserkov, No. 3, (Moscow, 1922), pp. 19-20; Golos Pravoslavnoi Ukrainy, No. 4 (Kharkiv, 1925), p. 4; Heyer, Kirche, p. 95; and Lypkivskyi, Istoriia, pp. 120-124.

19. See Sukhopliuiev, Ukrainski avtokefalisty, pp. 47-56; Lypkivskyi, Istoriia, pp. 124-137; Kommunist (Kharkiv), October 24, 1925; and V. Potiienko, "Tserkovna sprava na Ukraini," Knipro, August 1, 1925, p. 1.

20.Lypkivskyi, Istoriia, pp. 144-166; Vlasovskyi, Narys, pp. 198-207.

21. Izvestiia, November 22, 1929; Proletarska pravda (Kiev), December 22, 1929.

22. See Dmytro Ihnatiuk, Ukrainska avtokefalna tserkva i Soiuz Vyzvolennia Ukrainy (Kharkiv-Kiev, 1930), pp. 23-31.

23. For details, see this writer's "Soviet Church Policy in the Ukraine," pp. 288-295; Lypkivskyi, Istoriia, 173-175; Samoilovich, Tserkov, p. 123; Dnipro, January 15, 1934.

24. See this writer's "Radianska tserkovna po lityka i pravoslavna tserkva v Ukraini v roky 1929-39," in Samostiina Ukraina (Chicago, 1965-66).

25. Ibid.

26. Cited in Tserkva i zhyttia, No. 1, (1927), p. 120.

27. Ibid., p. 122.

28. Lypkivskyi, Istoriia, pp. 36-37.

29. Ibid., pp. 39-40; Chekhivskyi, Za Tserkvu.

30. Vlasovskyi, Narys, pp. 117-118.

31. Vseukrainska Pravoslavna Tserkovna Rada, Diiannia Vseukrainskoho Pravoslavnoho Tserkovnoho Soboru v m. Kyievi 14-30 zhovtnia n. s. 1921 r., 2nd ed. (Frankfurt a. M., 1946), pp. 3-4.

32. Ibid.

33. Ibid., p. 7.

34. Ibid., p. 14.

35. Ibid., p. 14-15.

36. Ibid., p. 15.

37. Ibid., p. 10.

38. Ibid., pp. 4-7. Cf. [Vseukrainska Pravoslavna Rada], Pidvalyny Ukrainskoi Pravoslavnoi Tserdvy, 2nd ed. (Tarniv, 1922), pp. 2-5.

39. Vseukrainska Pravoslavna Tserkovna Rada, Diiannia, pp. 7-12, 30-31.

40. Ibid., pp. 12-27.

41. Ibid., p. 8.

42. Sobor's resolution on the church's attitude towards the Soviet regime, reproduced in Michel d'-Herbigny, S.J., "Documents inedits. 'L'Eglise Orthodoxe Panukrainienne' crée en 1921 à Kiev," Orientalia christiana 1 (June 1923):119.

43. Vseukrainska Pravoslavna Tserkovna Rada, Diiannia, p. 9.

44. Interview with the late Metropolitan Ioann Teodorovych, Philadelphia, August 1958. Cf. Archpriest Viktor Solovii, "Rozlam V Ukrainskii Avtokefanii Tserkvi ta sproby ioho likvidatsii" in Na shliakhu do iedynoi UAPTs (Sydney-Melbourne, 1957), p. 17.

45. Lypkivskyi, Istoriia, pp. 48-52.

46. See Tserkva i zhyttia, Nos. 2-3 (1927), pp. 139-148.

47. These anxieties among some members of the UAPTs were exploited by the Soviet authorities which actively encouraged them during 1923-26 to secede from the UAPTs.

48. Lypkivskyi, Istoriia, p. 48.

49. The most comprehensive treatment of the autocephalist ideology appears in an article by Archbishop K. Krotevych, "Do ideolohii UAPTS," Tserkva i zhyttia, No. 1 (1928), pp. 14-28. Also important in this respect are Chekhivskyi, Za Tserkva; Lypkivskyi, Istoriia; as well as a series of articles by the Autocephalist bishops M. Pyvovariv, K. Maliushkevych, and M. Karabinevych which appeared in Tserkva i zhyttia during 1927-28.

50. Krotevych, "Do ideolohii," lists also a sixth principle, "the union of churches," which seems to reflect the UAPTs' eagerness to overcome its canonical isolation.

51. Archbishop M. Pyvovariv, "Tserkva v derzhavi i ikh vidokremlennia," Tserkva i zhyttia, No. 1 (1928), p. 25.

52. Ibid., p. 31.

53. "Pryliudna zaiava zibrannia 22-29 zhovtnia 1922 r. Vseukrainskoi Pravoslavnoi Tserkovnoi Rady Ukrainskoi Pravoslavnoi Avtokefalnoi Tserkvy," Pontificio Instituto Orientale Rome. (mimeographed, n.p., n.d.). According to Lypkivski, Istoriia, p. 128, this declaration--"written far too much in the spirit of 'class struggle' and 'dictatorship of the proletariat'"--was adopted in "order to rebut various

charges of counterrevolutionary activity, pro-Pet-
liura orientation, etc., which were directed [by the
regime] against the UAPTs." The adoption and announcement of this document "probably stopped further
arrests" of the Autocephalist leaders.

54. The Declaration was reportedly drafted by
Volodymyr Chekhivskyi, the principal lay ideologist
of the UAPTs, one of the former leaders of the
Ukrainian Social Democratic Party. Among the Autocephalist leaders were also such former Socialists
as Archbishops Oleksander Iareshchenko and Ivan Pavlovskyi, and layman Mykhailo Moroz who headed the
All-Ukrainian Rada from 1919 to 1924.

55. "Pryliudna zaiava," p. 5.

56. Cf. V. Potiienko, "Vidnovlennia ierarkhii
Ukrainskoi Avtokefalnoi Pravoslavnoi Tserkvy. Zapy-
sana doppvid na Zborkh Sv. Andriivskoho Ukrainskoho
Bratstva v Sosnovytsiakh, 1 sichnia 1944 r."

57. See Zhurnal moskovskoi patriarkhii, March,
1944, pp. 6-8.

58. See, e.g., "Iz 'Molitovnika' Arkhiep. Olek-
siia, Kievlianin, December 23, 1917. Cf. Lypkivskyi,
Istoriia, pp. 54-55.

59. Lypkivskyi, ibid., pp. 90-91. A leading
Ukrainian Communist V. Ellan (Blakytnyi), editor of
the official government daily Visti (Kharkiv), admitted in early 1922 that "we do not control the
spontaneous Ukrainianization, which is taking the
form of Autocephaly even in the workers' districts."
No. 77 (1922); cited in Ukrainskyi pravoslavnyi kal-
endar na 1958 rik [South Bound Brook, N.J., 1958],
p. 127.

60. Pidvalyny Ukrainskoi Pravoslavnoi Tserkvy,
pp. 8-10.

61. Ibid., p. 11.

62. Ibid., pp. 11-12.

63. Krotevych, "Do ideolohii," p. 18.

64. Lypkivskyi, Istoriia, pp. 101-102.

65. Ibid., pp. 107-117.

66. Pyvovariv, "Tserkva v derzhari," p. 31.

67. Krotevych, "Do ideolohii," p. 22.

68. An interesting illustration of this tendency can be found in Metropolitan Lypkivskyi's use of such terms as "popular-conciliar consecration" (of bishops), "popular hierarchy," "popular metropolitan," "popular church," "popular grace" (narodnia blahodat), or even "new Ukrainian grace." See Istoriia, pp. 44-45, 50, 52-53.

69. Note, for example, a resolution adopted in September 1922 by a conference of delegates to an abortive Ukrainian Orthodox Sobor in Kiev convoked by the Patriarchal Church but banned at the last moment by the Soviet authorities; the conference resolved in favor of an autocephaly, Ukrainianization, and conciliarism for the Orthodox Church in the Ukraine but the predominantly Russian episcopate of the Ukrainian dioceses refused to take any decisive action on these demands. Later, a group of Ukrainian bishops led by Feofil Buldovskyi of Lubny seceded in 1925 from the Russian Church and proclaimed themsleves as an autocephalous "Sobor of Bishops of the entire Ukraine" (see Ukrainskyi Pravoslavnyi Blahovisnyk [Kharkiv], no. 1 (1926), p. 9). The Renovationist Church in the Ukraine, though it remained largely Russian in leadership and orientation, also formally adopted autocephaly at its Kharkiv Sobor in May 1925 (see this writer's "The Renovationist Church in the Soviet Ukraine," pp. 59-67).

70. For the best available account of the wartime UAPTs, see Vlasovskyi, Narys, Vol. 4, Part 2, pp. 178-271.

71. On the rationale of the early Soviet policy with respect to the UAPTs, see an article in a March 1921 issue of the Kharkiv government daily, Visti, by Vasyl Ellan-Blakytnyi, "Tserkva chy shchos inshe?" reproduced in V. Ellan-Blakytnui, Tvory (Kiev, 1958), vol. 2, esp. p. 252.

72. Borot'bisty, the left wing of the Ukrainian Social Revolutionary Party, were forced to "dissolve themselves" in March 1920, with a number of them joining the Communist Party (Bolsheviks) of the Ukraine, among them Ellan-Blakytnyi, O. Shumskyi, and H. Hrynko who were offered important posts in the

346

Ukrainian Party-State apparatus during the "Ukrainianization" stage of the Soviet nationality policy in
the republic. Ukapisty (Ukrainian Communist Party,
formerly the left wing of the Ukrainian Social Democratic Party) continued in existence until their
"self-dissolution" in 1925, with a number of Ukapisty
joining the CP(b)U.

73. Lypkivskyi, Istoriia, p. 124.

74. Ukrainian national colors, repudiated by the
Soviet regime.

75. "Zle pryladzhena mashkara," reproduced in
Ellan-Blakytnyi, Tvory, pp. 271-272.

76. See this writer's "Soviet Church Policy in
the Ukraine," pp. 253-269.

77. Cf. Fletcher, Study, chapter 1.

78. Including the publication of a journal
Tserkva i zhyttia, a newsletter Tserkovni visti, and
a few books.

79. Izvestiia, November 22, 1929. This was a
completely unsubstantiated charge, according to
Lypkivskyi, Istoriia, p. 169.

80. Ibid., pp. 169-171.

81. Ihnatiuk, Ukrainska tserkva, pp. 27-31.

82. Pravda, March 15, 1930.

83. See Lypkivskyi, Istoriia, pp. 173-175;
Samoilovich, Tserkov, p. 123; and this writer's
"Radianska tserkovna polityka."

84. "The Classes and Parties--Their Attitudes
towards Religion," cited in V.I. Lenin, Religion
(New York: International Publishers, 1933), p. 25.

85. Cited ibid., pp. 37-38.

# Chapter 10
## MODERNIZATION AND LATIN RITE CATHOLICS IN THE SOVIET UNION

### V. Stanley Vardys

Difficulties of researching the condition of Roman Catholicism in the Soviet Union require a more precise definition of the scope of the current inquiry. Differences in the use of the concept of modernization make it necessary briefly to discuss the Soviet interpretation of its theory and practice. Therefore the consideration of the topic of modernization and the Catholic Church in the Soviet Union must be preceded by an explanation of the terms.

## LATIN RITE CATHOLICS IN THE SOVIET UNION

Latin rite Catholics constitute one of the smaller religious groups of the Soviet Union. They are scattered all the way from the Baltic sea in the West to the sea of Okhotsk in the East. In terms of ethnic background, the Latin rite church is a non-Russian and largely non-Slavic, composed mainly of the Lithuanians, Latvians, Poles, Belorussians, Ukrainians, Germans, and Hungarians. Some Armenians, Georgians, and diaspora Slovaks and Czechs also may be added to the list.

To a certain extent, the Catholics of the Soviet Union form a diaspora church, found in Leningrad and Moscow where the parishioners are mostly Lithuanians,

Poles and Latvians, and also in Central Asia where
many of the believers are of German background. Father Walter Ciszek, the American Jesuit who returned
from the Soviet Union after years of prison and pastoral work, reported the existence of a Catholic parish in Nikolayevka (Krasnoyarsk).[1] There it was composed largely of Lithuanian deportees. In 1976, news
reached the West through private channels that Ciszek's old church was legally reopened and is serviced
by a Lithuanian priest. Another Catholic church recently has been permitted in Odessa. A chapel was
authorized in Kiev.

The bulk of Latin rite Catholics in the Soviet
Union compactly inhabit the Lithuanian republic where
they do not constitute a diaspora but rather a majority of population. An East German source has estimated that 75 percent of Lithuania's inhabitants--or
two and a quarter million--in 1969 belonged to the
Catholic Church.[2] The second largest group is found
in Latvia, especially its Eastern part, the province
of Latgalia (Latgale) with an estimated 269,000 believers.[3] Islands of Roman Catholics further exist
in Belorussia and the Ukraine.[4] The total number of
Latin rite Catholics in the Soviet Union probably is
not larger than three and a half million.[5] Soviet
sources list six Catholic "religious centers" in the
country. These centers are not specified, and only
partly overlap with the total number of Dioceses.[6]
The two Latvian dioceses of Riga and Liepaja are administered as one and the six Lithuanian dioceses
currently are managed as four administrative units.
The administrator of Belorussia and Ukraine resides
in Poland. Thus, to study Latin rite Catholicism in
the Soviet system largely means a study of the Lith-

349

uanian and Latvian churches. Information of Latvian
Catholic developments, however, is mercilessly defi-
cient, and thus of necessity, and almost exclusively,
emphasis must be placed on the Catholics in Lithuania.
Largely through samizdat publications that include
the Chronicle of the Catholic Church of Lithuania[7] we
have a fair picture of changing church situation in
this former stronghold of East European Catholicism.

## MODERNIZATION IN SOVIET THEORY AND PRACTICE

After thus determining the topical scope of the
inquiry, it is necessary to explain further that in
this essay I will endeavor to study, first, the influence of modernization on particularly the Lithuanian Catholic Church and, second, the church's response to modernizing changes. The term of "modernization" of course denotes a complex social change
triggered off by industrialization and largely determined by its effects.[8] Despite the shortcomings of
this concept that render it useless when the theory
of modernization is employed as a substitute for
Marx's historical materialism, the concept of modernization helps in a comparative study of social change,
and more specifically, aids in the explanation of the
linkages between industrial development and societal
institutions, specifically, the impact this change
has on these institutions, including religion.
Strictly speaking, then, a study of the effects of
modernization on Catholicism in the Soviet Union can
provide information on the results that modernization
generally produces on Catholic churches in non-communist societies. The inquiry, furthermore, should
help in the discussion of such crucially important
questions as whether the admitted Communist hostility

350

to Catholicism or religion in general is characteristic only to a particular stage of advancing industrialization or endemic to the communist system itself. At the same time an analysis of responses by
the church should aid in the appraisal of the viability of continued church survival in such society.

The comparison of the impact of modernization on
religion in communist and non-communist societies unfortunately is limited by the heavy ideological-po-
litical component of the practice of Soviet modernization. In the Soviet Union, modernization is so
completely directed by the Communist Party that the
effects of industrialization are not only controlled
but even delayed, obstructed, or reversed by political means and for political purposes. Thus, for example, the Soviet economic mechanism can not operate
freely and various efforts made by economists to lib-
erate this process from the bureaucratic political
shackles were in the past either defeated or frustrated, as in 1965. The dictatorship of the political over the economic element makes it frequently
difficult to distinguish whether the position and the
role of religion in the Soviet Union has been affected by the growth of factories, rise of the cities,
and the working class--in other words, the forces of
modernization--or by the political decrees issued by
the absolute and arbitrary communist rulers. Similarly, the analysis of continued church viability in
communist society is impaired by the fact that the
Communist Party denies the use of important institutions of modernization (basically, the media of
communications) to the churches while on the other
hand using this technology against them. Thus, the
regime does its best to prevent, by legal and admin-

istrative means, the churches from modernizing themselves, that is, from revising and improving their
institutions to make them adequate to the needs of
technological urban society.  The Kremlin expects,
as a result, that the churches will wither away as
no longer functional and needed.

In Soviet literature, usually, "modernization"
refers to these latter church efforts of adaptation
and self renewal.  As the well known Soviet student
of Catholicism L. N. Velikovich writes, modernization is related to "the aspirations of the churchmen
newly to win over those whom the church had lost for
various reasons."[9]  The chief Lithuanian writer on
Catholicism Jonas Aničas acknowledges the modernization efforts of the Lithuanian church and identifies
them as, first, "adaptation to the new for the church
socio-political conditions" and second, "renewal of
her internal life."[10]  Western students of religion
stress the latter aspect of modernization.  According to Barbara Wolfe Jancar, "the Lithuanian Catholic hierarchy has been highly successful in its efforts to modernize; hence the frustration of its
priests and the continuing strength of Catholicism
in Lithuania.[11]  This author suggests, in effect,
that the recently demonstrated resurgence of Lithuanian Catholicism, that is, Lithuanian Catholic dissent, is a result of the church's modernization.  Her
view, however, is contradicted by Aničas who maintains that "modernization is a stick with two ends;
and both beat the church itself."[12]  These are important theses and this paper will concentrate on
their examination.

## SOCIAL CHANGE AND THE CHURCH IN
## HISTORICAL PERSPECTIVE

We may begin by tracing the church's radical
change in just little over a generation and by ap-
praising its once dominant position in Lithuanian society.  In the 1920s and 1930s the church served an
essentially rural population and as the Lithuanian
ethnicity itself, was deeply rooted in the life of
the village.  Its rural character was demonstrated,
among others, by the phenomenon of pastor-farmer that
prevailed in Lithuanian rural areas.  The church was
not a large landowner--parishes and monasteries
tilled less than one tenth of one percent of all
farmland--however, its ownership was conspicuous and
already in the 1930s, after about two decades of
slow-paced urban growth, the rising Catholic intelligentsia perceived it as largely producing for the
church more difficulties than benefits.  Stormy discussions that were triggered by suggestions that the
church distribute its lands to the poor or use them
for social welfare purposes did not produce volun-
tary disposal of church farms but sharpened the social consciousness of church leaders.  Above all, it
was symptomatic of the growing awareness of the necessity to modernize.  The otherwise conservative
hierarchy was nudged in the direction of reform by
Bishop Kazimieras Paltarokas, a professor sociology,
who after World War II had to carry the burden of
leadership of the decapitated and prostrated church.
Paltarokas had reformist allies among the young clergy and lay intelligentsia who worked within the
structure of Catholic Action movement.  This intelligentsia, educated under the jealous guardianship of
the bishops in Western Europe and in Lithuania it-

self, nevertheless allied itself with the young, already Lithuanian trained clergy and frequently came
forth not only as an associate of these clergymen but
also as their leader. The strength of this lay strata of church membership and its unwritten alliance
with the clergy considerably aided the church's survival under Soviet conditions.

Thus, when total secularization was imposed under Soviet auspices in the summer of 1940, it did not
meet with head-on opposition from either the hierarchy or the laity.[14]  In response to the communist
plans of nationalizing all church lands with the exception of six acres (3 ha.) that included the area
of church yards (that in Lithuania usually were rather large), the Archbishop of Kaunas, the then head of
the Lithuanian church province, did not protest but
politely requested that the reform leave the parishes
about 18 acres with an additional 7-8 acres for
church servants. The remaining land, he said, should
be used for social welfare purpose.[15]  Similarly,
Bishop Brizgys, his Auxiliary, asked for an exemption
for the convents on grounds that their land had been
not only acquired but also worked by the sweat of the
sisters themselves who supported many socially useful activities.[16]  On the other hand, the Soviet se-
verance of Lithuania's concordat with the Vatican
that had guaranteed to the church certain educational
rights and financial support was resented much deeper.
The bishops even refused to recognize the unilateral
Soviet rejection of provisions concerning education.
Yet the church rather quickly adjusted to the banish-
ment of religion teaching from schools by organizing
after-school instruction in churches.[17]  On the whole,
it may be said, secularization of the church's posi-

tion in society that now produced civil marriage and divorce, cut religion teaching in schools, caused the loss of church farms and of financial aid from the state did not provoke, though deeply angered, the Catholics. Some aspects of secularization, for example, civil marriage, even enjoyed support from segments of the reform-oriented young Catholic intelligentsia. The hierarchy though without illusions about Soviet objectives similarly did not go into active opposition as long as the Kremlin seemed to be satisfied with mere secularization. In the spring of 1941, however, Communist authorities struck out on a radical and unmistakenly hostile course and consequently met not only with criticism but also a fiery denunciation by the bishops.[18]

The story, in a way, was repeated in 1944-46, after Lithuania was reconquered by the Red Army. At first, in the wake of the victorious outcome of the war, the church's situation, despite some conflicts with the government, was even considered improved. Bishop Teofilius Matulionis, a prisoner of the Soviets in the twenties and the thirties and then exchanged by Lithuania's government for some native Lithuanian communists, in 1946 wrote to Mecys Gedvilas, the Chairman of the Council of Commissars of the Lithuanian SSR, that "The Catholic church of Lithuania has to acknowledge that the attitude and be behavior of Soviet government toward the church in 1944-45 is significantly different from 1940-41; it is better."[19] Matulionis therefore considered it possible frankly to consider some outstanding disagreements between the government and the church because in his view "the contact that was begun by Chairman Gedvila opens up wide opportunities" for their elimination. However, at the time the bishop wrote the commissar, the authorities already had decided on a different policy. They now applied pressure to the church's hierarchy at the top and middle levels demanding that the church reorganize itself in conformity to the Soviet law on religious associations. The hierarchy resisted, and as a result, Lithuania's bishops, with the exception of Paltarokas, were arrested, imprisoned, and banished. One of them, Bishop Borisevičius, was executed. Bishop Matulionis soon found himself in the prison of Vladimir and in the camps of Mordovia.

Stalin, needless to say, broke the church's organization but succeeded merely in limiting the church's role in society, not in destroying the church's internal solidarity. Loyalty to Catholic principles and to Rome remained unimpaired. Thus, while after the Twentieth Party Congress the church recovered to the degree that the parish pastor in the provinces would be seated together with the party secretary on public occasions, nevertheless the application of legal strictures in the atmosphere of fear and discrimination, coupled with intensified atheist activities, effectively reduced the church's social and moral influence. These government measures, furthermore, lessened the church's ability to cope with the rapidly proceeding industrialization. Lithuania's industrialization picked up after Stalin's death. Annually, about 1 percent of the total pupulation moved from collective farms to the cities. Yet while the cities grew and new towns were built, many city churches were closed down. In Vilnius, the capital, the authorities shut down twenty-three churches; in Kaunas, the second largest city of

300,000, the communists took over twelve churches.[20]
Establishment of new parishes was forbidden and the
increase in the number of city pastors not allowed.
This left very large masses, especially the youth,
with reduced opportunities for receiving any religious education or even for church attendance.

The stronghold of communist society is the city.
It is molded in the "international" way to blunt non-
Russian ethnicity and to disarm nationalism.  It is
jealously designed and built as an exclusive preserve
of communist ideological domination.  It is expected
to function as the heart of communist millenium.  The
Soviets therefore concentrated their efforts on push-
ing the church out of the expanding urban areas, an
effort which has not completely succeeded but which
left large urban segments virtually outside the per-
imeter of possible church service.

Some indices of social disorganization caused
largely by industrial urbanization further suggest
the decline of the moral influence of the church.
Thus, for example, the drop in Lithuania's birth rate
though caused by economic and social factors must be
at least partially attributed to the weakened church
influence.  It has been the church that in the past
had successfully sustained the idea of large families.  The prewar birth rate of 22.4 declined to 19.7
in 1963 and to 17 in 1972, giving the republic a net
growth rate of 7.9 in 1972 instead of 8.8 in 1939
and steadily dropping further.[21]  Divorce, rarely
known in independent Lithuania not only because it
was illegal but also because it was and still is
strongly opposed by the church, is quickly increasing.
In 1950, the rate of divorce (per 1,000 of the population) was a negligable 0.2.  It rose after the law

357

made it easier to qualify for separation, and in 1960 the rate jumped to 0.9. In 1973, it rose to 2.3 and continues to climb. This rate actually may be still higher because apparently not all court granted divorces are registered by proper authorities.[22] Divorces occur mostly in the cities where the church's moral influence is least felt. In 1972, the village divorce rate was still 0.9 (from 0.0 in 1950 and 0.3 in 1960) while in the cities it ran up to 3.5. The largest and religiously as well as ethnically most diverse city has the largest rate[23] (Vilnius: 3.8 in 1970). One fourth of family breakups are caused by an inordinate consumption of alcohol that represents one of the greatest social problems in the republic. An average alcohol consumption per capita is 10 liters of vodka (2.6 gal.), 14 liters wine (3.7 gal.), 30 liters (8 gal.) of beer and, as The Chronicle of the Catholic Church of Lithuania reports, "rivers of moonshine."[24] On November 28, 1973, second secretary of the Lithuanian Communist Party V. Kharazov blamed alcoholism, together with payoffs, favoritism, and falsified statistics for obstructing economic production.[25]

The church, furthermore, lost a percentage of practicing Catholics, especially in the cities which in 1973 constituted fifty-four percent of the republic's population. According to Soviet statistics, this loss is substantial. Nauka i religiia has reported that between 1958 and 1964, percentage of baptisms declined from 81 to 58 percent, percentage of church marriages from 79 to 38, with the largest alienation from the church occuring in large cities like Kaunas where in 1965, only 13 percent of all marriages were said to be contracted in church cere-

mony.[26]  These Soviet figures, to present a balanced
picture, must be offset by the large numbers of believers listed by the Chronicle of the Catholic
Church of Lithuania who receive the sacrament of con-
firmation or the masses of children who participate
in the first communion.  Furthermore, in Lithuania it
still happens that a member of komsomol marries in
church [27] or that a party member loses membership for
taking part in a religious funeral of one's own father or for allowing the god parents to baptize a
newly born party member's baby.[28]  In a testimony to
the International Sakharov Committee in Copenhagen
on October 17-19, 1975, former artistic director of
Kaunas drama theater, Jonas Jurasas, reported that a
secretary of the Central Committee of the Lithuanian
Communist Party told him that in the party's estimate, 71 percent of Lithuanian youth are church com-
municants ("participants in religious cults," as the
secretary put it).[29]  Secretary for propaganda A.
Barkauskas, speaking at the eighteenth conference of
the Lithuanian Komsomol in 1974, spoke about rising
"religious fanaticism," as he called it, and complained of how painful it was for him to say that not
only many average young people preferred church wed-
dings but also "a considerable part of Communist
youth and Communist party members."[30]  While atheist
beliefs have doubtlessly spread and are institutionalized in social behavior, it is not so much the hostility of professional propagandists as the attitudes
of the environment that characterize the treatment of
the church in uninhibited conditions of privacy and
in the domain of the inofficial political culture of
Lithuanian society.  Largely, it is not a hostile but
tolerant, friendly, and even solicitious attitude,

motivated possibly by compassion, feelings of guilt, nationalism, latent democratic beliefs, or personal ties. This change toward inofficial tolerance has been recently depicted in a short story published in the leading literary journal Pergale (Victory).[31] The author wrote about a young man who could not find his place in life, was finally thrown out of a theo- logical seminary, and found himself in the company of other artistically inclined restless "misfits." These included actors, former university teachers, artists, and designers. They establish a company for painting political commercials but quarrel and fall asunder. The hero of the story finds work on a restoration of a parish church. There, his boss is an atheist, a freethinker who before the war when Lithuania was independent tried to dynamite the very church building. The man was caught and served time. Now this same man, considerably older and more ex- perienced as a result of subsequent imprisonment by the communist regime, is helping to repair the church building he once attempted to destroy. "Romantic, isn't it?" asks J. Maciukvicius, the author of the story. Actually, as some recent cases show, the scenario is carved out of real life experience. This is the atmosphere in which one has to place the Lith- uanian youth unrest of 1972 that swept especially the central and southern part of Lithuania and culminated in a violent march through the streets of Kaunas. These thousands of young students and workers sought to honor Romas Kalanta, a 19-year-old member of the communist youth organization who self immolated for Lithuania's freedom in front of Mr. Jurasas' theater on May 14, 1972.[32]

It is nevertheless clear that the church has

sustained losses in membership and participation. Comparison of Catholic figures that the Vatican has given in its Annuario Pontificio annuals at the end of World War II and that the East German Catholics have published in 1969 allows an educated guess that the Lithuanian church has lost a membership it would have added in 25 years time. In other words, the church's growth has been stunted; it lost a generation of growth.

The Soviet side explains that this decline is part of a world wide phenomenon associated with the development of industrialized society that requires ideology and style of life different from the religious. A "progressive" Lithuanian priest is quoted as saying that for the diminished Lithuanian Catholic participation, "one can put the blame on the age of technology, the neckbreaking speed of life and the entirely different interests of the younger generation. Nowdays young people are much more concerned about concrete and material things, they have neither the wish nor the time for religious matters. Several years ago, together with a group of priests, I visited Hungary, Czechoslovakia, and stayed for some time in Italy. There I found similar problems. . . ."[33] In our terminology, this appraisal favors the thesis that modernization makes religion less needed and eventually therefore dysfunctional and obsolete. It also implies that in Lithuania, as in the rest of Europe, the Catholic church has not been able to adapt itself to this social change and integrate with the modern life style. Are the losses of the Lithuanian Church really attributable to the obsolescence of its institutions, irrelevance of its dogma and inadequace of its behavior?

## THE SECOND VATICAN COUNCIL AND THE CHURCH
## IN LITHUANIA

The beginnings of modernization in the Roman
Catholic Church are usually found in the idea of ag-
giornamento proclaimed by Pope John XXIII and concretely formulated in the decisions of the Second
Vatican Council. It may be said, however, that Jonas
Aničas, the already mentioned Lithuanian propagandist
who in January of 1976 was appointed chief of the
division that supervises school and culture in the
secretariat of the Central Committee of the Lithuanian Communist Party, is partially correct in asserting that the decisions of the Second Vatican
Council for the modernization of the entire Catholic
Church were already "in common practice" by the Lithuanian clergy.[34] The Lithuanian church did not stand
still during the period of its greatest freedom,
namely, in independent Lithuania. It grudgingly accepted secularization at a later time under Soviet
auspices, but it also found ways to live with it and
furthermore did not lose heart under the Stalinist
suppression.

Adaptation to new conditions indeed began before
the Second Vatican Council and belong to 1940-41 and
again the era of early destalinization. The council's decrees, however, constitute only a phase in
the Lithuanian church's self-renewal efforts and have
been neither fully implemented nor fully accepted.
Modernization of church's outlook was initiated mainly in three areas, the socio-political, the pastoral-
liturgical, and the communications with the believers. After the stormy Stalinist years, churchmen reconciled themselves to the existence of new social
institutions they had opposed and largely stopped

criticizing them. Instead of rejecting collective
farming as an "invention of the devil" they now coun-
seled the parishioners conscienciously to fulfill
their obligations. Similarly, while Bishop Teofilius Matulionis in 1945 publicly opposed Catholic youth
membership in communist youth organizations as contrary to church law,[35] after the Twentieth Party
Congress this opposition disappeared. Membership in
komsomol or in the Communist Party itself has not
been condemned by the dissenting Chronicle of the
Catholic Church of Lithuania either. The Chronicle
finds "good" people even in the party and worries
about their attitudes and behavior rather than institutional enrollment. It has never denounced anyone just because of party membership.

Second, the church liberalized its attitude
toward some heretofore strictly enforced religious
practices. It had, it should be noted, the Vatican's
authorization for changes. These included, for example, the laws of fasting; the keeping of the viati-
cum only in church and having it handled only by the
priests and deacons; the number of masses that could
be said daily; saying them not only in the morning
but also the evening so that working people could
attend; celebrating church feasts on state holidays;
avoiding conflict between church services and government sponsored activities. Thus, for example, in
1963, Tarybinis Mokytojas, the newspaper of the Lithuanian teaching profession, reported how Rev. Jonas
Kazokas, the pastor of a parish in Rikantai, in the
vicinity of Vilnius, explained his coexistence with
local atheist activists. Antireligious propaganda,
lectures, and other activities did not interfere
with church services, he said when asked by the news-

363

paper correspondent, because "when there is an anti-religious concert or meeting at the school or club, I change the time of the masses. From their gathering they [the people] go directly to church. . . ."[36]

Lithuanian priests, furthermore, worry very much about the condition of church buildings. Anicas has reported that of the 223 questions in a question-naire mailed out by the administrator of the Vil-nius archdiocese on the status of the kiocese, 128 concerned the condition of church buildings, litur-gical vestments, and liturgical vessels.[37] After Stalin's death, many pastors rushed to the repair and remodeling of their churches. Since then, even the state has helped with redecoration of some that had been declared national architectural monuments. Gen-erally, however, the authorities frowned upon the idea and successful repair work frequently indicated the pastor's ingenuity and close relations with many economic enterprises within the parish and outside of it. Without these contacts there would be no "defi-cit" materials needed for work. Many churches were equipped with electrical lights and even with micro-phones and loudspeakers. Similarly, the pastors have endeavored to keep the churches aesthetically attractive and have sought to enliven religious cere-monies with processions—so traditional in Lithuania and Latvia—in which young people and children would participate in national costumes. Finally, church-men sought closeness to the population and their needs. Generally, Lithuanian priests in the twen-tieth century were overwhelmingly sons of farmers, large and small, and already in 1940, at the first meeting of Lithuanian bishops that took place two weeks after Lithuania's occupation by the Red Army

the hierarchy claimed no less affinity with the working people than the pro-communist forces on grounds
that the Lithuanian clergy were of "the people's"
origins.[38]  This has remained true until the most recent years.  Thus, Catholic pastors easily identified
with popular attitudes and concerns.  This led the
clergymen to adopt the role of guardian of national
traditions--many of which were of religious character
anyway--and of the survival of the nation itself.
This identification is different from the officially
detested bourgeois nationalism in that the Lithuanian clergy show no active interest in restoring the
bourgeois social system.  At the same time, however,
the church clearly feels responsible for the future
of Lithuanian culture and ethnicity.  Dissident Catholic evaluation of the current condition is especially pessimistic, and The Chronicle of the Catholic
Church of Lithuania calls for determined resistance
to cultural assimilation by Russian Communists.  "Re-
gretfully," the journal's editors write, "the healthy
elements [of the Lithuanian nation] are being overwhelmed by the new winds; there pales the feeling of
national distinctiveness and moral strength, the
movement quickens toward the acceptance of common
form without distinct content.  Moscow's pliers seek
to squeeze out the Lithuanian's spirit, to let die
the Lithuanian thought. . . .  Will we surrender?
Will we allow the wind from the East to bury our
small land?  Will the Prussian fate be ours?"[39]

In pastoral activity, the clergy since destalinization sought direct contact with their parishioners,
especially with the youth.  In the late 1950s and
1960s Soviet newspapers carried many a story "exposing" this relationship.  Thus, in 1959, the kom-

somol newspaper <u>Komjaunimo Tiesa</u> reported that while
"the principal is repairing the school, his students
are working on the repairs of the church."[40]  The
culprit responsible for allegedly luring away the
students was the local pastor H. Vaicius.  In another
parish, high school students helped to install electric wiring into the local church.  During vacations,
these same students were found playing soccer in its
yard.[41]  In 1960, <u>Ogonek</u> reported that Lithuanian
priests have discovered new methods for keeping contact with the people; one pastor (Rev. A. Kerpaus-
kas of Batakiai) organized sports clubs, another
sponsored dances (Rev. Pukenas in Lentvaris), still
another priest led a book reading group (Rev. Masys
in Birzai).[42]  Such cases though no longer as numerous are still reported by the <u>Chronicle of the Catholic Church of Lithuania</u>.

Such pastoral communications, as will be explained, did not pan out.  The pastors ran into stubborn opposition from the government that in 1966 made
any such activity an expressly criminal violation of
the laws guaranteeing freedom of religious cults and
the separation of the church from public institutions.[43]

Thus, in the early 1960s, at the time of the
Second Vatican Council, the Lithuanian church was
rather advanced in seeking changes in the situation
that had tied down the traditional church to the
status quo, to the existing social institutions, that
had made institutional formalities the criterion for
judging a person's religious commitment.  Even the
dialogue with the atheists promoted from Cardinal
Koenig's office in Vienna was not a new discovery because this dialogue had been going on in Lithuania

366

for a considerable length of time. It was not institutionalized, as proposed by the Church in Rome,
but rather sporadic, local; it was not always in discussion form, but frequently involved reasoned appeals on the part of the churchmen or the faithful
and a broadside from the government. Sometimes, such
dialogue would be even published in newspapers, as
was an appeal by a "Lithuanian Catholic" who protested indiscriminate attacks against the moral integrity of all the clergymen and confessed to an ultimate commitment to the faith. She was answered by
J. Ragauskas, an ex-priest and then the chief atheist
propagandist in Lithuania, who insisted that "scientific inquiry" would convince the young lady to
abandon religion.[44] Because of the atheist stress
on science as the force that denies religion, Lithuanian clergymen in the 1970s are especially concerned with the relationship between science and religion, a problem on which the Second Vatican Council did not dwell very extensively. In Lithuania
there still rages a laicist, positivist battle between the "scientific" and "religious" approach to
the philosophy of life, a struggle fought in Western
Europe in the nineteenth century. Atheists--and the
government--insist on their incompatibility. Actually, under the label of "science" the Communist Party
attempts to sell much of its own propaganda. However, "science" is the trump card atheists employ in
the war of ideas and apparently it still has an impact on large sections of the population, though less
and less among the young people and among the intellectuals. The portrayal of the ideological weakness
of atheist efforts at persuasion has found its way
into literature. In 1969, Jonas Milelinskas, a well

367

known writer of the middle generation published a
narrative entitled "Three days and three nights" in
which he pictured a school inspector from the ministry on a visit to a local parish priest while check-
ing the performance of a provincial school.[45]   The
priest, the inspector discovers, is an old high
school friend and conversation therefore is frank and
uninhibited.  The inspector is surprised to find the
priest's library shelves bulging with all sorts of
books, beginning with Aristotle and including Marx
and Lenin.  He also discovers that his old friend
the pastor is the calmest and most decent man in the
entire environment that is otherwise characterized
by drunkenness, violence, deceit, and hypocrisy.  To
his chagrin, the inspector is disarmed in the discussion of the merits and nature of religion.  The
priest suggests that "the pastor of the twentieth
century must not be armed with a stick but with a
book."  That is the reason the priest's library is so
complete.  "Naturally," the priest continues, "it is
necessary for us to know our opponent, his theses,
his assertions, his reasoning, his arguments and mo-
tifs, the entire arsenal of his wisdom.  Unfortutun-
ately, we do not always have the possibility to pro-
pagate our truths and in case of need to defend
them."  "What about using the pulpit?" suggests the
inspector.  "The pulpit?"--asks the priest, at the
same time curious and surprised.  "Blessed naiveté!
We don't live in times, my friend, before Gutenberg's
invention of the printing press.  How much can
preaching from some dozens of pulpits mean against
the flow of lava from the press, schools, television,
radio, movie theaters, organization activities, lecture halls, various festivals, and speakers' stands?"

"Frankly speaking," the priest continues, "I am sorry
for the person who is trying to prove the atheist
point of view in the press or from the speaker's
stand but never reflects that the king, as Anderson
has said, is naked, that is, that his opponents' lips
are chained.  There is not much honor in being right-
eous over a dumb and deaf person.  That's why I believe that a thinking person should not become an
atheist at least until the time someone very powerful
and just will not say:  let us hear out the other
side as well--audiatur et altera pars."

The discussion of the two friends finally leads
to the appraisal of religion's merits to society.
"They [meaning the atheists]" says the priest to the
now confused and doubting inspector, "reduce everything to earthly concerns; with a lantern they search
for the social roots of religion; they try to explain this emotion as an expression of man's weakness when confronted with the elements, et cetera.
They call it a remnant, superstition, but the thought
does not occur to them that faith is the man's road
to eternity, to the absolute, that it embodies man's
natural thirst for extending his existence beyond the
grave.  This may be an illusion, but it is a holy illusion that reflects man's nature, his essence, that
helps him to exist and to avoid becoming an animal."
After an exchange in which the inspector suggests
that atheists do not degrade man by changing the concept of freedom to that of willfulness (Dostoevski's
"Esli boga netu tak znachit vse dozvolene" finds its
place in the conversation), the inspector finally
asks whether his friend has no doubts about his
priestly vocation.  The priest answers affirmatively
and then explains the raison d'etre for himself and

369

the clergy in a modern scientific, even a communist
society. "If there were anyone who could clear my
doubts, I would immediately take off my soutane.
But there is no such person, and there won't be. No.
We [the priests] will be needed so long as man will
remain mortal and yet will dream about immortality
and strive toward it. And if, with the help of science, to his own misfortune he will tame immortality,
we will leave the scene without a murmur. Until this
does happen, it is our duty to remind the man:
sursum corda (lift up your hearts).

Nevertheless, the intellectual enrichment of the
faith remains a problem, especially that doors are
shut to the treasures of Western ideological and phil-
osophical-sociological writings and that religious
intellectual experimentation is banished from social
and educational activities. Intellectually, the
church has fallen behind. The existing theological
seminary offers little help because its students have
no access to new or even extensive old writings, and
discussions are discouraged. Students learn, basically, from notes they take during classes and the
seminary's leadership since the early sixties en-
courages administrative rather than intellectual aspects of pastoral training. In Lithuania this intellectual void is filled later, partly by the introduction of secular civil rights philosophy which sup-
ports the church's right of intellectual investigation and communication with the believers. In Latvia,
Soviet observers have noted the Catholic clergy is
promoting ideas of the new Christian hunanism of
Jacques Maritain, Etienne Gilson, and Teilhard de
Chardin.[46]

The dialogue with the atheists in Lithuania had

been going on before the Second Vatican Council became concerned with it, but so far it has led nowhere though the Lithuanian churchmen sought it and would welcome the terms for the dialogue as proposed by Cardinal Koenig's office. However, if this idea of the council was accepted though found currently unrealistic, the council's propagation of inter-church ecumenism has been considered with suspicion. The only known ecumenical service in Lithuania has been held on the occasion of the eightieth birthday of the chairman of the consistory of the Evangelical Lutheran Church. This was the first such service in Lithuanian history altogether.[47] The Catholics, nevertheless, have not shown enthusiasm for the idea. In one respect, Lithuanian churchmen perceive of it not as an instrument of Christian unity and modernization but a threat to the Lithuanian church. Lutheranism is not considered dangerous or even inimical. Neither are the Orthodox rites though traditionally many Lithuanians identify them with tsarist suppression and efforts of forcible conversion to Orthodoxy. Lithuanian Catholic clergymen--at least those who are sympathetic to The Chronicle of the Catholic Church of Lithuania--have spoken up for the Uniate Ukrainian church to which they feel bound by ties of dogma and experience. They also seek and apparently maintain improved relations with the Jews. However, all fear the leadership of the Russian Orthodox Church. The fear is grounded in the belief that the development of close ties to this church might induce the Vatican to transfer the Lithuanian dioceses to the jurisdiction of the Orthodox Patriarch in Moscow. This could be done for the sake of ecumenical unity, in hopes of winning current concessions with the Kremlin, and future _rapprochement_ with Russian Orthodoxy. The Lithuanians, it appears, think that in case they are abandoned to Moscow's patriarchate, they would lose direct ties to Rome and to the West, and thus would be delivered to the Kremlin's total mercy.

The other even more far reaching reform of the Second Vatican Council, that of liturgy in the vernacular, similarly has been received without elation although for entirely different reasons. The Vatican reform makes sense for societies where the church has at its disposal modern means of communications. In Lithuania not only would the new liturgy require considerable changes in the physical church layout that are not easy to introduce in a system where every little church repair has to be approved by local government agencies, but it would be very difficult to say the mass in vernacular without the congregation having the needed texts. As a result, the vernacular, that is, Lithuanian or respectively Latvian or Polish are used in the administration of the sacraments and church singing, but not in the main Latin Catholic liturgy, the mass. Until now, the Soviets have allowed only the publication of a volume of the Vatican Council decrees, a liturgical volume with texts for the administration of the sacraments (in three languages) with a church song book, a prayerbook, and in 1972, a new edition of the New Testament and the psalms.[48] These latter volumes have been translated from Latin or Greek in impeccable modern Lithuanian, much improved over the old editions, thus showing the church's desire to be "up to date," as well as its ability to secure the necessary intellectual talent for the task. However, these works have been published in small editions, partly exported to Lithuan-

ians abroad, and thus locally available only on an
extremely limited basis. This is insufficient for
the daily or weekly liturgy of the mass. For use in
this liturgy, the church would need periodically to
provide rather numerous texts printed in large quan-
tities. Currently, this appears to rest beyond the
realm of possibility.

## CONTROL OF COMMUNICATIONS AS KEY TO SOVIET AND CATHOLIC MODERNIZATION

This problem reveals the character of the Soviet
model of modernization. While stressing technology,
insisting on scientific approach to philosophy and
application of science to daily existence, the Soviets deny this to the churches, the only, as they
say, legal institutions of opposing ideology in the
country. Thus, Soviet modernization is ideologically
prejudiced. The Catholic Church is striving to modernize, but is held up, frustrated, or simply forbidden by the official government policy. This prohibition covers especially the means of communications. In the past, clergymen have tried to find
their way into communist press, but have been up-
braided for doing so. For example, in 1962, the Rev.
V. Ślevas, pastor of Endrejavas in western Lithuania,
wrote a letter to Tiesa, the Lithuanian version of
Pravda, suggesting that a place be made for religion
teaching in schools. Instead of publishing this letter as usually would be the case, the newspaper
passed it on to the publication of the teaching profession, Tarybinis Moktojas (Soviet Teacher), where
the letter was not printed but answered by comparing
religion to garbage. Rev. Ślevas, for his desire to
"invade" the school which is regarded as an exclusive-

ly atheist possession was transferred to a new place of work. Six years later this priest of the Telsiai diocese stubbornly continued efforts of establishing lines of communications with the communist rulers. In 1968, however, he complained and made proposals not to the newspapers but directly to Chairman Kosygin in Moscow. He thus began the Lithuanian petition drive that in 1972 culminated in the Lithuanian Catholic letter of 17,000 addressed both to Kurt Waldheim of the United Nations and Leonid Brezhnev of the Soviet Union.[49]

Another priest, the Rev. Aleksandras Maraitis, a Jesuit, met with a worse fate. After apparently many attempts to respond to the various distortions of religious dogmas and clerical life that were published in the Lithuanian press, in 1960 he finally succeeded and had a short letter printed by the literary weekly Literatūra ir menas (Literature and Art). In his missile Markaitis complained of what he considered distorted and obsolete interpretation of the Middle Ages. The editors of the weekly answered the priest's criticisms but their author shortly afterwards was deported to a camp in Mordovia from which he later returned a mentally broken man.[50] Markaitis was accused of producing "anonymous" letters to the press that "unjustly" slandered communist authors on religious subjects.

At one time, nevertheless, the government itself suggested that the bishops start a Catholic publication. Negotiations concerning such a publication, however, did not produce results. A Soviet writer explains that the government had consented but that the diocesan administrators would not agree among themselves and the project fell through.[51] It is likely that the churchmen refused because of stringent limitations the authorities planned to impose on the journal. Such a periodical, apparently fashioned after Zhurnal moskovskoi patriarkhii, could not have brought much improvement into the religious situation though it would aid claims of Soviet propaganda. Lithuanian church leaders insisted on a publication that is free and broad in scope of discussion and contents. Demand for the right of publication remains very high on the list of grievances that Lithuanian clergymen and believers since 1968 have periodically submitted to communist authorities.[52]

Finally, the government has opposed the modernization of pastoral methods and, as noted earlier, in 1966 (in Lithuania, on May 12, 1966) expressly forbade a variety of practices as criminal violations of Article 143 of the Lithuanian criminal code that deals with the separation of church and state.[53] At the same time, the authorities intensified the enforcement of prohibition against a systematic teaching of religion. Similarly, they cut the number of theological students and further impeded their admission. In addition, a drive was begun to compel all congregations to sign contracts with the local soviets as was the practice elsewhere in the Soviet Union and to drive a wedge between the "reactionary" and "progressive" clergy, discriminating against the first and promoting the latter group. It also became clear that through strict regulation of the dvatsatka membership and through hierarchical appointments the government sought to win the internal control of church organization.

All of these limitations, especially the pressure to eliminate religious teaching (catechization)

and further curtail the supply of new priest, finally
brought the simmering discontent to a boil and pro-
voked Lithuanian Catholic protests and dissent.  It
may be said that the Lithuanian Catholics reacted
against the prohibition to communicate with the believers.  While in 1972-76 this reaction produced
some improvement, the Communist Party shows no desire
to accept the church as a legitimate institution of a
modern urban society.  The current appointment of
Anicas as the party appartchik in charge of schools
and culture shows the communist determination to pursue the same old policy.[54]

Returning to the Soviet thesis that modernization makes religion obsolete, in the case of Latin
rite Catholics we must say that the Latin rite church
of Lithuania, as Barbara Wolfe Jancar has suggested,
has been a modernizing church.  If it has lost ground,
it was not because it did not adapt itself to the age
of technology and science but largely because it has
been forbidden to employ technology and science in
its service.  This certainly shows the domination of
politics over technology and its social consequences
in the Soviet case.  Stated in different terms, this
case hardly offers evidence that modernization as
such is inimical to Latin Catholicism as Jonas Anicas
has insisted.

NOTES

1. Walter J. Ciszek, S.J., With God in Russia
(New York: McGraw-Hill, 1964), pp. 248-49.  Paul
Mailleux, S.J., rector of the Pontifical Russian
College in Rome in 1971, cited the existence of Latin
rite Catholic churches in Moscow, Leningrad, Tbilisi,
Odessa, Kishinev, two in Lviv, and a chapel without
a resident priest in Kiev.  See his "Catholics in
the Soviet Union," in Marshall, Aspects of Religion,

p. 366.

2. Begegnung, No. 1 (1969), pp. 14-15.

3. Segretaria di Stato, Ufficio Centrale di Statistica della Chiesa. Raccolta di Tavole Statistiche 1969 (The Vatican: Tipografia Poliglotta Vaticana, 1971), p. 113. If this number is correct, it indicates an approximately fifty percent decline in membership since the end of World War II.

4. On Belorussia see A. Drujski, Religious Life in Byelorussia (n.p., n.d.). On the Ukrainian and other Latin rite Catholics, see Paul Mailleux in Marshall, Aspects of Religion, and Bohdan Bociurkiw, testimony, in U.S. Congress, House, Committee on Foreign Affairs, Hearings before the Subcommittee on Europe. 93rd Cong., 2nd Sess., July 25, 1974, esp. p. 352; also Bociurkiw's "Catholics in the Soviet Union Today," in A Symposium, Religion in the USSR, 1975, a "private use" publication of Radio Liberty conference papers, pp. 35-74.

5. In 1973, in a private report to the Anglican church committee studying religion in the USSR this writer has estimated the number as approximately three and a half million. It was arrived at by the use of Annuario Pontificio, the calculation of demographic changes that have occurred after World War II, and the probable losses of Catholic commitment under Soviet rule (p. 3). Bociurkiw gives an estimate of "over three million." See his paper at Radio Liberty symposium, p. 39.

6. A. I. Ivanov, P. K. Lobazov, Politika sovetskogo gosudarstva po voprosam religii i tserkvi (Moscow, 1973), p. 52. Actually, the application of this number is not clear.

7. Twenty-three issues of this publication totalling approximately 1,300 singlespaced folded sheet pages have appeared until the fall of 1976. A dozen issues have been translated into English and published in individual copies by the Lithuanian Roman Catholic Priests' League of America.
Excerpts, sometimes very complete, in English translation are found in The Violations of Human Rights in Soviet Occupied Lithuania, reports since 1972, publ. by the Lithuanian American Community; also, translations appeared in the quarterly Lituanus (Chicago); Religion in Communist Lands (London); and

377

Elta (New York).  In German, several issues have been published by Acta Baltica (Taunus).  In French, excerpts have appeared in Cahiers du samizdat.  In Italian, excerpts are published by Russia Cristiana (Milan) and in Elta (Rome).

8. On Soviet concept of modernization, see an interpretation by John A. Armstrong, "Communist Political Systems as Vehicles for Modernization," in Political Development in Changing Societies, ed. Monte Palmer and Larry Sterr (Lexington:  Heath Lexington, 1971), pp. 126-158; also see V. Stanley Vardys, "Modernization and Baltic Nationalism," Problems of Communism (Sept-Oct., 1975) pp. 32-33.

9. L. N. Velikovich, Krizis sovremennogo katolitsizma (Moscow, 1967), p. 74.

10. Jonas Aničas in Nauka i religiia, No. 8 (1975), p. 12.

11. "Religious Dissent in the Soviet Union," in Dissent, pp. 22-23.

12. Nauka i religiia, No. 8 (1975), p. 12.

13. Data from Anicetas Simutis, The Economic Reconstruction of Lithuania After 1918 (New York:  Columbia University Press, 1942), p. 2; Jonas Aničas, Katalikiskasis klerikalizmas Lietuvoje 1940-1944 metais (Vilnius, 1972), p. 29; M. Gregorauskas, Tarybu Lietuvos žemes ukis (Vilnius, 1960), p. 78.

14. Soviet view of secularization in Anicas, Katalikiškasis, pp. 32-33; Western Lithuanian view in J. Savasis, The War Against God in Lithuania (New York;  Manyland Books, Inc., 1966), pp. 16-17.

15. Archival document among Bishop Brizgys papers.

16. Archival document among Bishop Brizgys papers.

17. Minutes of the Lithuanian Bishops conference on July 2-3, 1940.

18. Memorandum of the Lithuanian Bishops of May 1941.

19. Letter by Bishop Matulionis to Chairman

Gedvila.

20. Cf. The Chronicle of the Catholic Church of Lithuania, No. 18 (August 1975); also J. Savasis, Kova prieš Dieva Lietuvoje (Putnam: Immaculata Press, 1963), p. 53.

21. Centrine statistikos valdyba prie Lietuvos TSR Ministru Tarybos, Lietuvos TSR Ekonomika ir kultura 1972 metais (Vilnius, 1973), p. 17; also Lietuvos statistikos metrastis, vol. 12 (Vilnius: Centralinis Statistikos Biuras), p. 17.

22. Pranas Dičius, Santuoka ir Šeima Tarybu Lietuvoje (Vilnius, 1974), p. 184.

23. Ibid., p. 186.

24. The Chronicle of the Catholic Church of Lithuania, No. 9, in Lietuvos Kataliku Baznyčios Kronika, vol. 2 (Chicago, 1975), p. 77.

25. Facts on File, 1973, p. 1098 B-C.

26. V. Pomerantsev, "Vchera i segodnia," Nauka i religiia, No. 4 (April 1966), pp. 5-6.

27. Tiesa, March 13, 1976, p. 2.

28. Laikas ir ivykiai, No. 2 (1975), pp. 9-10.

29. Lithuanian text in I Laisvę, No. 63-64 (August 1975), p. 65.

30. Reported by The Chronicle of the Catholic Church of Lithuania, No. 9, in Lietuvos.

31. Pergale, No. 2 (February 1975), pp. 53-54.

32. New York Times, May 22, 26, 1972 and June 14, 1972.

33. J. Rimaitis, Religion in Lithuania (Vilnius, 1971), p. 29.

34. Nauka i religiia, No. 8 (1975), p. 23.

35. Previously cited letter by Bishop Matulionis.

36. Tarybinis mokytojas, June 6, 1963, cited in Savasis, War Against God, p. 110.

37. Jonas Anicas, "Realizatisiia reshenii II Vatikanskogo sobora i katolicheskoi tserkvi v Litve," in Katolitsizm v SSSR i sovremennost', ed. Jonas Aničas (Vilnius, 1971), p. 91.

38. Minutes of the meeting of Lithuanian Bishops on July 2-3, 1940.

39. The Chronicle of the Catholic Church of Lithuania, No. 17 (1975), p. 32.

40. Cited by Savasis, Kova prieš Dieva, p. 61.

41. Ibid.

42. V. Prival'skii, A. Uzlian, "Sviataia rumba," Ogonek, No. 39 (September 1960), pp. 20-21.

43. Baudziamasis kodeksas (Vilnius, 1970), pp. 143-44; 281-82.

44. Tiesa, December 22, 1960.

45. Pergale, No. 12 (December 1968), pp. 19-78.

46. E. Balevits, "'Novyi khristianskii gumanizm' v propovedicheskoi deiatel'nosti katolicheskogo dukhovenstva v Latviiskoi SSR," in Aničas, Katolitsizm v SSSR, pp. 127-28.

47. Aničas, in "Realizatsiia,", p. 90.

48. Zhurnal moskovskoi patriarkhii, No. 4 (1974), pp. 72-76; V. Stanley Vardys, "Catholicism in Lithuania," in Marshall, Aspects of Religion, p. 394.

49. Arkhiv samizdata, No. 1092; New York Times, July 23, 1972.

50. Cited by Savasis, Kova prieš Dieva, pp. 62-64.

51. J. Aničas and J. Rimaitis, Tarybiniai įstatymai Lietuvoje apie religinius kultus ir sažines laisve (Vilnius, 1970), p. 52.

52. Some have been reported in the Western press;

English translation of the most important documents in the previously cited The Violations of Human Rights in Occupied Lithuania.

53. Baudžiamasis kodeksas, pp. 281-82.

54. Sovetskaia Litva, January 23, 1976, p. 1.

Chapter 11
PROTESTANT SECTARIANS AND MODERNIZATION
IN THE SOVIET UNION

Andrew Blane

Lest they mislead, the terms in the title of
this essay require explanation.  Some ten years ago
I began to use the phrase "Protestant sectarians"
as a general rubric for the various adherents of a
religious movement common to modern Russian history.
They have in the past known a number of different
names:  "Stundists," "Baptists," and "Pashkovites"
in the late nineteenth century, "Evangelical Christians" and "Baptists" in the early twentieth century,
and since 1944--when their descendants merged into a
common body--"Evangelical Christians-Baptists."
This latter is still their official name, even though
their ranks were expanded in 1945 and 1947 by the
merger of certain Pentecostals and again in 1963 by
the addition of various Mennonites.  Outside the Soviet Union it is common to speak of "the Russian
Baptists."  Inside the parlance is more varied:  the
larger Soviet populace calls them "sectarians" or
"Baptists," whereas they themselves say "Baptists"
or "Evangelicals" or, often as not, simply "believers."

Since the late nineteenth century specialists
in Russian religious history have treated these believers as a branch of the larger religious phenom-

enon known as "sectarianism." But the terms employed
have been many. The most frequent practice has been
to designate them in contradistinction to other sectarian peoples, e.g., "rationalist sectarians" (versus "mystical sectarians"), "Evangelical sectarians"
(versus "Spiritual sectarians"), "sectarians of foreign origin" (versus "sectarians of native origin").
None of these rubrics is to my mind satisfactory.
In their stead I have employed "Russian Protestant
sectarians" and appropriate derivatives. Each element and the order of elements have their specific
purposes. The order distinguishes these peoples
from the sectarian Protestants of the radical wing
of the sixteenth century Reformation in Western Europe. The noun "sectarians" identifies them as an
integral part of Russian sectarianism; the adjective
"Protestant" expresses, although it does not describe, the historical and ideological connection
between these Russo-Ukrainian believers and the descendants of the Radical Reformation, as well as dif-
ferentiates them from the myriad of Russian sectarians who have no similar linkage; the adjective "Russian" serves as a geographical (rather than an ethnic) modifier, with the geography incorporating the
whole of late imperial or Soviet Russia.[1]

It is somewhat more difficult to explain "modernization." I first encountered the term in reference to Russian history when I read Cyril Black's
essay on "The Modernization of Russian Society." It
was published in 1960 as the concluding piece to the
important symposium, The Transformation of Russian
Society.[2] My most recent encounter was in The Modernization of Japan and Russia, a book in which once
again Cyril Black had a hand. It appeared in 1975,

the collective product of eight scholars, representing the fields of history, economics, sociology, and
political science.[3] In the fifteen years that separate these two studies the term "modernization" has
undergone notable refinement. The broad definition
remains the same, i.e., "the process by which societies have been and are being transformed under the
impact of the scientific and technological revolution."[4] However, much descriptive detail and many
disclaimers have been added. Aware of the criticisms
and controversies that have arisen over the meaning
of "modernization," the authors of The Modernization
of Japan and Russia are careful to avoid terms such
as "traditional," "Westernization," and "progress"
because their use in the past "tended to confuse
many discussions of modernization."[5] Moreover, for
their own explication they prefer description to definition. A modernized society, they note, is characterized by a high use of inanimate power, a high capacity to coordinate and control resources, a high
level of production and urbanization, a low birth
rate, long lifespans, widespread education and the
broad dissemination of knowledge, to cite only the
more prominent indices. "Modernization," they find,
"is a continuous process that has no self-defined
stages." However, for the purposes of description
and analysis three historical phases can be abstrac-
ted: gestation, transformation, and high modernization.[6] It is this broad historical process that is
meant when I use the term "modernization" in this
essay.

There is yet another term in the title that
needs clarification--the connective between "Russian
Protestant sectarians" and "modernization." I have

not in this essay attempted a study in "religious modernization," however useful that might be. "Modernization" and "religious modernization" are in my understanding quite distinct. And their difference is not simply the modifier "religious." Whereas "modernization" by definition is integral to the modern period of history, "religious modernization"-- i.e., the process of adapting or updating religious life and thought is as old as history itself. In the modern era, "religious modernization" has been a small though not insignificant part of the encompassing process of modernization. Similarly, the adaptions of Russian Protestant sectarian life and thought to the social transformations of modern Russian history are but a part, although an important part, of the larger relation between Russian Protestant sectarians and "modernization." It is the larger relation that is my concern in this essay.

The collective work on The Modernization of Japan and Russia also provides a convenient point of entry to my subject. This study notes that Japan and Russia from divergent pasts have been successful latecomers in the process of modernization. It sets out to discover how this came about, and why, and what this suggests about the general process of modernization. Of the many stimulating observations offered, three have particular relevance to the historical life of the Russian Protestant sectarians. The authors claim that (1) the process of modernization in Japan and Russia can be periodized in coterminus stages: circa 1700-1860, the laying of the foundations of modernization, circa 1860-1940, the transformation to modernity, circa 1940-present, the entry into high modernization; (2) the historical experience of Japan and Russia suggests that latecomers to modernization require, especially in the period of transformation to modernity, greater political control and coordination than did the early modernizers, with Russia resorting to coercion more often and in greater measure than Japan; (3) the ability to adapt foreign institutions to domestic purposes and to borrow extensively from abroad, without losing a sense of national identity, are among the components which contributed to successful modernization in both Japan and Russia.[7] The pertinence of these generalizations to the historical life of the Russian Protestant sectarians should become apparent as in the course of the essay I first discuss their origins and then their relations with the state.

Peter the Great's grandaughter, Elizabeth, was the first monarch to devise a program to attract immigrants from Europe to Russia. Its implementation, however, had to await the reigns of Catherine II and Alexander I. The intent of the program was to provide European Russia with a protective shield against Turkic tribes by populating the vast uninhabited areas along the Volga River and in the southern Ukraine. To encourage settlers Catherine offered an attractive list of rights and privileges in a manifesto dated July 22, 1763. Many responded and moved to Russia. Among them were Mennonite families whose faith and mode of life had incurred the disfavor of their European home states. One authority estimates that the total number of Mennonites immigrating to Russia between 1788 and 1870 was 10,000 individuals in 2,300 families. These believers, however, "never constituted more than a minority of the total number of immigrants coming to Russia from Germany and many other countries."[8]

While granting certain rights and privileges, Catherine also imposed certain restrictions on the new settlers. "All the nationalities of the Mohammedan faith living within Russia can be persuaded to accept the Christian religion without any restriction," proclaimed the Manifesto of 1763, but "everyone is warned that none of the Christian believers residing in Russia should under any pretext be persuaded or misled to accept or join the faith and the church" of any of the immigrants from outside the borders.[9] How important this proviso proved remains an open question. Mennonite scholars note that neither "the first agreement of 1788 nor any of the following contains a clause restricting mission work in Russia," and they conclude that "it is likely very few Mennonites who settled in Russia ever heard of the restricting clause of the Manifesto of 1763."[10] Whatever the actual or perceived legal conditions, the German settlers made no efforts to proselytize the Russian or Ukrainian peasantry until the 1850s when a pietist awakening in southern Germany crossed over into Russia and kindled the German colonists with a missionary passion.[11] The spread of this pietist revival into the Ukraine, facilitated if not inspired by the forces of modernization, was one of the contributing factors to the birth of Russian sectarianism.

A second contributing factor, even more intimately connected to the process of modernization, was the extraordinary social ferment which began in Russia during the Crimean War and culminated in the emancipation of the serfs in 1861. Reform followed reform, until the whole of Russia was convulsed by

change. Freed from the mooring of serfdom, some of
the peasant masses were prepared to break with the
mooring of Orthodoxy. A larger number, however,
sought to fasten themselves more securely to the
Orthodox pier lest they find themselves adrift in an
unknown sea. Many sought haven in religious zeal,
often accompanied by moral transformation. For some
the awakening was nourished and intensified by the
personal sharing of religious experiences in small,
intimate companies. In the Ukraine several native
peasants shared in the pietist revival which swept
their German neighbors.[12]

A third factor which promoted the rise of the
Protestant sectarian movement, also closely linked
to the larger process of modernization, was the
growth of literacy among the masses and the publication of a Bible in the vernacular. The translation
of the Bible into common Russian was initiated by
the British and Foreign Bible Society, whose operation in Russia began in 1810. The work of translation commenced in 1816; the Four Gospels were completed in 1818; the entire New Testament in 1822.
Work on the Old Testament was in progress when, in
1826, the Russian Bible Society was closed by the
state and its assets turned over to the Holy Synod.
This slowed but did not stop the translation work.
However, the entire program was halted in 1836, and
much of the completed material was destroyed. Count
Protasov, Ober Prokurator of the Holy Synod and the
official responsible for the decision, successfully
and prophetically argued that the distribution of the
Bible in a country with as many sects as there were
in Russia would only result in further proliferation.
Twenty-two years later, after the death of Protasov,

two Orthodox scholars gained permission from the
authorities to launch the project anew. Portions of
the Gospels soon came out, and after 1863, with the
formation of "The Society for the Dissemination of
the Holy Scriptures in Russia," began to reach many
hands. In 1876 the entire Bible appeared in Russia
for the first time in the vernacular.[13]

A fourth factor, doubtless contributing to the
emergence and spread of Russian Protestant sects,
was the long and active tradition of religious dissent in Russia. The initial manifestation took place
in the fourteenth century; the most dramatic and con-
sequential outbreak was the "great schism" of 1666-
1667.[14] Thereafter religious dissent was a regular
feature of Russian social history, appearing most
markedly during periods of national or regional crisis. Like its causes, the characteristics of Russian
religious dissent were complex and varied. One no-
ticeable constant was conflict with the state. Because church and state in Russia were bound together,
an open break with one usually led to hostilities
with the other. At one time or another most Russian religious dissenters suffered from state discipline. One such instance, the exile of Molokane
to Siberia and the Transcaucasus during the reign
of Nicholas I was to prove of significant import to
the birth and growth of the Protestant sectarians.[15]

In an environment seeded and ripened by these
social, psychological, and ideological factors, a
number of Russians and Ukrainians of varied social
background, dissatisfied with the established forms
of religious life and desiring a more personalized
expression of faith, during the third quarter of the
nineteenth century turned to Evangelical Christian-

389

ity. Their conversions occurred in three widely separated regions of the empire--the Caucasus, the
Ukraine, and in St. Petersburg. I have elsewhere
more fully recounted the various strands of this
story.[16] It should be enough here to record the concluding lines:

> They held a common antipathy to traditional
> religion as they know it. They had an aver-
> sion to the priesthood, icons, the sacramen-
> tal system, fasting, and the veneration of
> the Virgin and the saints. They found lit-
> tle meaning in the mysterious and the litur-
> gical; they responded more deeply to the sim-
> ple and the concrete. They held a common be-
> lief that salvation must be directly and con-
> sciously experienced. They had a common
> trust in the Bible as the sole authority in
> religious life. They know a common impera-
> tive that each believer must share his faith
> with his neighbor. This latter proved the
> source of their strength and the root of
> their troubles.
>     The three groups knew equally obvious
> differences. The Caucasian movement spread
> predominantly among the settlements of the
> Molokane, although a beachhead was established
> quite early within the various mountain tribes
> and non-Russian nationalities. Their cadres
> were petty bourgeois and the movement reflec-
> ted this character. Almost from the outset
> they organized themselves effectively on the
> principles (of the German Baptist Union)
> brought them. . . .by their redoubtable lea-
> der, Pavlov. Distant from the center of pub-
> lic affairs, they labored without serious
> disturbance until 1887. In these calm con-
> ditions their movement flourished and expan-
> ded. From the very first days the Caucasian
> sectarians willingly took the name of Bap-
> tist.
>     The background of the Stundists in the
> Ukraine was entirely peasant and wholly Orth-
> odox. They emerged in three successive
> phases: moral reform within the confines of
> the Orthodox Church, then a break with Orth-
> odoxy and the formation of isolated communi-
> ties, and finally the slow crystallization

of an alliance between their various groups. For many years the movement remained diffuse and chaotic in character. The name Baptist was but one among several which they accepted; the name Stundist, foisted upon them by their opponents, was accurate to the extent that it pointed to their common German pietist origins, but for the rest was inexplicit. From the very beginning they ran into difficulty with the authorities. Nevertheless, they grew steadily, and in so doing they heightened the concern of those who opposed them.

The Pashkovites in St. Petersburg were for the most part aristocrats. Highly educated, their conversion was inspired by an Englishman who delivered his sermons in French. Although Orthodox in name, their intellectual tradition stemmed as much from the ideologies of the Masonic Order and the Russian Bible Society, both of which had flourished in the capital a half century earlier, as from the established faith of the land. High position gave them influence disproportionate to their numbers. A formal organization was unnecessary among so few, besides personal contact was a daily affair. Their concern focused on the saving of souls in evangelical meetings, and the serving of mankind through philanthropic and social enterprises. The informal cohesiveness in which they operated made them reluctant to take a name. When pressed for response they simply replied "the faithful," or "the children of God," or "the open brother."[17]

This, then is how the Russian Protestant sects emerged on the historical scene. Certain connections between the factors contributing to their emergence and the process of modernization have been noted in passing. However, when examined in the context of Russia as a latecomer to modernization, the most interesting link is the foreign stimulus which was everywhere present at their inception. This is not to claim, as has often and mistakenly been claimed, that the Protestant sects are "sects of foreign origin." Such a claim ignores the predominant native aspects in their origins. It is simply to note that foreign influence and foreign borrowing, described earlier as a component contributing to the successful modernization of Russia, also played an important role in the birth and growth of these evangelical sects. Still more noteworthy to my mind is the coincidence between the gestation period of Russia's modernization and entry into the transformation period, on the one hand, and the gestation period and birth of the Russian sectarians, on the other.

There are many facets to the history of the relations between the Russian Protestant sects and the state. When examined from the point of view of legal change and the fluctuating attitude of the authorities to the implementation of the law, this history can be divided into eight segments. The most complex was the first, coinciding roughly with the reign of Alexander II. From his father he inherited a body of religious law that was fiercely discriminatory against religious dissidents, in particular the Old Believers and the sectarians.[18] Periodically under the rule of Alexander liberalization of these laws came under discussion, but few alterations were actually made. The single change of consequence was introduced only at the end of his reign, through a law of March 27, 1879 which declared that "Baptists, on the basis of Article 44 of the Fundamental State Laws, without hindrance may preach their dogmas and fulfill the religious rites peculiar to their tradition."[19] Of greater significance than Alexander's failure to loosen the laws restricting religious nonconformity, was his relative unconcern to implement them. As a result, the Old Believers and most of the sectarians enjoyed a period of comparative peace through neglect.[20] One exception to this rule existed, namely, the brief though sustained attack on certain new sects which emerged in the late 1860s. Chief among these were the Stundists, a pioneer branch of the Russian Protestant sectarians.

In the conservative reaction that followed Alexander's assassination, the pendulum of religious toleration once again swung adversely for religious dissidents. The chief instigator of this reaction was K. P. Pobedonostsev, the lay Ober Prokurator of the Holy Synod of the Russian Orthodox Church.[21] Pobedonstsev's first success was a new law which altered the legal position of the dissenters. On the surface, the law of May 3, 1883, could be called a progressive measure. Its provisions were more liberal than those of the law which it replaced, and it omitted the classification of sects according to their level of harmfulness. However, assessed as a whole and in the context of the times, the new law was a repressive act against the Old Believers and the sectarians.[22] First, the existent law had not been applied for more than two decades; second, the new law contained broad stipulations which could be manipulated to the detriment of the dissenters. In the decade that followed its introduction, this happened on a large scale.[23] But the results do not seem to have satisfied the authorities, at least so far as the Stundists were concerned. On July 4, 1894, "the Committee of Ministers. . . .decreed that the Minister of Internal Affairs, acting together with the over Prokurator of the Most Holy Synod, might declare the whole sect to be 'especially dangerous, and might forbid the Stundists to hold group

prayer meeting." This was duly done."[24] Only after
the turn of the century did the pressure on the Stundists, as also on other religious dissenters, begin
to abate. The cause was the dramatic deterioration
of domestic conditions leading to the revolution of
1905.

The most eloquent index of the improved status
of Russian religious dissenters was the series of
government decrees, beginning in 1903, which led to
a radical alteration in their legal position. Far
and away the most important was the imperial ukaz of
April 17, 1905 which proclaimed the principle of religious toleration in Russia and decreed measures
for its implementation.[25] Although this edict, as
also the governing regulations of October 17, 1906,
reserved for the Orthodox Church alone the right of
propagandizing among other faiths, there is no doubt
that, judged in its entirety, the new law of religious toleration dramatically improved the legal
position of both the Old Believers and the sectarians.[26] In implementation, however, the state proved
discriminatory. For although the law of 1905-1906
extended considerably wider privileges to both the
Old Believers and the sectarians, over the next years
"the official policy was. . . .[on the one hand] one
of wooing the Old Believers and of reducing to a minimum the restrictions upon them. . . .whereas, [on
the other hand] the authorities, both ecclesiastical
and secular, remained hostile to the sectarians, and
in spite of the changed conditions continued to make
trouble for them."[27]

The need to rely upon ad hoc measures to limit
the activity of the sectarians could not satisfy
long. In 1909 and 1910 aided by the conservative

tide that had begun to flow throughout the country, the imperial government issued a number of highly restrictive circulars to govern the life of the sectarian communities.[28] Once again the pendulum of religious toleration had swung against the Protestant sects. The outbreak of war in 1914 made matters still worse. In an atmosphere charged by the passions of military conflict, opponents of the sectarians developed new suspicions and voiced fresh denunciations on the grounds that the sects threatened the security of the state. That these accusations found resonance at the highest levels of the government is evidenced by a speech given in the Duma on August 3, 1915. "I must say," observed the Minister of Internal Affairs, Shcherbatov, "that among. . . . [the Baptists], along with those who are sincere believers there are not a few undoubted tools of the German government. Concerning this there are facts beyond all doubt."[29] Contrary evidence supplied to the Minister by his employees was ignored.[30] As the war progressed the hardships suffered by the sectarians at the hands of the authorities mounted. It was not until the collapse of the autocracy in February 1917 that the new era of trial came to an end.

The brief and chaotic era of the Provisional Government did little to improve the legal status of religious sectarians. A law of July 17, 1917 recognized full religious freedom for all citizens with the right to change religion or to profess no religion at all.[31] This, however, was little more than reconfirmation of the Act of Toleration of April 17, 1905 and it did nothing to abrogate the highly restrictive measures of 1909-1910. More significant for the Protestant sectarians was the lack of in-

395

terest or machinery on the part of the Provisional
Government to enforce these edicts. As a consequence, in practical reality the sects entered a
period of considerable religious liberty. The Bolshevik coup in October 1917 did surprisingly little
to alter this. In conformity with the revolutionary
aims of the new leaders, a series of enactments in
1917-1918 introduced an entirely new corpus of religious legislation,[32] but their impact on the life
of the Protestant sectarians was relatively mild.
Neither the nationalization of property nor the dis-
enfranchisement of the clergy were serious blows,
for as compared with the Orthodox majority they had
few possessions and were essentially a lay movement.
Only the deprivation of the right of juridical person to their congregations incurred real loss. This
itself, however, needs to be weighed in the light
of the various advantages which the new laws provided as compared with the imperial legislation of
1909-1910 which they superceded. Though in a formal
sense these were many, in fact they added nothing to
the practical liberties enjoyed by the sectarians
since the collapse of the monarchy. Where Bolshevik
legislation brought real and tangible benefit was in
the realm of religious equality. The decree that all
religions were equal under the law removed with a
stroke the manifold privileges which for centuries
had belonged to the Orthodox Church.[33] In the favorable conditions of the 1920s evangelical activity
was to reach a high point unknown in their history,
before or since.

This relatively happy state of affairs under
the atheist rulers lasted for a decade. When a
change came, it came with fury. The change coincided

with the abandonment of the NEP and the launching of the First Five Year Plan. "In the eyes of the regime," according to the testimony of the Smolensk archives, "the church interposed an obstacle to the successful fulfillment of the new program of collectivization and rapid industrialization, and a frontal assault was launched to diminish the power and influence of all forms of religious organization."[34] On April 8, 1929 an omnibus new "Law on Religious Associations" was adopted. It codified all earlier regulations and introduced many new restrictions. "Religious associations," states Article 17, "are forbidden: (a) to create mutual aid funds, cooperative or commercial associations, or in general to use property at their disposal other than for the satisfaction of religious needs; (b) to give material support to their members; (c) to organize either special prayer and other meetings for children, young people, and women, or general meetings, groups, circles, and departments for Bible, literary, handicraft, religious education and other work, or to arrange excursions and set up children's playgrounds, open libraries and reading rooms, or organize sanatoriums and medical care. Only books necessary for the conduct of religious services may be kept in houses of prayer and church buildings."[35] On May 18, 1929 Article 124 of the Soviet constitution was amended whereby "freedom of religious propaganda" was replaced by "freedom of worship." The constitution no longer permits, said an official commentator, "the winning of new groups of toilers, especially children, as adherents of religion" or "any kind of propaganda on the part of the Churches and religious persons."[36] "These activities must be

397

qualified according to Articles 58-10 and 59-7 of
the Criminal Code."[37] Implementation of the new
laws on religious associations was as swift as they
were fierce. Moreover, in the feverish atmosphere
engendered by the national rush to industrialization
and collectivization it was not infrequent that Draconian measures far exceeding legal stipulation were
employed in the assault on believers. By the end of
the 1930s all organized religious life in the Soviet
Union was virtually extinct.

The war changed everything. Mortally threatened
by a powerful military foe, the Soviet state called
a halt to the attack on religion. In the new circumstances it could not afford the alienation of any
of its citizenry, and every resource was needed to
mount the war effort. As with the rest of the populace, religious believers on the whole rallied to
the defense of the nation. The All-Union Council of
Evangelical Christians, the only central organ of
the Protestant sectarians still functioning, addressed its followers in a circular shortly after
the German armies crossed the Soviet border: "Now
brothers and sisters, the days have come to show in
deeds and not in words our true relation to the
fatherland and to the events being experienced by our
country. The time has arrived for us, believers in
the Lord Jesus Christ, to show in acts our love for
our dear fatherland. Many brothers will be called
to the defense of their country. We urge them to
fulfill their duty to the end. . . ."[38] Cooperation by the religionists in the war effort step by
step led to a rapprochement in church-state relations. The new reality was given institutional expression in October 1943 and in June 1944 with the

establishment first of a Council for the Affairs of
Religious Cults.[39]  In the field of law, however,
there was little change.  A modicum of improvement
was registered through decrees permitting the ac-
quisition of property and exemption from certain
taxes,[40] but the "Law on Religious Associations" of
1929 remained the fundamental law governing religious
life.  Where change was radical was in the disin-
terest of the state in adhering to this law.  It was
as if the excesses of implementation in the 1930s
were to be balanced in the 1940s by laxities.  In
this new environment, the Protestant sectarians set
about the arduous task of reconstructing and expanding community life.  Their previous history would
suggest that the new state of affairs would not be
permanent.

Toward the end of the 1950s "the strange alliance" between church and state that evolved during
the war came to an end.  Under the banner of destalinization, Khrushchev launched a massive attack on all organized religion.  In October 1958
the tax exemptions and economic rights granted to
monasteries were revoked.[41]  In October 1960 by means
of Article 227 of the Criminal Code a new crime was
established--creating, leading, or drawing minors
into a group which under the guise of preaching religious beliefs causes harm to health (or, as expanded in 1962, "induces citizens or minors to re-
fuse social activity or the performance of civic
duties").[42]  That this provision was drawn up with
the sectarians in mind was revealed in its application.  On March 16, 1961 as a sign that the omnibus
"Law on Religious Associations of 1929" was no longer to be honored in the breach, a new set of instruc-

tions for implementation was issued.[43] Then, on December 19, 1962 in a legislative act as striking for its magnitude as its secretiveness, some twenty-nine of the sixty-four articles of this law were amended. The thrust of the changes was to limit religious activity further and to bring state control deeper into religious life.[44] Concomitant with these legislative acts, officials of the state set about by means of administrative measures to impose strictures on the religious communities far beyond the dictates of law.[45] With the fall of Khrushchev in October 1964, this practice of <u>administrirovanie</u> more or less came to a halt.[46] Nevertheless, the combative era of church-state relations which he inaugurated continued in force, with law the basic weapon. In December 1965 partly to curb the lawlessness of lower organs of the state, the two Councils which since the war had been responsible for church life were combined into a single Council for Religious Affairs and given broader powers.[47] Then in March 1966 three edicts were issued to clarify and yet again broaden the legal limits on religious activity. Once again most proscriptions were patently tailored for the sectarians.[48] Since the edicts of 1966, the boldest legislative act of the religious front has been the publication on June 23, 1975 of an amended version of the "Law of Religious Associations of 1929." Its chief significance was in bringing to public light the legal amendments introduced but not published in 1962 under Khrushchev. Beyond this there is a further granting of powers to the Council for Religious Affairs and--in effect--the right of juridical person to religious communities.[49] The publication of this revised law offers fresh

evidence that the militancy against religion rekin-
dled in the late 1950s continues to be the policy
of the state today, although since Khrushchev the
only weapons sanctioned are propaganda and law.  How
long this pattern of church-state relations will
last is for the future to reveal.  Viewed in historical retrospect, the most "favorable" periods in the
relations between the Russian Protestant sects and
the state were 1855-1881, 1905-1911, 1917-1928, and
1941-1959.  During those times the evangelicals enjoyed a considerable growth and spread in their membership, their religious and missionary activity was
marked by inventiveness and elan, their organizational network proliferated with the establishment
of new churches, the training of preachers, and the
publication of religious materials, and their contacts with co-religionists abroad expanded and
strengthened.  The most "difficult" periods were 1881
1881-1905, 1911-1917, 1928-1941, and 1959-1964 (extending in some respects to the present).  In each
of these spans their organizational life underwent
contraction, including the closure of large numbers
of churches, their leaders suffered arrest, imprisonment, even death, many of their members were subjected to harassment and fines, and (with the exception of the most recent period) their relations
with co-religionist in other lands diminished or
ended.[50]  What effect these hostile times had on
their growth and spread is difficult to judge for
lack of data.  Prison and exile often meant the introduction of their faith to new terrains.  The hardships of 1881-1905 and 1911-1917 slowed but apparently did not halt their growth.[51]  The assault of 1928-
1941 cut deeply into their ranks, although there is

401

some evidence that many members simply took their religious life underground. It is hard to explain their extraordinary growth during the war and in the immediate post-war years apart from the return to open religious life by many who were previously keeping it hidden.[52] In 1959-1964 they seem once again to have suffered some decline in their numbers.[53] But whether this was another instance of tactical withdrawal or a permanent apostacy is yet to be ascertained.

My excursus into the history of the relations of the Russian Protestant sects with the state is not without reason. The state, I would contend, has been the most critical force in the historical life of the sectarians, more so than the traditional forces associated with the process of modernization such as industrialization, urbanization, or education. It would seem, however, that their checkered encounter with the state is itself linked with the modernization process. Latecomers to modernization, as noted, require greater political control and coordination than did the early modernizers, most especially during the period of transformation to modernity. Russia was late to enter the moderniztion process. It seems hardly coincidental that the difficult history of the relations of the Protestant sects with the Russian state outlined here is practically coterminus with the historical transformation of Russian society to modernity.


NOTES

1. Although I have used the term "Russian Protestant Sectarians" for over a decade, and in this time seen it taken up by others, I have never been

entirely satisfied with the term.  I am not troubled
by the modifier "Protestant."  It may be true that
in historic fact these believers are not Protestants,
yet across the centuries "Protestant" has become a
sufficiently expansive and flexible word that with
the qualifiers I use I find it appropriate.  More
disturbing is the term "sectarians."  It can carry,
and often does carry, a perjorative connotation.
However, this is not a necessary element and I in-
tend no negative sense in its usage.  (It is the same
when I use the word "Baptist," which at various
places has been employed perjoratively--e.g., in the
1890s when in the Russian Empire it became a heated
and threatening issue as to whether or not it was
against the law to bear the name "Baptist.")  Though
infelicitous to the ear the word "sectarian" may
sound, it has long been used in Russian religious
historiography and among specialists has taken on a
technical meaning.  (One contemporary analogy to this
phenomenon is the use of "dissidents" to describe
members of the Soviet human rights movement.  Since
"dissident" can convey a negative nuance, it is not
an altogether neutral choice, yet its frequent use
over the past decade has given it the weight of
tradition which will not be easily or singly over-
turned.)  Most troubling of all is the adjective
"Russian."  For more than a century this has been a
convenient and conventional modifier to embrace the
past and present life of many peoples who were not
and are not ethnic Russians, but whose destinies
have been encompassed in the life of the Imperial
Russian state, from its antecedants to the time of
Kiev, to its sucessor in the Union of Soviet Socialist Republics.  With the advance of historical and
ethnographic knowledge, as well as the rise of the
unassailable claims of minority peoples, such sweeping use of the word "Russian" is less and less tena-
ble.  I continue its use in reference to the Protestant sectarians with reluctance only because I have
found that any term which seeks to preserve the
many ethnic variants in the movement is hopelessly
clumsy.

2. Cyril E. Black, The Transformation of Russian
Society (Cambridge, Mass:  Harvard University Press,
1960), pp. 661-80.

3. Cyril E. Black, Marius B. Jansen, Herbert S.
Levine, Marion J. Levy, Jr., Henry Rosovsky, Gilbert
Rozman, Henry D. Smith, II, S. Frederick Starr, The

4. Ibid., p. 3.

5. Ibid., pp. 7-10.

6. Ibid., pp. 4-6.

7. Ibid., pp. 10-22, and ff.

8. The Mennonite Encyclopedia, vol. 4 (Scott-dale, Pennsylvania), p. 384.

9. Ibid., p. 385.

10. Ibid.

11. Bratskii vestnik, No. 3 (1957), pp. 5-51.

12. Ibid.

13. The full story is told in Ia. Christovich, Istoriia perevoda Biblii na russkii iazyk (St. Petersburg, 1872-1873).

14. The Strigolniki, who in the fourteenth century broke with the Orthodox Church in a dispute over fees charged for ordination and the sacraments, as well as certain other differences, are traditionally designated the first Russian sect. The "great schism" of the seventeenth century occurred when a large body of Orthodox believers refused to accept the liturgical and church reforms of Patriarch Nikon. From this the schismatics came to be known as the Old Ritualists or Old Believers.

15. The Molokane, or Milk Drinkers (so-called because they rejected fasts and drank milk during Lent), first appeared in the Province of Tambov in the last quarter of the eighteenth century.

16. Andrew Blane, ed., The Religious World of Russian Culture, 2 vols (The Hague: Mouton, 1975), 2:268-76.

17. Ibid., pp. 276-78.

18. I. S. Berdnikov, Kratkii kurs tserkovnago prava, 2nd. ed. (Kazan, 1913), pp. 1114-1161.

19. Polnoe sobranie zakonov, vol. 54, no. 59452.

20. Berknikov, pp. 1163-1187.

21. I. V. Preobrazhenskii, Konstantin petrovich Pobedonostsev, ego lichnost' i deiatel'nost v predstavlenii sovremennikov ego konchiny (St. Petersburg, 1912), p. 8.

22. K. K. Arsen'ev, Svoboda sovesti i veroterpimosti (St. Petersburg, 1905), pp. 142-201.

23. See Blane, Religious World, pp. 282-84.

24. Curtiss, Church and State, p. 166, as based on Zavlialov, ed., Tsirkuliarnye ukazy sviateishago pravitel'stvuishchago sinoda 1867-1895 gg. (St. Petersburg, 1896),pp. 261-262.

25. Sobranie uzakoneii i rasporiazhenii pravitel'stva (St. Petersburg-Petrograd, 1863-1917), no. 526 (1905).

26. For details, see this author's doctoral thesis, "The Relations Between the Russian Protestant Sects and the State, 1900-1921" (Duke University, 1965), pp. 41-48.

27. Curtiss, Church and State, pp. 334-335.

28. Tserkovnyia vedomosti, May 1, 1910, pp. 146-148, and February 26, 1911, pp. 43-44.

29. Missionerskoe obozrenie, January, 1916, p. 137.

30. Blane, Religious World, pp. 300-01.

31. Sobranie ukaz, Vol. 1, Part 2, No. 1079.

32. The most important of these were a decree of February 2, 1918 which established the principle of a secular state by declaring the separation of the church from the state and the school from the church (Dekrety sovetskoi vlasti, vol. 1 (Moscow, 1957):271-74), the Constitution of the Russian Federated Soviet Republic (RSFSR) of July 10, 1918 which affirmed the principle of the separation of church and state (ibid., vol. 2, pp. 550-66), and the instruction of the People's Commissariat of Justice (NKIu) of August 24, 1918 which gave directions for the implementation of the decree of separation of

church and state (P. V. Gidulianov, ed., <u>Otdelenie</u>
<u>tserkvi ot gosudarstva v S.S.S.R., polny sbornik</u>
<u>decretov, vedomstvennikh rasporiazhenii i opredele-</u>
<u>nii verkhsuda RSFSR</u>, i.t.d., 3rd ed. (Moscow, 1926),
pp. 622-32.)

33. See Andrew Q. Blane, "Protestant Sectarians
in the First Year of Soviet Rule," in Marshall, <u>As-</u>
<u>pects of Religion</u>, pp. 302-22.

34. Merle Fainsod, <u>Smolensk under Soviet Rule</u>
(Cambridge, Mass.:  Harvard University Press, 1958),
p. 434.

35. <u>Sobranie uzakonenii i rasporiazhenii</u>, no.
35 (1929), text no. 353.  The new law also provided
the state authorities with comprehensive rights of
intervention and control.  See, for example, Article
64.

36. N. Orleanskii, <u>Zakon o religioznikh obedi-</u>
<u>neniakh RSFSR i destvuiushchie zakony, instruksii</u>
<u>c otdelnymi kommentariami</u> (Moscow, 1930), p. 47.

37. <u>Bezbozhnik</u>, II, 1930, p. 6.

38. <u>Bratskii vestnik</u>, No. 1 (1954), pp. 6-7.

39. <u>Izvestiia</u>, October 8, 1943, and July 1, 1944.

40. Gerhard Simon, <u>Church, State, and Opposi-</u>
<u>tion in the U.S.S.R.</u>, trans Kathleen Matchett (Berke-
ley:  University of California Press, 1974), p. 68;
Kuroedov and Pankratov, <u>Zakonodatel'stvo</u>, p. 106.

41. <u>Postanovlenie soveta ministrov SSSR</u>., October 16, 1958, No. 1159; <u>Postanovlenie soveta minis-</u>
<u>trov RSFSR</u>, November 6, 1958, No. 125.

42 Harold J. Berman, intro. and trans., <u>Soviet</u>
<u>Criminal Law and Procedure, The RSFSR Codes</u> (Cam-
bridge, Mass.:  Harvard University Press, 1966), pp.
60, 63, 201, and 230.

43. Duroedov and Pankratov, <u>Zakonodatel'stvo</u>,
pp. 150-60.

44. Ibid., pp. 83-97.

45. Brief but useful discussions of the "admin-

istrative" aspect of Khrushchev's campaign against religion are in Struve, Christians, pp. 291-335, and Simon, pp. 69-88.

46. Blane, "Year of Drift," pp. 9-15.

47. Izvestiia, August 30, 1966; Administrativnoe pravo, Moscow, 1967, pp. 509-10.

48. Vedomosti verkhovnogo soveta RSFSR, No. 12, March 24, 1966, ordinances 21, 219, and 390; Rosemary Harris and Xenia Howard-Johnston, eds., Christian Appeals from Russia (London: Hodder and Stoughton, 1969), pp. 92-143.

49. Ibid., No. 27 (873), July 3, 1975, pp. 487-91. The amendments are dated June 23rd.

50. For details of examples of a "favorable" (1905-1911) and a "difficult" (1911-1917) period, see Blane, Religious World, pp. 287-95 and 297-304.

51. Ibid., pp. 283, 298-99, 303.

52. E. F. Murav'ev and Iu. V. Dmitriev express this in a different way: "Before the Great Patriotic War our antireligious press sometimes assessed the growth of atheism among the working people of the USSR incorrectly. Successes in separating the masses from religion in our country were indeed considerable at that time. But these successes were overestimated. Most important, this separation was not always permanent, and in the period of the Great Patriotic War and in the postwar period there were sometimes relapses into religious belief" ("O dondretnosti v izuchenii i preodolenii religioznykh perezhitkov," Voprosy filosofii, No. 3 (1961), p. 64).

53. Cf. Yakov Zhidkov, "Russia," in Baptist World Alliance, Golden Jubilee Congress, (London, 1955), p. 261, and A. V. Karev, "O zhizni i deiatel'-nosti soiuza evangel'skikh khristian-baptistov v SSSR," Bratskii vestnik, No. 6 (1966),p. 17.

# INDEX

410

ABOUT THE CONTRIBUTORS


Alexandre Bennigsen, Directeur d'études à l'école pratique des hautes études, Sorbonne, VIeme section and Professor of History, University of Chicago. Co-author with Ch. Lemercier-Quelquejay of Islam in the Soviet Union (1967) and The Evolution of the Muslim Nationalities of the USSR and Their Linguistic Problems (1961).

Andrew Q. Blane, Associate Professor of History, City University of New York, Lehman and Hunter. Co-editor with Thomas E. Bird and Richard H. Marshall, Jr. of Aspects of Religion in the Soviet Union 1917-1967 (1971) and editor of The Religious World of Russian Culture, 2 Vols (1975).

Bohdan R. Bociurkiw, Professor of Political Science, Carleton University, Ottawa, Canada. Co-editor with John W. Strong of Religion and Atheism in the USSR and Eastern Europe (1975) and author of numerous article on church-state relations, religion and atheism, and Soviet internal problems.

Dennis J. Dunn, Associate Professor of History and Director of the Institute for the Study of Religion and Communism, Southwest Texas State University, San Marcos, Texas. Author of The Catholic Church and the Soviet Government 1939-1949 (1977) and of various articles dealing with church-state relations in the Soviet Union.

William C. Fletcher, Professor and Director of Slavic and Soviet Area Studies, University of Kansas. Author of Religion and Soviet Foreign Policy, 1945-1970 (1972), The Russian Orthodox Church Underground, 1917-1970 (1971), A Study in Survival: The Church in Russia, 1927-1943 (1965), and of many other books and articles on church-state relations in the Soviet Union.


413

Zvi Gitelman, Associate Professor of Political Science, University of Michigan. Author of Jewish Nationality and Soviet Politics (1972) and of many essays on Soviet politics.

Alfred Levin, Professor of History and Director of the Russian Studies Program, Kent State University. Author of The Second Duma: A Study of the Social-Democratic Party and the Russian Constitutional Experiment (1940, 2nd ed., 1966), The Third Duma, Election and Profile (1973), and of many articles on Russian history.

Sidney Monas, Professor Slavic Languages, University of Texas at Austin. Author of The Third Section: Police and Society in Russia under Nicholas I (1961) and of many articles on various aspects of Russian History.

David Powell, Research Fellow, Russian Research Center, Harvard University. Author of Antireligious Propaganda in the Soviet Union: A Study of Mass Persuasion (1975) and of articles on Soviet politics.

Walter Sawatsky, Mennonite Research Fellow, Keston College, England. Author of a number of articles on Russian religious history.

Donald W. Treadgold, Professor and Chairman of History, University of Washington, Seattle. Author of The West in Russia and China, 2 Vols. (1973), Twentieth Century Russia (4th Ed., 1976), and of many other books and articles on Russian history.

V. Stanley Vardys, Professor of Political Science, University of Oklahoma. Editor of Portrait of a Nation: Lithuania Under the Soviets and of the forthcoming The Baltic States at War and Peace.